The Cairo Conference of 1943

The Cairo Conference of 1943

Roosevelt, Churchill, Chiang Kai-shek and Madame Chiang

Ronald Ian Heiferman

McFarland & Company, Inc., Publishers
Jefferson, North Carolina, and London

LIBRARY OF CONGRESS CATALOGUING-IN-PUBLICATION DATA

Heiferman, Ronald Ian.
    The Cairo Conference of 1943 : Roosevelt, Churchill, Chiang
Kai-shek and Madame Chiang / Ronald Ian Heiferman.
        p.   cm.
    Includes bibliographical references and index.

    ISBN 978-0-7864-4804-3
    softcover : 50# alkaline paper ∞

    1. Cairo Conference (1943)   2. World War, 1939–1945—
Diplomatic history.   3. Roosevelt, Franklin D. (Franklin Delano),
1882–1945.   4. Churchill, Winston, 1874–1965.   5. Chiang,
Kai-shek, 1887–1975.   6. Chiang, May-ling Soong, 1897–2003.
7. World War, 1939–1945—China.   8. World War, 1939–1945—
Asia.   9. Western countries—Relations—China.   10. China—
Relations—Western countries.   I. Title.
D749.H45   2011
940.53'141—dc22   2010049126

British Library cataloguing data are available

© 2011 Ronald Ian Heiferman. All rights reserved

*No part of this book may be reproduced or transmitted in any form
or by any means, electronic or mechanical, including photocopying
or recording, or by any information storage and retrieval system,
without permission in writing from the publisher.*

Front cover: Chiang Kai-shek, Franklin D. Roosevelt, Winston
Churchill and Madame Chiang Kai-shek pose for cameras at the
Cairo Conference, November 25, 1943 (courtesy of the Franklin D.
Roosevelt Library and Museum, Hyde Park, New York)

Manufactured in the United States of America

*McFarland & Company, Inc., Publishers
    Box 611, Jefferson, North Carolina 28640
        www.mcfarlandpub.com*

For my wife,
Dr. Judith Davis Miller,
without whose encouragement, good humor, and help,
I would not have completed this project.
This book is dedicated to her.

Acknowledgments

This project began years ago as a doctoral dissertation at New York University under the direction of Professors Marilyn Young and the late McGeorge Bundy. More recently, a number of people have been helpful to me in writing this book and I would like to acknowledge four of them. Ms. Lisa Nguyen, modern Chinese history project archivist at the Hoover Institution Library and Archives at Stanford University, was generous with her time in answering my queries and helping me locate materials in the Chiang Kai-shek Diaries, the T. V. Soong Papers, and other collections at Stanford, many of which were unavailable when I wrote my dissertation. Mr. Fei Yan, a graduate student at Stanford, assisted me with translations of entries in Generalissimo Chiang's diaries. Mr. Matthew Hanson, archives technician at the Franklin D. Roosevelt Presidential Library, escorted me through the vast photographic collection at that library and helped me locate the photographs of the Cairo Conference which appear in this book.

Last, I would like to thank Ms. Courtney Phillips, adjunct assistant professor of computer science and interactive digital design at Quinnipiac University, who helped me with the formatting and preparation of this manuscript. Although I am not quite a Luddite, like some geriatric scholars more at home using old manual typewriters than their laptops, my computer skills are quite limited. Ms. Phillips cheerfully answered all of my technical questions with great patience and kindness. I can only hope that I have been as kind and understanding with my students!

Table of Contents

Acknowledgments	vi
Preface	1
Introduction: The War in China, 1937–1942	3
1. Roosevelt's Envoys in China: 1942	9
2. Madame Chiang's Public Diplomacy	21
3. T. V. Soong's Private Diplomacy	34
4. Chiang and Roosevelt Plan a Summit	49
5. November 21–22, 1943: The Cast Assembles	60
6. November 23, 1943: The Play Begins	70
7. November 24, 1943: The Plot Unfolds	81
8. November 25, 1943: The Second Act Begins	92
9. November 26–27, 1943: End of the Second Act	105
10. November 28–29, 1943: Interlude in Teheran, Part I	117
11. November 30–December 1, 1943: The Teheran Interlude, Part II	129
12. December 2–7, 1943: Cairo. The Final Act	139
13. A Postscript on the Cairo Conference	154
Chapter Notes	171
Bibliography	189
Index	195

Preface

While studies of World War II summit conferences are quite numerous, none of these studies have focused entirely on the Cairo Conference and the interaction of the allied leaders who met there: Churchill, Roosevelt, Chiang Kai-shek, and Madame Chiang Kai-shek. When the Cairo Conference is discussed, it is usually as a preface to the Teheran Conference which immediately followed the talks at Cairo. Even then, the description of what happened at Cairo is usually presented from an Anglo-American perspective rather than from the Chinese point of view, despite the fact that the focus of the discussions in Cairo was the China-Burma-India theater of war and the future of Sino-Western relations.

That the Cairo Conference has been overshadowed by the wartime summits at Teheran and Yalta is understandable given the start of the Cold War in Europe almost immediately after the German surrender in May 1945. To understand the collapse of relations between the Anglo-American allies on the one hand and the Soviet Union on the other, it is important to look at the conferences at Teheran and Yalta, the interactions between Churchill, Roosevelt, and Stalin, the understandings they reached, and their misunderstandings. That said, the Cairo Conference also marked an important turning point in the relations between the allies in the war against Japan—China, Great Britain, and the United States—the consequences of which were critical to the defeat of Japan and the extension of the Cold War to East Asia.

Albeit less studied, the interaction of Churchill, Roosevelt, and Chiang in Cairo is every bit as compelling from a human interest perspective as the interplay between Churchill, Roosevelt, and Stalin at Teheran and Yalta and offers a sobering reminder of what can happen when policy is made at the very highest level by individuals who know relatively little about the culture of their partners and are not able to separate myths and stereotypes from realities. Summit conferences may make for good theater, but do not necessarily result in good policies, as an examination of the Cairo Conference reveals.

Each of the parties at the Cairo Conference came with their own agendas, frequently contradictory. Generalissimo and Madame Chiang hoped to obtain a commitment to make the China-Burma-India theater the focal point

1

in the war against Japan, a matter not only of strategic importance to them but also of poetic justice. Roosevelt hoped to buoy the ego and spirits of Chiang and to insure that the Kuomintang regime would not make a separate peace with Japan, thus allowing the Japanese to redeploy the nearly one million troops they had stationed in China. Churchill had no real interest in meeting with Chiang and his wife at Cairo at all, but felt obliged to humor Roosevelt and to make sure that no agreements would be reached in Cairo that would in any way prejudice British colonial interests in Southeast Asia in the postwar era. The contradictory agendas of Churchill, Roosevelt and Chiang were exacerbated by the bad chemistry between three of them: Churchill, Generalissimo Chiang, and Madame Chiang. Even when good chemistry seemed to prevail, as between Roosevelt and the Chiangs, the failure to reconcile conflicting priorities at the Cairo Conference contributed to tensions, which would have important consequences after the war was over. It is fair to say that none of the principals left Cairo with a sense of "mission accomplished." While the tripartite alliance of China, the United Kingdom, and the United States against Japan may have remained intact after Cairo, it was beginning to fray.

A unique aspect of the Cairo conference was the presence and participation of China's first lady, Madame Chiang Kai-shek. As her husband's chief confidant, she was present at almost all of the meetings between Chiang, Churchill, and Roosevelt. Since Generalissimo Chiang did not speak or understand English, Madame Chiang often served as her husband's translator, making sure that he understood the comments of Churchill and Roosevelt and that his thoughts were clearly presented to them. But Madame Chiang was more than a translator; she was Chiang's partner in articulating China's foreign policy. Neither Clementine Churchill nor even Eleanor Roosevelt had such an influence on their husbands. In an age when women did not participate in policy making at the highest level, Madame Chiang's participation at the conference changed the gestalt of this summit in interesting and important ways, a factor often left out of previous studies of the Cairo Conference.

This study of the Cairo Conference addresses the issues outlined above, using sources often overlooked by previous scholars. The book focuses on the China-Burma-India theater of war and Sino-American relations rather than issues relating to the war in Europe because these issues were the reason Roosevelt arranged to meet with Generalissimo Chiang in November 1943 and were the principal focus of attention of the discussions at Cairo.

From the time of the Cairo Conference until the early 1970s, the Wade-Giles system of transliterating Chinese into English was the standard. That being the case, I have decided to use the Wade-Giles system (but deleting the apostrophe in "Kai-shek") instead of the Pin-Yin system, the current standard. The reader will not have to grapple with one system of transliteration in passages from period documents and a second in the body of this text.

Introduction:
The War in China, 1937–1942

When the Japanese attacked Pearl Harbor on December 7, 1941, the Sino-Japanese War was already four years old with no end in sight. Fighting alone with little or no outside assistance, the Chinese Nationalists were forced to evacuate much of China proper and retreated to Southwest China and established a wartime capital in Chungking in 1938, where the government of Free China remained until the Japanese surrender in 1945. The Japanese occupied China's major coastal cities, Manchuria, and much of northeast China with as many as 100,000,000 Chinese citizens living under Japanese occupation. Such was the state of affairs in China when the United States joined the war against Japan.

Chiang Kai-shek's Nationalist regime had been reluctant to confront Japanese aggression before 1937, but when Japanese armies invaded China proper, the Kuomintang armies fought long and hard between 1937 and 1939. Japanese leaders, who had anticipated solving the "China Incident" in three to six months found themselves bogged down in China, their early successes against Chinese armies providing no clear-cut victory in China. This involvement cost the Japanese hundreds of thousands of casualties and tied down almost one million Japanese troops in China for more than seven years. However costly this proved to be for the Japanese, the Chinese fared even worse.

By the time that war broke out in Europe in September 1939, the war in China had become a stalemate. Ensconced in their southwest retreat in Szechwan and Yunnan provinces, the Chinese Nationalist regime stubbornly refused to accept Japan's conditions to end the war in China. With geography as his most reliable ally, given the fact that much of Free China was beyond the reach of Japanese land and naval forces, Chiang Kai-shek hoped to hold on until the United States joined the war against Japan, an eventuality he believed was inevitable.[1] Chiang's only other ally, and an unreliable one at that, was the Chinese Communist Party.

The outbreak of war in Europe brought no relief for the Chinese. Indeed, after September 1939, the situation worsened for the government of Chiang Kai-shek. What little aid had been forthcoming from the Soviet Union ceased while the British and French, fearful of Japanese retaliation against their colonies in Southeast Asia, went out of their way to avoid provoking a conflict with Japan, agreeing to Japanese demands to close the lifelines to Free China from Burma and Indochina. With the Haiphong-Yunnan Railway and the Burma Road closed, the situation in China became critical. Were it not for some belated assistance from the United States in 1940 and 1941, including surplus weaponry and the American Volunteer Group or Flying Tigers, the end might have been in sight for the Kuomintang regime.

Japan's attack on Pearl Harbor changed the nature of the war in China, or so the Chinese Nationalist leaders believed. For the first time in four years, China had allies. Within weeks of the attack on December 7, 1941, and the subsequent Japanese offensives in Burma, Malaya, the Netherlands East Indies, and the Philippines, the China-Burma-India (CBI) theater of war was established with Generalissimo Chiang Kai-shek as the "Supreme Commander" of the war effort in China. Chiang and his associates assumed this would mean that China would be the site of the ultimate victory over Japan, poetic justice for the suffering of the Chinese people. They were wrong.

The creation of the CBI and the designation of Chiang Kai-shek as the commander of Allied forces in China solved few problems and actually created headaches for Chiang and his American allies. From the outset of the alliance, both sides pursued contradictory courses which would ultimately result in hostility, recriminations, and a legacy of bitterness and frustration. The Chinese wished to see China as the main stage in the war against Japan. The United States and Great Britain had other ideas, seeing China as a holding action and a third priority sideshow. Complicating matters even further were misunderstandings based on vague promises, clashes of personalities, and the logistical nightmare of supplying the war effort in China.

A good part of the blame for these misunderstandings can be placed on the shoulders of the respective leaders of China and the United States, Chiang Kai-shek and Franklin D. Roosevelt, each of whom clung to beliefs and stereotypes that proved incompatible with the realities of the war. Because Sino-American diplomatic and political relations were conducted at the very highest level of government between Chiang and Roosevelt, neither of whom was particularly knowledgeable about the culture and political reality of the other, and both of whom were loath to fully share their thoughts and commitments with their subordinates, the mythology of Sino-American relations would begin to unravel soon after the wartime alliance commenced.

Franklin Delano Roosevelt shared the romantic view of China popularized by American missionaries and their advocates in the government and media. Such people believed that it was the moral obligation and responsibility of the United States to bring the blessings of modern civilization to China and to educate the Chinese in the democratic process. By the beginning of the twentieth century, thousands of American missionaries were running hospitals and mission schools while hundreds of Chinese students came to the United States to study at elite colleges and universities like Columbia, Harvard, and Yale. Upon their return to China many of these students would play a major role in the Kuomintang regime. It was such modern men and women, the fruits of American efforts in China, that Roosevelt and many Americans assumed represented the future of the Chinese nation.

Roosevelt's view of China also reflected the history of the Delano family which made its fortune in the China trade, in large measure from the opium trade. His maternal great-grandfather, Captain Warren Delano, was a principal in the firm of Russell and Company, the most important American trading company in China. Roosevelt's grandfather, Warren Delano, Jr., also became a partner in Russell and Company, representing the company in Canton, Hong Kong, and Macao. Roosevelt's mother, Sarah Delano, travelled to China with her family before marrying James Roosevelt and lived at the Delano mansion in Hong Kong, Rose Hill, as a young woman. In short, Roosevelt was raised on a pabulum of China lore and surrounded by Chinese artifacts brought back to the United States by his great-grandfather, grandfather, and mother.

Although Franklin D. Roosevelt never visited China himself, it is clear that he felt an affinity for China and an understanding of the Chinese people. In a discussion of China policy with Henry L. Stimson, Herbert Hoover's secretary of state, in January 1933, Roosevelt told Stimson that he had "a personal hereditary interest in the Far East."[2] In 1934, responding to a memorandum received from Henry Morgenthau, his friend, neighbor, and secretary of the treasury, concerning China's finances, Roosevelt responded to Morgenthau with the following observation: "Please remember that I have a background of little over a century in Chinese affairs."[3] In 1951, Sumner Welles, another friend of the president and under secretary of state from 1937 to 1943, would later recall, "No one close to the President could have failed to recognize the deep feeling of friendship for the Chinese people that he had inherited from his mother's side of the family."[4]

Whether Roosevelt's family history made him an expert on China is debatable given the fact that much of what he learned from his mother and his maternal grandfather was folklore filtered through decades of telling and retelling stories, a tradition which the president continued with relish. Indeed, when discussing China policy with his subordinates, Roosevelt often lapsed into this storytelling mode rather than discussing the matters at hand. General Joseph Stilwell experienced this at firsthand when he had a meeting with Roosevelt shortly after being appointed commander of American forces in the CBI and before leaving for China. Armed with a litany of questions to discuss with the president, Stilwell noted in his diary that Roosevelt was more interested in discussing his family's history in China than the details of the war in China.⁵ For Stilwell, who had served as a military attaché in China and was one of the very few American officers who spoke Chinese, this was not a good omen of things to come.⁶

If Roosevelt fancied himself an old China hand, Chiang Kai-shek believed he knew a thing or two about American attitudes toward China despite the fact that he had never visited the United States. Like Roosevelt, whose family history influenced his view of China, Chiang's family associates would shape his views of the United States. Madame Chiang Kai-shek (Mayling Soong) had been educated in America, graduating from Wellesley College with honors. Her older brother, T. V. Soong, graduated from Harvard and did graduate work at Columbia University. Her two sisters, Ailing Soong and Chingling Soong, were also educated in the United States as was Ailing's husband, H. H. Kung, one of the generalissimo's closest advisors. Chiang's wife and in-laws spoke fluent English and had excellent contacts in the United States, a fact that was not lost on the generalissimo.

The Soongs moved in important circles, networking with influential American friends of China including Henry Luce and Pearl Buck. Luce and Buck were both born in China, the children of American missionaries, and did more to shape American views of China than any other people of their generation. Pearl Buck's novels, particularly *The Good Earth*, were read by millions who would otherwise have had little or no knowledge of Chinese culture. Her sympathetic portrayal of the Chinese countered many of the previous negative and racist stereotypes of China and the Chinese commonplace in the United States. Concentrating more on Chinese politics than culture, Henry Luce did much the same in his magazines, *Time* and *Life*, presenting Generalissimo and Madame Chiang Kai-shek as America's friends and China's saviors.⁷ Luce may have abhorred Roosevelt, but he shared many of the president's romantic views of China.

Madame Chiang and T. V. Soong sought to influence American public opinion and bring pressure on the Roosevelt administration to aid China in the war against Japan, using all of their connections in the United States to advance Chiang Kai-shek's cause. Although no such aid was forthcoming until after 1940, given the limitations placed on the president by the Neutrality Acts passed by the Congress of the United States in 1935, 1936, and 1937, Roosevelt welcomed Chiang's representatives to the White House and used the bloody pulpit of the presidency to call attention to Japan's aggression. But there were limits to how far the president could go, as he learned after delivering his Quarantine Speech in Chicago in 1937.

Japanese atrocities in the early months of their invasion of China did more to influence American opinion than anything Chiang or Roosevelt could have accomplished on their own. Still photos and newsreels of the Battles of Shanghai and Nanking shocked the conscience of most Americans. The bombing, looting, and pillaging of these cities was captured forever by print and photojournalists on the scene. The rapine behavior of Japanese forces in Nanking after the retreat of Chinese forces from the city may have been hidden from cameras by Japanese military censors, but American and European diplomats, journalists, merchants, and missionaries painted the pictures the cameras could not capture. Even John Rabe, a prominent German businessman and the head of the Nazi Party branch in Nanking, tried to intervene with the Japanese military to stop the atrocities.[8]

From the beginning of the war in China in 1937, Chiang Kai-shek corresponded with President Roosevelt on a regular basis, pleading for aid, and pointing out that the United States had a vested interest in stopping Japanese aggression. Roosevelt was sympathetic to the generalissimo's pleas but political realities dictated that the United States remain neutral in the Sino-Japanese conflict. With his eye on an third run for the presidency in 1940, Roosevelt could not afford to be labeled as an interventionist or a warmonger. The president was no isolationist, but he understood that his best chance to win an unprecedented third term was to avoid any rhetoric suggesting involvement in the European or East Asian wars.

Roosevelt had every reason to believe that the Republicans would nominate an isolationist conservative in 1940 and to steer clear of the war. But much to his surprise and the surprise of many others, the nominee of the GOP was Wendell Willkie, a liberal Republican who shared many of the same views as FDR and was even more internationalist in his policies than the president dared to be. During the campaign Willkie argued quite forcefully that the United States had an obligation to come to the aid of the victims of German and Japanese aggression. Willkie's candidacy was supported enthusiastically by Henry Luce who trumpeted Willkie's views in *Time* and *Life*, criticizing Republican isolationists like Senator Taft and suggesting that President Roosevelt was "incapable of leading the nation through the world crisis."[9]

Willkie's candidacy provided cover for Roosevelt and negated many of the hostile comments from the Republican right, making it easier to take action after winning the 1940 election. It is no accident that even before taking the oath of office for a third time, the Roosevelt Administration prepared to submit the Lend-Lease Act to Congress, which would provide a vehicle to aid America's friends while maintaining the illusion of neutrality. The debate over Lend-Lease was acrimonious, but the legislation was ultimately passed with Roosevelt signing it into law in March 1941. Willkie supported the bill, as did his friend and mentor Henry Luce. Their support was critical to the president when it came time for Congress to vote the measure up or down.[10]

Although the Lend-Lease program was primarily intended as a device to help Great Britain, Chinese officials immediately grasped the significance of the program and requested American aid. Roosevelt was sympathetic but clearly had different priorities than Generalissimo Chiang. Delivering aid to Great Britain was the president's first priority. Delivering aid to China was a secondary priority. Moreover, even after the United States declared war on Japan in December 1941, the logistical difficulties of moving large quantities of munitions to China were so considerable that it is unlikely that Roosevelt could have satisfied Chiang's requests even if the president placed Chiang's needs ahead of Churchill's. All Roosevelt could do was placate Chiang by sending such limited military aid as could practically be delivered to China and a string of personal emissaries to China to humor the Generalissimo and ensure that the Chinese would remain in the war.

1

Roosevelt's Envoys in China: 1942

Even before the Japanese attacked Pearl Harbor, the United States was involved in the East Asian conflict, sending aid and advisors to China under the Lend-Lease program and, before that, through a variety of other subterfuges. Since the United States was technically a neutral country and did not wish to provide the Japanese with a cause for breaking diplomatic relations or commencing hostilities, American aid to China had be discretely managed, often by non-governmental agencies and operatives. From the outset, American involvement in the Sino-Japanese war was conducted through private individuals and groups, and even after the passage of the Lend-Lease Act and the Japanese attack on Pearl Harbor, this practice continued, much to the consternation of officials in the State Department and the War Department.

Secrecy in the conduct of Sino-American relations was not only a necessity before Pearl Harbor, it was President Roosevelt's preferred method of operation. Many historians have pointed out that Franklin Roosevelt had a penchant for such operations and operatives. His mistrust of career diplomats and the State Department is well documented and nowhere did the president bypass the formal foreign policy apparatus more regularly than in the conduct of China policy. As others have pointed out, Roosevelt was his own secretary of state and his *de jure* secretary of state, Cordell Hull, was little more than a figurehead who played virtually no role in matters relating to China.[1] Rather than rely on Hull or his subordinates at the China Desk in the State Department, FDR preferred obtaining information from confidants and personal emissaries like Lauchlin Currie, Wendell Willkie, Harry Hopkins, and Henry Wallace.

It is interesting to note that Generalissimo Chiang Kai-shek also preferred the private management of Sino-American relations by trusted allies and subordinates like his brothers-in-law, T.V. Soong and H.H. Kung, and his wife, Madame Chiang. These people, as opposed to Chinese ambassador to the United States Dr. Hu Shih and the Foreign Ministry, were charged with shaping Sino-American relations. It is true, however, that after Pearl

Harbor, individuals like Soong and Kung were given appropriate cabinet-level positions in the Chinese government, but they held power only so long as the generalissimo retained confidence in them. Roosevelt, on the other hand, never felt it necessary to regularize his surrogates.

On the eve of the Japanese attack on Pearl Harbor, the United States was represented in Chungking by Ambassador Clarence Gauss, a career diplomat who had served in consular posts in China before the war. Although Ambassador Gauss had lived in China for many years, he had no knowledge of the Chinese language and little knowledge of Chinese history. Despite his years of service in China, Gauss had few close contacts within the Kuomintang leadership and limited rapport with Chiang, the Soong family, and military leaders in Chungking.[2] From their point of view, Gauss was not a person to trust or use as a conduit to the Roosevelt administration. When the United States entered the war, Chiang hoped to have Gauss replaced as ambassador or to have Roosevelt send a personal representative to Chungking.

Dr. Hu Shih was China's ambassador to the United States when the war began. He had been serving in this post since 1938. Unlike Ambassador Gauss, who had limited knowledge of China and the Chinese language, Hu Shih was bilingual, had studied and lived in the United States for many years, and was held in high esteem by the Roosevelt administration and the American public. Unfortunately, Hu Shih did not have the full support of Chiang Kai-shek and the Kuomintang leadership, who considered him to be aloof and sometimes hostile to their efforts. Although Ambassador Hu had been a good press agent for China during his years in Washington, in Chungking it was felt that he did not push hard enough to advance China's interests and that at times he did not convey the essence of Chiang's thoughts to American leaders.[3]

Shortly after the United States entered the war, the Chinese government requested the dispatch of a special presidential representative to Chungking and sent their new foreign minister, T.V. Soong, to Washington, where he remained much of the next two years. The permanent residence of China's foreign minister in the United States rendered Ambassador Hu Shih's position redundant and suggests just how important the Chinese considered their American allies. Despite his occasional differences with Chiang Kai-shek, T.V. Soong was a close associate of the generalissimo with good personal connections in the United States where Soong had been serving as Chiang's personal emissary to FDR from 1940 to 1942. In Kuomintang politics, titles were often irrelevant—what counted was closeness to Chiang and his inner circle.

Like Hu Shih, T.V. Soong was quite familiar with American ways, having obtained his B.A. from Harvard and completed his graduate studies at Columbia. Unlike Hu Shih, Soong had entry into the innermost circles of the Kuomintang, and powerful connections in the United States. In many ways, Soong was the perfect Chinese operative in Washington. He understood how to play politics and enjoyed the social obligations and interaction necessary to gain the confidence of congressional leaders and confidants of the president.

Soong's mission was to extract the maximum commitment of American economic and military aid, to establish China's position as a great power among the allies, to serve as Chiang's surrogate at important meetings with Roosevelt and Churchill, and to create and cultivate a pro-China lobby in the United States. Although he was occasionally assisted in these efforts by other high-ranking Chinese operatives, such as H.H. Kung, Soong's operation was largely a one-man show. As for Ambassador Hu Shih, his role was a largely ceremonial one, limited to delivering public addresses about China's culture and history to fraternal, political, and social organizations throughout the United States.

Shortly after T.V. Soong was elevated to the post of foreign minister and returned to the United States, Lt. General Joseph Stilwell was dispatched to China. Like Soong, Stilwell wore many hats and had multiple responsibilities. He was to command American forces in the CBI theater, serve as chief American Lend-Lease administrator in China, and assist Chiang Kai-shek in the reshaping of China's armies, serving as the generalissimo's chief of staff. Although Stilwell was not the personal representative of President Roosevelt that the Chinese had requested, he came close to filling that role, but unlike T.V. Soong who maintained cordial relations with American political leaders, Stilwell did not cultivate good relations with the Kuomintang leadership. His tenure in China was frustrating to both the Chinese and himself. The story of Stilwell's problems in China has been told many times and it is not my intention to repeat it in this study.[4] However, because Stilwell knew a good deal about China and had the confidence of Marshall and Stimson, it is important to note his perspective on the China tangle.

Based on two previous tours of duty in China, Stilwell had come to conclude that Chiang Kai-shek lacked the will to commit his military forces to an all-out war against Japan. He attributed this to the generalissimo's insecurity about his position at the top of the Kuomintang hierarchy and his obsessive concern about the Chinese communists. As Stilwell often pointed out, Chiang was more concerned about the threat posed by the Chinese communists than the threat posed by the Japanese.[5] Unless Chiang could be pressured to commit his troops to a real effort against Japan, Stilwell believed that he would hold them in reserve for eventual use against the communists.[6]

In Stilwell's opinion, the only way to deal with Chiang was to extract a quid pro quo for every significant American effort to aid the Chinese. Nothing less would suffice to force the generalissimo to abandon his phony war against the Japanese.[7] Stilwell warned against the use of hyperbole to puff up Chiang's ego, but his warnings fell on deaf ears at the White House where the president seemed concerned that Stilwell's suggested method of doing business with Chiang would drive the generalissimo into the arms of the Japanese.[8]

Stilwell made no secret of his view of the situation in China and within a few months after his arrival in Chungking, Chiang Kai-shek was considering asking for his recall. He chose not to do so at that moment because he did not wish to alienate powerful supporters of Stilwell in Washington, such as Secretary of War Stimson and General George C. Marshall. Frustrated by Stilwell's refusal to defer to his authority and Ambassador Gauss' ineffectiveness, the generalissimo and his subordinates hoped to clarify their position by requesting that an intimate of the president be sent to China on a fact-finding mission.

On June 1, 1942, T.V. Soong hand-delivered a message from Chiang to Harry Hopkins for transmission to President Roosevelt. In this note, the generalissimo indicated that he was most anxious to discuss the situation in China with the president, but could not leave China to do so. That being the case, Chiang requested that FDR send Harry Hopkins to China so "I could acquaint him with the situation and consult you intimately through him."[9] Even as this message was being delivered to Hopkins and the president, Madame Chiang sent a cable to Dr. Lauchlin Currie, special assistant to the president on matters relating to China and Lend-Lease, urging his help in persuading Roosevelt to send Hopkins to China and asking Currie if he could accompany Hopkins to Chungking.[10] The appeals of Generalissimo and Madame Chiang were made at the urging of T. V. Soong, who was keeping the Chiangs appraised of the situation in Washington.[11]

Currie, who had visited China in February 1941 to ascertain China's need for Lend-Lease supplies, forwarded Madame Chiang's cable to the president with the comment that he believed Chiang's request was more for morale boosting than for consultation, but urging FDR to give serious consideration to sending Hopkins to China.[12] Two days later, Curry submitted a lengthy memorandum to Roosevelt elaborating on the reasons why he thought the president should honor Chiang's request. At the end of this memo, Currie suggested that if Hopkins could not be spared for such a mission, he could be sent in Hopkins' place. Not one to be shy about his ability, Currie argued that he was already familiar with China, was a "true friend of China," and had "all the necessary vaccinations and inoculations and could leave at a moment's notice."[13]

Roosevelt was already aware that the Chinese felt left out of allied policy councils. He was also aware, thanks to T.V. Soong, that the Chinese did not feel that America's diplomatic and military representatives in Chungking were adequately informing the Roosevelt administration of the real situation in China. Chiang's request for the dispatch of a presidential envoy to Chungking provided FDR with an opportunity to both boost Chinese morale and get a better sense of the China tangle from a person of his own choosing. Yet he did not want to have Hopkins away from Washington for a prolonged period. The solution was to take Currie up on his offer to be a stand-in for Hopkins.

On June 26, 1942, Currie cabled Madame Chiang that Roosevelt could not spare Hopkins but that the president was sending him instead.[13] Madame Chiang replied enthusiastically, indicating that she and the generalissimo looked forward to his visit.[14] Madame Chiang's enthusiasm about the Currie visit was not shared by her brother, T.V. Soong. According to Currie, when he told Soong about the president's decision, Soong replied that "nothing could be served by my going" and that he would take the matter up with the president.[15] Although Soong never spelled out his reasons for opposing Currie's visit to China and no record exists of Soong's conversation with Roosevelt about this matter, one may surmise that Soong was disappointed that Hopkins, the closest confidant of the president and a good friend of his, was not being sent and that a relatively low-ranking subordinate with little influence was being sent instead.

On July 3, 1942, Secretary of State Hull informed Ambassador Gauss of Currie's mission, including the fact that the Chinese had originally requested that Hopkins be sent. Gauss was also told that Currie would proceed "without publicity" and the ambassador was instructed to cooperate with Currie after he arrived in Chungking. Since T.V. Soong had been told of Roosevelt's decision and had presumably kept Chiang abreast of Currie's plans, Gauss was advised that the embassy was not to get involved in planning Currie's itinerary. The embassy's role was to provide whatever assistance Currie requested.[16]

Ambassador Gauss may not have liked being excluded from planning the Currie visit, but by the summer of 1942, Gauss was largely a bystander in the conduct of Sino-American relations and recognized this himself. In a cover letter to a memorandum of a conversation with General Stilwell, which Gauss sent to the State Department on July 11, 1942, he admitted that since T.V. Soong had gone to Washington in his capacity as foreign minister, most high level contact with the United States took place through Soong's office. Gauss also observed that he was often not even informed of conversations between Soong and members of the Roosevelt administration.[17]

Lauchlin Currie arrived in Chungking on July 21, 1942, and remained there until August 7. During this period, he met with Generalissimo and Madame Chiang fourteen times at their villa just outside of the city. This was Currie's second visit to Chungking, the first having taken place in February 1941. In his notes on his meetings with the Chiangs in 1942, Currie observed that Chiang had changed since they had last met. He found the generalissimo "more worried and discouraged" and characterized his meetings with Chiang as "trying, at least at first."[18]

Currie attributed the malaise in Chungking to the fact that there was no definite plan on which the Chinese and Americans seemed to be working. "The atmosphere," he said, "was one of drift."[19] This was compounded by the fact that China had been oversold to Americans who had an erroneous picture of the situation in Chungking while the Chinese, for their part, had been oversold on America's productive capabilities and had an exaggerated ideas of "U.S. love for China."[20]

During the course of his meetings with Generalissimo and Madame Chiang, Currie came to the conclusion that both China and the United States had chosen poor diplomatic and military representatives to deal with one another. He was particularly critical of T.V. Soong whom Currie suggested, in his report, did not keep the Chinese government well-informed of his activities in Washington and did not always present Chiang's views accurately. It is interesting to note that although Currie accused Soong of failing to keep Chiang adequately informed, he cited no examples in his report to illustrate this accusation. Ambassador Gauss would also be criticized by Currie for his "lack of contacts" in Chungking and failure to cultivate such contacts.[21]

On August 5, 1942, Currie raised the problem of T.V. Soong's methods of operation with the Chiangs, stating that Soong had "resorted to bargaining and pressure which have caused an estrangement of relations" and suggesting that President Roosevelt was not well disposed to Soong. Once again, Currie provided no specifics to prove this allegation nor is there any indication that Chiang or his wife asked him for such information.[22]

Currie went on to point out that officials at the War Department were even more hostile to Soong because of his "aggressive behavior and failure to respect protocol."[23] He also pointed out that another consequence of Soong's "meddling" in Washington was that the prestige of Ambassador Hu Shih had declined considerably because American officials believed that he did not have influence with the generalissimo.[24]

Currie states that he suggested to Chiang that it might be prudent to recall Hu Shih and replace him as ambassador with someone closer to the Kuomintang leadership, even going so far as to suggest H.H. Kung as a suitable replacement. If Kung or someone comparable were dispatched to Washington, Soong could be recalled to Chungking where China's foreign minister ought to be based.[25] According to Currie, Chiang was noncommittal with regard to Soong, except to point out that China had a shortage of men with Soong's English language skills and experience.[26] Soon after Currie left China, Hu Shih was recalled and replaced as ambassador by Wei Tao-ming, but the reasons for this change had little to do with Currie's suggestions.[27]

At some point during their conversation on August 5, Currie suggested to Generalissimo and Madame Chiang that one way to overcome the misunderstandings that plagued Sino-American relations was to arrange a personal meeting between Chiang and Roosevelt.[28] Their reaction to this proposal is not recorded and nothing more seems to have been said of this idea during Currie's remaining days in Chungking. It should be noted that upon his return to the United States, Currie made this same suggestion to FDR, who leaned toward such face-to-face encounters and had intimated the need for a Sino-American summit in a previous communication to Chiang.[29] But for the moment, no plans were made for the generalissimo and the president to meet.

While in Chungking, Currie met with Ambassador Gauss once or, perhaps, twice, but told Gauss little about his discussions with Generalissimo and Madame Chiang. Nor did Currie consult other officials at the embassy.[30] As would more often than not be the case during the war, the American embassy in China was peripheral to the conduct of Sino-American relations at the highest level, much to the dismay of the embassy staff.

Currie left Chungking on August 7, 1942, stopping in India and North Africa before returning to Washington. Upon his return, Currie drafted a lengthy report (43 pages) on his mission, which was given to Roosevelt on August 24. This report was surely one of the most thoughtful memoranda on China submitted to the president during the war and more realistic than many of the reports on the situation in the CBI Roosevelt was given to read. Of particular significance was Currie's assessment of Chiang as a leader who had limited power and was as much "a prisoner of the cliques and factions which surround him as their warden."[31] Curry also pointed out that Chiang was "pathetically dependent upon America" for economic and military aid not to say anything of recognition of his place as the legitimate head of a world power.[33]

Currie concluded his report with some very specific recommendations. He urged the President to remove General Stilwell and Ambassador Gauss, suggesting that if these men were recalled, Chiang might reciprocate by recalling T.V. Soong and replacing Hu Shih.[34] Currie also urged Roosevelt to be more sensitive to Chiang's pride. "The old forms really matter to him," Currie suggested, "and it would pay large dividends for us to keep this in mind and make a point of consulting him on any of the moves we proposed in the Far East."[35]

It is not clear if President Roosevelt actually read Currie's full report, although others in the administration certainly did.[36] By the time Currie returned to the United States and submitted his findings to Roosevelt, the president was already involved in sending another envoy, Wendell Willkie, on a visit to Chungking. Whether the Willkie visit was merely an effort to plump up Chiang's ego or represented a logical sequel to Currie's visit is uncertain.[37] What is clear, however, is that the Willkie visit to China represented a very public effort at private diplomacy.

On August 21, 1942, three days before he received Currie's report, Roosevelt informed Chiang that he hoped to have Willkie visit Chungking sometime in early October on his return to the United States from the Soviet

Union. "I particularly want him to meet you and your good wife," FDR stated, "for I know that much good will come there from. I want him to realize your many and great problems and to tell you something of our problems as well."[38] On August 24, Ambassador Gauss received a cable confirming Willkie's impending visit from Secretary of State Hull and urging him to get in touch with the generalissimo about arrangements.[39]

Unlike Lauchlin Currie who was little-known outside of Washington, Wendell Willkie was one of America's most prominent political leaders and the leader of the "loyal opposition." He also happened to be out of work and willing to undertake a mission for the president. Given Willkie's political stature in America, his visit to Chungking was sure to be closely watched and his activities in China would be widely reported by American journalists. The media value of the Willkie visit was not lost on Chinese officials and propagandists either.

The announcement of Willkie's visit was forwarded to Chiang Kai-shek by T.V. Soong who also informed the generalissimo and other Kuomintang leaders that Willkie was more than just another American envoy. He might be the next president of the United States! Thus, all efforts were to be made to make Willkie's visit a productive one.[40] Translated into simple terms, this meant that it was imperative that Willkie see China in a positive light so as to maximize the public relations opportunities that his visit might offer.

Soong's message was well-heeded by his colleagues in Chungking. As the most prominent American to visit wartime China to that point, Willkie's tour was carefully orchestrated and planned. When his plane touched down at Urumchi on September 28, 1942, after a long flight from Tashkent, Willkie was greeted by several special representatives of the generalissimo, including Hollington Tong, Chiang's chief press representative and translator. Tong stayed with Willkie from that moment until his departure from China on October 9.

Of all Chiang Kai-shek's subordinates, Tong was the most savvy about public relations and had good rapport with most foreign journalists in China. Furthermore, Tong understood how American politicians operated. He was a very good choice as an escort for Willkie. Not only did Tong arrange and manage Willkie's itinerary well, he made a great impression on Willkie, who later described him as "the kind of aide any great leader would like to have."[41]

The very public nature of Willkie's visit became clear immediately upon his arrival in Chungking on October 1. As his car proceeded from the airport some distance from the city center to the capital, the streets were crowded with people waving small Chinese and American flags. Willkie was clearly impressed. In his account of his journey, Willkie noted:

> Before we reached the middle of the city, the crowds stood packed from curb to storefront. Men, women, young boys and girls, bearded old gentlemen, Chinese with fedora hats, others with skull caps, coolies, porters, students, mothers nurs-

ing their children, well dressed and poorly dressed—they packed eleven miles of road over which our cars slowly moved on our way to the guesthouse in which we were supposed to stay.[42]

Willkie must have felt quite at home in this environment. Such political parades had been a common experience for him during the 1940 presidential election campaign. Still, there was something very different about this first experience in Chungking. "It was perfectly clear," Willkie later pointed out, "not all of these people, many of whom were barefoot or dressed in rags, had any clear idea of who I was or why I was there ... but in spite of my efforts to discount it, this scene moved me profoundly."[43]

Whereas Lauchlin Currie had entered Chungking without fanfare or press coverage in July and left just as quietly in August, Willkie's triumphal entry into Chungking was a media event of epic proportion and the first of many such public events and meetings. Hollington Tong and the others who arranged Willkie's visit proved quite adept at combining private interludes with Chiang and other Kuomintang leaders with expertly staged occasions that provided good footage to American newsreel cameramen and good copy to American journalists. The value of a good press was well understood by the generalissimo's subordinates in Chungking.[44]

Willkie spent six days in Chungking, during which time he had several lengthy conversations with Generalissimo and Madame Chiang at the villa. Except for the occasional presence of Hollington Tong, who provided Madame Chiang with some relief in translating for the generalissimo and Willkie, no one else was present at these meetings. As Ambassador Gauss lamented in a memorandum to Secretary of State Hull, Willkie did not request the use of an American translator nor did he seek "information or guidance from the Ambassador or the Embassy."[45] As had been the case during Currie's visit, the ambassador and the embassy were irrelevant to the discussions taking place. Indeed, Willkie not only declined Gauss' invitation to stay at the embassy, he did not even visit the embassy while he was in Chungking.[46]

According to Willkie, his discussions with the Chiangs were wide-ranging, including such matters as long-range goals for China's post-war economic development, China's more immediate economic and military needs, Sino-Russian relations, Sino-British relations, personnel problems in the CBI theater, and the personalities of other allied leaders.[47] During the course of these conversations, Willkie also had the opportunity to take the measure of Chiang and his wife. His observations in this regard are most interesting and provide a marked contrast to the views of Lauchlin Currie.[48]

Whereas Currie came away from his contact with Chiang with the impression that the generalissimo was "troubled" and in a somewhat precarious position vis-a-vis other Kuomintang political cliques and military leaders,⁴⁹ Willkie seems to have come to a different conclusion. To Willkie, the generalissimo was "a strangely quiet, soft spoken man" with "a reflective manner, a quiet poise."⁵⁰ Willkie found Chiang "bigger than his legendary reputation" and commented that the generalissimo had come to power "the hard way" and held power because of the loyalty of his subordinates and the talents of his in-laws, the Soong family.⁵¹ In Willkie's mind, Chiang was in a very strong position.

In addition to his conversations with Generalissimo and Madame Chiang, Willkie met with other important Chinese leaders including General Ho Ying-chin, China's minister of war, H.H. Kung, Chiang's chief financial advisor and brother-in-law, Ch'en Li-fu, minister of education and a leader of the CC clique of the KMT, and Chou En-lai, chief communist representative in Chungking. His impression of these men, particularly Chou En-lai, was quite positive. Willkie later remarked that Chou "left me with the feeling that if all Chinese communists are like himself, their movement is more a national and agrarian awakening than an international or proletarian conspiracy."⁵²

Little of Willkie's time in Chungking was spent in talking with American diplomats or military personnel. He did, however, spend some time with General Claire Chennault and was much impressed by the commander of the fabled Flying Tigers. Willkie was "shocked by the paucity of material he had to work with" and shared Chennault's "sense of bafflement" at the failure of American officials to support his air strategy and increase his supplies.⁵³ Willkie also noted that Chennault was "the most popular American in China!"⁵⁴

During the course of his stay in Chungking, Willkie seems to have concluded that Generalissimo and Madame Chiang were correct in being concerned about the picture of China's war effort being disseminated in the United States. At a dinner party hosted by H. H. Kung and his wife on October 3, Willkie suggested that if the generalissimo could not leave China to meet with President Roosevelt, Madame Chiang should consider going to the United States on a speaking tour to tell Americans the truth about China. When Kung asked Willkie if he was serious about this suggestion, Willkie replied:

> I believe it is vital for my countrymen to understand the problems of Asia and the viewpoints of its people ... Madame would make the perfect Ambassador. Her great ability—and I know she will excuse me for speaking so personally—her great devotion to China are well known in the United States. She would find herself not only beloved, but immensely effective. We would listen to her as no one else.⁵⁵

According to Ambassador Gauss, who was also present when Willkie invited Madame Chiang to visit the United States, she asked Willkie if such a visit would result in more supplies for China's armies and Chennault's air force to which he replied, "Her visit would get all the planes that Madame Chiang might desire."[56] The generalissimo, Gauss relates, made no comment but seemed to consider Willkie's proposal to be a serious one.[57]

Willkie concluded his stay in Chungking on October 7, but before leaving China he was flown to Sian to observe Chinese military forces in action against the Japanese. Hollington Tong accompanied Willkie. When they arrived at the battlefield, they were met by Captain Chiang Wei-kuo, the son of the generalissimo, who guided them along the front where units from one of Chiang's crack divisions were holding a river line against enemy forces.

During the course of this inspection tour, Willkie addressed 9000 of the Chinese soldiers in the blazing sun, assuring them that America would not forget their efforts.[58] All in all, Willkie was much impressed by what he observed. Shortly after his return to the United States, Willkie wrote that the old image of China's military impotence and incompetence were no longer valid:

> Military China is united; its leaders are trained and able generals; its new armies are tough fighting organizations of men who both know what they are fighting for and how to fight for it.[59]

From the perspective of Chiang Kai-shek and the Kuomintang leadership, Willkie's visit had been a great success. Even before Willkie left China, the generalissimo cabled Roosevelt praising Willkie and suggesting he had learned much from him about the overwhelming problems the president faced.[60] H.H. Kung was even more expansive. "Never," Kung stated, "have I seen such a spontaneous and heartfelt welcome given to a foreign visitor.... Despite his short stay, Mr. Willkie has done much by his infectious enthusiasm to invigorate China's war effort."[61]

Willkie left China on October 9, 1942, and arrived back in the United States four days later. After resting and recuperating from his 31,000 mile journey, Willkie briefed the president who then cabled Chiang that he was grateful that the visit had gone well and that he had learned much about the situation in China from Mr. Willkie.[62] Roosevelt also cabled H.H. Kung, acknowledging the warm reception that Willkie had received and stressing the value of such face-to-face exchanges of information and points of view.[63]

Although there is no written record to indicate the nature of Roosevelt's conversation with Willkie about his visit to China, one may surmise that Willkie's analysis of the situation in China made an impression on the president. Roosevelt preferred such personal reports to lengthy memoranda and he respected Willkie more than some of his subordinates and many of the professionals in the State Department. Since Willkie's ideas about the world situation were in harmony with FDR's own world view, Willkie's impressions of the situation in China undoubtedly had a greater impact on Roosevelt than Currie's more dispassionate observations and the reports the president received regularly from American officials in the CBI theater. Roosevelt's continued optimism about China was at least, in part, a response to what he heard from Willkie.

2
Madame Chiang's Public Diplomacy

Nineteen forty-two did not prove to be an auspicious year in the CBI theater. British forces were driven from Burma and the anticipated advantages of American involvement in the war against Japan did not materialize as Chinese leaders had hoped. The loss of Burma was an important setback for the Chinese. More important, however, was the conflict between Chinese and American planners over strategy in the CBI, which led to tension and growing frustration beneath the facade of cooperation in the war against Japan. This conflict was due to the diametrically opposing views of Chinese and American leaders as to how best to secure the defeat of the Axis powers.

Chiang Kai-shek and his associates had predicted the inevitability of America's entry into the war and believed that once this happened, China would become the main battleground in the struggle against Japan. They were to be sorely disappointed after Pearl Harbor when it became apparent that Roosevelt and his advisors were making the war against Germany their first priority and relegating the war against Japan to a secondary status. They became alarmed when it became clear that the Americans seemed to see China as little more than a holding action in the war against Japan.

Even if Roosevelt and his advisors had considered Japan to be America's number one enemy, the logistical problems of providing the kind of assistance that the Chinese wanted were such that it was impossible to do more than keep Free China alive. Geography dictated American options, a fact which seemed lost on Chiang and his subordinates in Chungking. They remained convinced that once they had won the president's ear, he would revise American policy and make China a first priority theater of war.

During the visits of Lauchlin Currie and Wendell Willkie to China in 1942, Generalissimo and Madame Chiang sought to inform them of China's misgivings over the priorities of America's military planners and hoped to have them convey this message to President Roosevelt. Chiang, who had never been out of East Asia, had little appreciation of the power of Hitler's Germany, the resources that the Nazis could draw upon from the territories they occupied, or the pressure being brought to bear on Roosevelt by Stalin for some relief from the German onslaught. The generalissimo was preoccupied with his own problems and had a limited grasp of geo-political realities. For Chiang, Japan was the main enemy and the place to defeat Japan was China. This was the message he wanted to convey to Roosevelt.

Converting Currie and Willkie to the Chinese line was but one part of Chiang's effort to change American policy and rally public opinion in the United States to the cause of China. The generalissimo and his associates also mounted an aggressive campaign to influence the president, congressional leaders, and influential private citizens in 1942 and 1943. This campaign was spearheaded by Madame Chiang and her brother, T. V. Soong, with Madame Chiang presenting China's case to the public while her brother continued to work behind the scenes in Washington.

Willkie had suggested that Madame Chiang should visit the United States to lobby for China when he was in Chungking in October 1942, and she and the generalissimo took him up on his invitation. From February 17 to April 4, 1943, Madame Chiang barnstormed the United States on a triumphal speaking tour arranged by prominent American members of the China lobby, many of them children of missionaries stationed in China, who had been assiduously courted by the Kuomintang leadership and were sympathetic to Generalissimo and Madame Chiang. They were aided and abetted by members of the Roosevelt administration who provided logistical assistance in setting up Madame Chiang's itinerary.

Madame Chiang first arrived in the United States in November 1942. The initial purpose of her visit was to seek medical attention at Presbyterian Medical Center in New York City for a rare dermatological condition, urticaria, which her doctors believed might be caused by nervous stress and tension.[1] There was also a possibility that she might be afflicted with cancer of the skin. Although cancer was not found, Madame Chiang remained in the hospital for several months. Shortly after her release from Columbia-Presbyterian Hospital, Madame Chiang commenced her public tour.

When Madame Chiang left Chungking in November 1942, she was accompanied to the United States by Hollington Tong, vice-minister for information of the Chinese government. As had been the case during Willkie's visit to China when he organized Willkie's tour, Tong was to coordinate and help plan Madame Chiang's speaking tour so as to maximize her exposure in the American media. If he had been helpful in turning Willkie's visit to China into a series of media opportunities, Tong helped make Madame Chiang's visit to the United States into a media spectacular. No other wartime leader of America's allies to visit the United States received the kind of reception and coverage that Madame Chiang generated, not even Churchill.

Madame Chiang's official tour began on February 17, 1943, when she arrived in Washington D.C. When her train pulled into Union Station, she was greeted by President and Mrs. Roosevelt, representatives from the Chi-

President Roosevelt chats with Madame Chiang en route from Union Station, Washington, D.C., to the White House, February 17, 1943. Courtesy of the Franklin D. Roosevelt Library and Museum, Hyde Park, New York.

nese Embassy, and hundreds of well wishers. As the presidential entourage proceeded to the White House, throngs of people cheered Madame Chiang on, waving Chinese and American flags. Everywhere she went, Madame Chiang would generate similarly large and enthusiastic crowds.

On February 18, Madame Chiang went to the United States Capitol where she addressed members of the Senate in their chamber followed by an address to members of the House on their side of the capital. This marked the first time that a private citizen had been invited to speak before the Congress of the United States. Madame Chiang took advantage of these opportunities to present her husband's case and argue for increased American assistance to China.

In her speech before the House of Representatives, Madame Chiang stressed the need to press the war against Japan as vigorously as the war against Germany. "Let us not forget," she said, "that Japan in her occupied areas today has greater resources than Germany."[2] She went on to point out that "China has borne Japan's sadistic fury unaided and alone."[3] While praising American victories at Midway and the Coral Sea as steps in the right direction, she went on to express her concern that "the prevailing opinion seems to be to consider the defeat of the Japanese as of relative unimportance and that Hitler is our first concern."[4] This, Madame Chiang suggested, was not borne out by the facts.

Madame's Chiang's address before the House of Representatives was broadcast live throughout the United States by the major radio networks. With this in mind, her speech was carefully crafted and revised with the help of Hollington Tong. Madame Chiang was a compelling speaker. The combination of her charm and her knowledge of the English language thrilled audiences all over the United States. "China's First Lady," as she was often referred to, was the perfect ambassador of good will for her government. Even those who did not necessarily share her point of view could be beguiled by her. Secretary of War Henry L. Stimson, who was one such person, warned a subordinate "not to be vamped by her and to watch out for what she said."[5]

Secretary Stimson may have had reservations about Madame Chiang's purpose and the regime she represented, but he was in the minority. Her address to the House of Representatives was followed by an avalanche of favorable comments from administration leaders and the press. Typical of these was the lead editorial in the *New York Herald Tribune* on February 19, 1943:

> The extraordinary ovation which greeted Mme. Chiang in the House of Representatives—at her entrance and for sentence after sentence of her moving speech—was, after all, a personal tribute to a great individual. The gallantry of her long journey in wartime, her wisdom, her dignity, her loveliness have won admiration throughout America. Far more than that, in her serenity and candor she stood as the symbol of a great nation. The 160 years of friendship between our two peoples means much to Americans. They represent not simply a diplomatic calm; they speak of generations of mutual understanding, of a spiritual kinship that has transcended every obstacle of cultural diversity and language.[6]

On February 19, the day after her visit to the capital, Madame Chiang and President Roosevelt held a joint press conference at the White House. As was Roosevelt's custom, the conference was held in his office. Normally, a relatively small number of reporters would have been present at a presidential press conference. On this occasion, more than 150 journalists packed the oval office.

At the beginning of the news conference, President Roosevelt promised to increase aid for China "as soon as the Lord will let us."[7] Madame Chiang broke into the conversation to remind the president, "The Lord helps those who help themselves."[8] Reporters noted that Roosevelt laughed heartily at this rejoinder and that this was one of the few times they had witnessed the president being outwitted in such an encounter.[9]

During the course of the press conference, a reporter asked Madame Chiang whether the Chinese government was making use of all available manpower against the Japanese as opposed to hoarding the best Kuomintang units for future use against domestic foes. She answered that question by

A very somber Eleanor Roosevelt and an equally somber Madame Chiang visit George Washington's estate at Mount Vernon, Virginia, February 22, 1943. Courtesy of Franklin D. Roosevelt Library and Museum, Hyde Park, New York.

pointing out that China was committing all resources to the war, but she argued, "The Chinese people should not be expected to fight virtually barehanded in the future as they had in the past six years."[10]

On February 24, Madame Chiang held another joint press conference, this time with Mrs. Roosevelt. This conference was limited to the female reporters who covered national news from Washington. Madame Chiang once again pointed out the need to send more munitions to China, but, at the same time, she made it clear that China was not looking for charity. "What China was doing to resist Japanese aggression," Madame Chiang suggested, "was not only in her own self interest, but in the interest of the democracies of the world."[11]

In between her public appearances, Madame Chiang met privately with congressional leaders and members of the Cabinet. In these private sessions as in her public statements, Madame Chiang pressed for increased aid and urged a re-examination of American war aims and priorities. Among those with whom she met was Secretary of War Stimson, who noted in his diary that she was a "most attractive and beguiling little lady."[12] Stimson also noted that he tried to avoid discussing specific requests for aid because he did not want to make promises that the United States could not keep.[13] Stimson's caution was characteristic of other members of Roosevelt's Cabinet and inner circle.

Madame Chiang and her party left Washington on February 28, 1943, bound for New York City. Upon her arrival in New York the next morning, she was greeted by Mayor Fiorello H. La Guardia and a reception committee of distinguished members of the Chinese-American community in the city. Before taking up residence at the Waldorf Astoria Hotel, her headquarters during her New York stay, Madame Chiang delivered a speech on the steps of City Hall in which she once again stressed one of the themes she had defined in Washington, namely that China's struggle for justice and freedom was part of a larger world effort:

> If we thought we were fighting alone, if we thought we were fighting only for China, to be very frank with you, China would not be the China of today, but would have been a conquered China. But we realized that justice would prevail and the people of America knew and realized what was at stake.[14]

The highlight of Madame Chiang's stay in New York took place on the evening of March 2, when she addressed a crowd of almost 20,000 people in Madison Square Garden. In addition to those who filled every seat in this vast indoor arena, there were dozens of dignitaries seated on the stage, including the governors of New York, New Jersey, Pennsylvania, and the six New England states. Also present were the "corporate sponsors" of Madame Chiang's tour, Thomas J. Watson, founder and president of IBM, and John D. Rockerfeller, Jr., the heir to the Standard Oil fortune.[15] Friends and family, such as Wendell Willkie and T.V. Soong, filled the remaining seats on the stage.

The rally at Madison Square Garden had all of the trappings of a Broadway extravaganza. Before Madame Chiang gave her address, there was a parade of Chinese-American children dressed in native costumes followed by bands and color guards representing each of the armed services. Hollington Tong and his associates meticulously planned the gala at Madison Square Garden, allowing plenty of photo opportunities and insuring that a lively and enthusiastic audience filled the hall. In addition to the thousands who filled Madison Square Garden that night, millions more listened to the event, which was also carried by the major radio networks.

Before Madame Chiang was called to the microphone, the audience was warmed up by Governor Thomas E. Dewey of New York and General Henry A. Arnold, commanding officer of the United States Army Air Force. In his opening remarks, Governor Dewey urged more aid to China. "To the intrepid people of China," the governor stated, "we in America can pledge no less than a full partnership. For our sake and theirs we shall send them every help at our command."[16] Not to be outdone, General Arnold stated, "Mere words won't kill Japs. You've got to shoot them or bomb them to bits—stamp out each one the way we stamp out termites."[17]

After General Arnold concluded his remarks, Madame Chiang was introduced to the audience by Wendell Willkie. Willkie noted that it was his pleasure to present Madame Chiang in New York just as she had introduced him a few months before in Chungking. He extolled her virtues in the following words:

> I have met a good many war leaders and it is not inappropriate for me to say that she is the most fascinating of all and the most beloved of her people. We speak of her wit and charm, and her beauty, but you miss the point of her if you think of her only as an angel—though she is one, an avenging angel.
> It was China which first understood the true nature of this war and Madame Chiang is one of the two driving forces behind this great nation. She is a leader of 450,000,000 people.[18]

Following Willkie's ebullient introduction, Madame Chiang delivered her address. First she thanked the American people for their warm hospitality. Next she acknowledged what the United States had done to aid China. Then she elaborated on the reasons why dictatorships and tyrannical governments were historically short-lived, likening the leaders of Axis nations to tyrants of old who treated the inhabitants of conquered lands as slaves. "Was it this cruelty of the conqueror toward the conquered," she asked, "which contributed to the fall of dictatorships whose leaders strutted about in a frenzy of exhibitionism during their short day as invincible conquerors and masters?"[19]

"The swift and mighty tide," Madame Chiang went on to point out, "is toward universal justice and freedom."[20] This, she suggested, is what China had bled for the past six years. China would not capitulate to the Japanese. Nothing short of total annihilation would prevent the Chinese from struggling against "wanton domination."[21] China repudiated the philosophy that "a slow and humiliating death by strangulation was more horrendous than surrender to the enemy."[22]

Madame Chiang concluded her remarks with an appeal for unity among the nations united against the Axis powers, which would facilitate the defeat of these dictatorships and pave the way for the realization of a better world. She illustrated this point by relating to her audience the experience of China during the Warring States period (403–221 B.C.), when Ch'in Shih Huang-ti, the king of the state of Ch'in, attacked neighboring kingdoms whose leaders failed to cooperate in the face of Ch'in aggression and fell prey to Ch'in conquest. "Do we want history to repeat itself?" she asked rhetorically.[23] The answer was self-apparent.

As had been the case when Madame Chiang addressed the House of Representatives, her speech at Madison Square Garden was crafted to appeal to Americans. Her use of terms like "democracy" and "tyranny" was no accident. What she attempted to do was to tell China's story in a manner that all Americans could relate to, stressing values that were part of the political vocabulary of most Americans. At the urging of Hollington Tong, she also sought to impress her audience with China's antiquity and the wisdom to be gleaned from her ancient past, much as Pearl Buck had presented China to her readers and Hollywood was now presenting Charlie Chan to millions of moviegoers. Tong was convinced that this dual approach would be quite successful.[24]

Although Madame Chiang and Hollington Tong were not unaware that some of this rhetoric was hyperbolic, their purpose was to "accentuate the positive and eliminate the negative," a characteristic of much of wartime propaganda. If good press coverage was to be obtained, image was as important as reality.

Madame Chiang left New York City on March 5 and spent the next several days at Wellesley College, her alma mater. Following three days of rest at the college, she continued her public tour, addressing a capacity crowd at Symphony Hall in Boston on March 9. Madame Chiang's success in persuading Americans that the Chinese and American governments were fighting a common enemy to preserve common values was illustrated in the introductory remarks of Boston's mayor, Maurice J. Tobin, who told that crowd at Symphony Hall, "Every word she utters is as American in every way as the words of Thomas Jefferson, Abraham Lincoln, and George Washington."[25] In Boston, as in New York, Madame Chiang was already speaking to the converted. They needed little persuading that China's cause was just.

Chicago was the next stop on Madame Chiang's itinerary. Madame Chiang and her entourage arrived in Chicago on March 19 and spent the next three days in the city. The highlight of her visit to Chicago was a rally at Chicago Stadium on March 22, which was attended by over 20,000 people. In her speech before this crowd, Madame Chiang once again stressed common goals and ideals, as the following excerpt from her text suggests:

> Some of your Presidents like Jackson and Lincoln came from the backwoods—products of the people. Some of the greatest emperors of China also came from peasant stock. Both our peoples have been fortunate enough not to decry poverty. Though our two countries have widely varied backgrounds, histories, cultures, and traditions, both recognize the inherent ability of the individual as an individual with powers to sway, to contribute to, and to help mold the destiny of a nation.[26]

Madame Chiang left Chicago on March 23; her next stop was to be San Francisco. When she arrived in Oakland on March 25, she was greeted by Governor Earl Warren and a crowd of dignitaries. From Oakland, Madame Chiang went immediately to San Francisco's Chinatown, the largest Chinese community in the Americas, where she was treated to a parade and pageant in her honor. Not to be outdone by the mayors of New York, Boston, or

Chicago, San Francisco's mayor, Angelo J. Rossi, praised her as a "gracious and lovely lady who ... through her magnetic and dynamic personality has truly won her way into the hearts of the American people."[27]

Responding to Mayor Rossi, Madame Chiang told an attentive crowd that she felt right at home in San Francisco. With "tears in her eyes and in a voice choked with emotion,"[28] she said,

> As I look out at San Francisco's beautiful Civic Center, my mind flies back to the modern Civic Center we were building in Shanghai before the war. It is in ruins now. But China, like the mythical phoenix, always arises anew from its ashes. And I pledge that the China which will arise again will be a great China and a friend of America.[29]

On March 25, Madame Chiang held a press conference at her hotel. These press conferences were at the heart of her American tour and afforded her the opportunity of reaching even larger audiences than her speeches. Although some reporters asked questions about political issues, many of the journalists were more interested in human interest stories, which Madame Chiang was only too happy to provide. Stories about families torn asunder, the heroism and sacrifice of thousands of nameless and faceless individuals, and the ability of a people to survive intolerable conditions may not have appeared on the front pages of such prominent papers as the *San Francisco Chronicle*, but they were carried in local papers and magazines which were read by even more people than the more prestigious dailies. The value of such coverage was well known to Hollington Tong and Madame Chiang.

The most important event of Madame Chiang's visit to San Francisco was her speech to more than 10,000 people at the Civic Auditorium on March 27. Governor Warren escorted Madame Chiang to the stage and introduced her. A reporter for the *Chronicle* noted that Madame Chiang had to wait for almost five minutes after Governor Warren's introduction for the applause to subside before beginning her address.[30] Never one to lose an opportunity, Madame Chiang reiterated some of the themes that had become the hallmark of her speeches before American audiences:

> Today we are both threatened by the lowering clouds of evil forces which, if they could, would deprive us not only of our beloved lands, but would uproot from our hearts the traditions we treasure and erase from our minds the principles we cherish.
> China has been able to withstand the vicissitudes of ages because her thinking people have learned the wisdom of storing up valuable truths which are to be had if one will take the time and trouble to cultivate their inner self. You, too, realize the importance of cultivation of the mind and spirit.[31]

By emphasizing the common values and goals of Chinese and Americans, Madame Chiang hoped to create a climate in America that would make it difficult for Roosevelt and other political leaders to ignore or postpone dealing with China's request for increased economic and military aid. Her message was getting through, as the following remarks made on the occasion of Madame's speech at the Civic Auditorium by San Francisco's mayor illustrate:

> Let us hope that Madame Chiang's visit to the United States has aroused the people of this country to the importance of cooperating with China.... The barbarous Japanese warlords must be stopped—and stopped now. Generalissimo Chiang K'ai-shek and our own heroic General MacArthur can do the job if we will give them the guns and the planes. Intelligent self-interest dictates that America must now overcome every obstacle and place in the hands of MacArthur and Generalissimo Chiang K'ai-shek those guns and planes with which to defeat the warmongers of barbaric Japan.[32]

Madame Chiang left San Francisco on March 30 bound for Los Angeles, the culmination and grand finale of her tour. It was a fitting place to end the crusade. Los Angeles' political leaders and Hollywood's movie moguls provided the backdrop, organization, and theatrical expertise necessary to turn her visit to the city into a spectacular rivaling *Gone with the Wind*.

Madame Chiang's visit to Los Angeles was a series of media events. Upon arrival at Union Station, Madame Chiang was greeted by the mayor and David O. Selznick, co-chairman of the welcoming committee. Madame Chiang was driven to City Hall along a route jammed with spectators enjoying the event and the balmy weather. As had become almost *de rigueur*, Madame Chiang was given the keys to the city and delivered a variant of her by now well-rehearsed response to such hospitality.

The day after her arrival in Los Angeles, Madame Chiang was the guest of honor at a reception sponsored by the movie industry and attended by more than two hundred stars and moguls, including Charlie Chaplin, Barbara Stanwyck, Joan Bennett, Claudette Colbert, Fred Astaire, Ginger Rogers, Louis B. Mayer, Harry Warner, Howard Hughes, Harry Cohn, and Samuel Goldwyn. She was introduced to this group of luminaries by Tyrone Power, who was dressed for the occasion in his marine uniform. James Cagney and Greer Garson were among the featured speakers at the reception.[33]

In between her meetings with Hollywood celebrities, Madame Chiang also visited the Chinese community in Los Angeles. Such visits to Chinatowns had also been arranged in the other cities on her itinerary. Although these visits attracted less attention than other events on her schedule, they served to cement the ties between the Chinese-American communities and the Kuomintang regime. Considering that Chinese-Americans remitted considerable amounts of money to China, it was important that they not be overlooked—nor were they. Madame Chiang received an enthusiastic reception in every Chinese community she visited.

However colorful and newsworthy Hollywood's reception for China's first lady proved to be, the main event of her stay in Los Angeles was the giant rally at Hollywood Bowl which took place on April 4, 1943. This was the largest such event of her tour with over 30,000 people jamming the Bowl. The start of the rally was heralded by trumpet blasts after which Spencer Tracy, acting as master of ceremonies, opened the gala. Madame Chiang was then escorted to the rostrum by nineteen of Hollywood's best known actresses led by Mary Pickford, Marlene Dietrich, and Ingrid Bergman.[34]

Following this parade of stars, units from the army, navy, and marine corps marched around the Bowl while military bands played the anthems of the U. S. armed forces and the Chinese army marching song. After this, a costumed pageant, narrated by Walter Huston, outlined the history of China with over 500 Chinese-Americans in the cast. When this was over, Madame Chiang walked to the microphones amidst "a tremendous round of applause."[35]

Madame Chiang's speech was impassioned. First, she reminded the audience that China had fought against the Japanese for seven years and at a great cost. Next, she reminded the audience that the Chinese had resisted against great odds, receiving little outside help, but struggling on in pursuit of a noble cause:

> And what did China have? We had no navy to speak of, only an embryo air force and an infantry equipped mainly with rifles, machine guns, and outmoded artillery pieces. But we had manpower, which willingly volunteered its flesh and blood. We had fighting spirit, for we knew we were struggling for justice and righteousness.[36]

Even in China's darkest hour, Madame Chiang suggested to her audience, the Chinese people did not despair because they had faith that America and the other democratic powers would realize that China was fighting for more than her own survival.[37] She then went on to praise President Roosevelt for taking "decisive measures to enable America to become the Arsenal of the Democracies."[38] Although she made no explicit appeal for increased American aid, Madame Chiang left no doubt that such aid would be most welcome.

Madame Chiang closed her address with a restatement of China's war aims and a vision of a happier future:

> We take pride in the fact that, amid all the stern and never ending demands of war, we are preparing for a just and permanent peace and for the strenuous world-building that lies before us.... We shall not be cozened of an equitable peace. We shall not permit aggression to raise its satanic head and threaten men's greatest heritage: life, liberty, and the pursuit of happiness for all peoples.[39]

The Hollywood Bowl rally marked the end of Madame Chiang's formal speaking tour of the United States, a tour designed to rally American public opinion and influence the policy of the Roosevelt administration. She spent another two months in the United States during which time she engaged in more private diplomacy. She left the United States at the end of June 1943.

Before returning to China, Madame Chiang had the opportunity to meet with President Roosevelt for a series of discussions. Although Roosevelt was noncommittal on the question of increased American aid for China and made no promise to reconsider U.S. policy in the CBI, he did suggest that such matters could best be taken up at a meeting with the generalissimo which might be arranged in the autumn.[40] Roosevelt reiterated this idea in a cable sent to Chiang on June 30, 1943, in which he summarized his meetings with Madame Chiang:

> I have concluded a series of very satisfactory talks with Madame Chiang Kai-shek, which she will tell you about. I have told her of my anxiety to meet you sometime this fall. I think it is very important that we get together. If you agree with this, I suggest some place midway between our two capitals. I would appreciate very much hearing from you relative to this proposal.[41]

Roosevelt did not have to wait long for a response to his invitation. On July 9, Chiang sent the president a cable accepting his suggestion for a summit. "For many years," Chiang told Roosevelt, "I have been wishing that we could discuss together in person various problems of mutual interest."[42] The date and place of such a meeting could be worked out by T.V. Soong and the president's men. Chiang's only request was for "at least a fortnight's" notice.[43]

Chiang had good reason to hope for an early meeting with Roosevelt. Despite the success of Madame Chiang's tour from a public relations perspective, her mission was far from an unqualified success because she received few specific promises of increased American aid and no concrete assurances that the Roosevelt administration was willing to rethink its wartime strategy. The American people may have been charmed and influenced by Madame Chiang, but important advisors of the president remained quite skeptical of her motives and the message she had delivered to her listeners.

While Madame Chiang had painted a vivid portrait of the heroic resistance of the Kuomintang regime in every speech she delivered during her American tour, the realities of the situation in China as portrayed by American diplomats and intelligence operatives in China were quite at odds with the situation described by Madame Chiang. They described a government plagued by factionalism, unwilling to wage a real war against the Japanese, husbanding its resources for use against the Chinese communists, and waiting for the United States to win the war for them.[44] Such negative comments were also beginning to appear in dispatches filed by American journalists in China.[45]

Although Madame Chiang managed to rally the American people to her cause, she was less successful in converting people like Morgenthau and Stimson who were privy to the increasingly bad news coming from the military and political fronts in China. She had not anticipated that so many of Roosevelt's intimates would be so hesitant to support her husband's government and returned to China quite disappointed with the reception she had received from the Roosevelt administration.

Reporting to Secretary of State Hull from Chungking on the blue mood of Madame Chiang and her entourage, George Atcheson, assistant secretary of state for Far Eastern affairs, suggested that Madame Chiang and Tong may have been misled by Wendell Willkie as to what to expect might be gained from a trip to the United States.[46] Because she did not get "all she wanted and Willkie had promised," Madame Chiang was alleged to be in something of an anti–American humor.[47] Still, Madame Chiang's tour had brought pressure to bear on the Roosevelt administration to increase aid to China.

Hundreds of thousands of people had attended the rallies, banquets, parades, pageants, and press conferences at which Madame Chiang had pleaded China's cause. Millions more listened to her speeches on the radio and followed her activities through accounts in their local papers. She received more attention in the broadcast and print media than any other wartime leader of an allied nation. Now it remained for her brother, T.V. Soong, to lobby behind the scenes to effect a change in American policies and arrange for a summit between Chiang and Roosevelt.

3

T. V. Soong's Private Diplomacy

Shortly before the Japanese attack on Pearl Harbor, T.V. Soong was elevated to the office of foreign minister by his brother-in-law, Chiang Kai-shek, and sent to the United States, where he remained for much of the duration of the war except for an occasional return trip to Chungking. The permanent presence of China's foreign minister in Washington was recognition of the fact that China's only real ally in the war against Japan was the United States, which was also China's only source of external economic and military assistance. While the Chinese government maintained diplomatic relations with other allied nations, the relationship with the United States was special, a diplomatic and military umbilical cord.

T.V. Soong was well suited for his new role as Chiang Kai-shek's personal emissary to the Roosevelt administration. His family ties with Chiang insured Soong's access to the inner circles of the Kuomintang. His connections in the United States, where he had been educated and sometimes represented the Bank of China, ensured his access to Roosevelt's aides and congressional leaders. His command of the English language and understanding of the American political process made him an effective public spokesman and enabled him to shape American public opinion.

Whereas his sister, Madame Chiang Kai-shek, was a very public representative of the Chinese government, T.V. Soong most often operated privately, negotiating with administration and congressional leaders behind the cameras and microphones and reporting on his conversations directly to Chiang Kai-shek. The day-to-day operations of the Foreign Ministry were left to underlings in Chungking. Although they reported on all matters to Soong, his chief mission was to lobby the United States government.

The rhythm of Soong's activities in the United States was established within the first few months of his tenure in Washington. Almost immediately after his arrival in September 1941, Soong initiated relationships with key members of the Roosevelt administration, including Secretary of War Stimson, Secretary of State Hull, and Secretary of the Treasury Morgenthau. He also penetrated the White House inner circle through his contacts with Harry

Hopkins and other presidential assistants. For the next three years hardly a week went by without his meeting with one or more of these individuals, except for those periods when he was abroad or back in Chungking for a brief visit.

Members of Roosevelt's Cabinet were not necessarily fond of T.V. Soong, nor appreciative of his methods of operation, but they allowed him access to them because they understood the president's interest in China and the importance he placed on Chinese participation in the war against Japan. Since Roosevelt allowed Soong relatively free access to his office, they could not easily deny him entry into theirs. On the other hand, men like Stimson and Morgenthau resented his closeness to Roosevelt and the president's tendency to humor Soong by making obscure and veiled promises of assistance while leaving it to them to implement these promises or, as was more often the case, explain why the president's promises could not be realized.

From the moment he arrived in Washington until the end of the war, Soong was primarily a supplicant for arms and economic aid, but he was also involved in obtaining a "rightful" place for China in allied diplomatic and military councils. Frequently, these aims were intertwined, with Soong equating increased aid as a tangible symbol of Allied recognition of China as a full partner in the war against the Axis powers and using the reception he received from administration and congressional leaders as a barometer of the good intentions of the United States.

Soong's style was apparent in his initial contacts with the Roosevelt administration in November and December 1941. In a diary entry dated November 6, 1941, Secretary of War Stimson describes one of his first meetings with Soong. At the start of the session, Soong discussed a meeting he had with the president on the previous day to discuss China's desperate need for arms. Soong described Roosevelt's reaction as very sympathetic, paraphrasing the president's remarks as follows:

> It is a pathetic situation. I want so much to give these poor men who have been fighting for four years everything we can and I feel that in this case it is of more strategic value than stuff we are pouring into Russia will ever be by the time we get it there.[1]

Having recounted the president's reaction, Soong asked Stimson what the War Department was prepared to do to help the Chinese. Stimson's answer could hardly have been satisfactory. He had to tell Soong that the re-arming of China was impossible for the moment because of the crisis in the Philippines, but promised to "see what we could scrape up."[2]

Soong met again with Stimson on December 2, 13, 30, and 31, 1941. At these sessions, an additional theme was added to Soong's agenda: the matter of Chinese representation on Allied war councils. Having been told by Stimson and other administration leaders that more military aid would not be

President Roosevelt, Postmaster-General Frank Walker, and Chinese Foreign Minister T. V. Soong celebrating the issuance of China War Relief stamps in the Oval Office at the White House, July 8, 1942. Courtesy of the Franklin D. Roosevelt Library and Museum, Hyde Park, New York.

immediately forthcoming, Soong pressed the secretary of war to act on a more easily realized objective of the Chinese government, greater consultation between Washington, London, and Chungking. At the same time, Soong gave Stimson a lesson on the meaning of "saving face" in Chinese diplomatic protocol, suggesting that Chiang was "getting a little peeved by thinking he was being left out in the cold."[3]

One way of assuring Chiang that his opinion and counsel were wanted and ensuring against his "loss of face" was to appoint an American military representative of high stature and with political clout in Washington to Chungking. For Chiang, this appointment would be a litmus test of the good intentions of the United States. That being the case, Soong spent much of his time and energy lobbying for a satisfactory appointment. Although administration leaders were aware of the symbolic importance of this appointment, the ultimate selection of General Joseph Stilwell as commander of American forces in China and chief military representative of the president in Chungking proved to be a poor one from the point of view of the Chinese government.

As the effort was made to select an appropriate military liaison officer to serve in Chungking, T.V. Soong was very much a part of the process and conferred routinely with appropriate officials in the War Department. Throughout January and February 1942, Soong met regularly with Stimson and served as a conduit between the War Department, President Roosevelt, and Generalissimo Chiang. When Stilwell's name was brought up as a possible representative, after a number other candidates were discussed but dismissed, Soong "seemed to be thoroughly satisfied with the choice" and was reported to have advised Secretary Stimson that he would urge Chiang to signal his approval of the Stilwell appointment.[4] This assessment exaggerated Soong's enthusiasm for the Stilwell appointment and is an example of how Chinese and American officials often misread each other.

Within weeks after his conversations with Soong, it became clear to Stimson that Soong felt that Stilwell was less than an ideal choice to serve as Roosevelt's military representative in Chungking. He did not learn this from Soong himself but, rather, from comments that Soong made to others about Stilwell's lack of tact and Chiang's feeling he could not work well with Stilwell. When these comments were relayed to Stimson, he was livid. In a conversation with Secretary of the Treasury Morgenthau, he warned him to be wary of Soong:

> Well, you can't trust T.V. Soong. In my experience of Orientals, if you say something to them as a proposal, they will always say "yes," but they will get the word to you in some roundabout way that they really meant "no" which often makes you think that they have double-crossed you.[5]

Stimson was correct when he told Morgenthau that Chinese diplomats preferred not to say no in response to initial proposals. What he did not understand was that they said no in other ways. Had the Secretary of War listened more carefully to the reservations Soong expressed about Stilwell in their January and February meetings, rather than trying to impress Soong with the confidence that General Marshall and others in the War Department had in Stilwell, a good many future problems might have been avoided.[6]

With the selection of Stilwell a *fait accompli*, Soong turned his attention to other matters in the spring and summer of 1942. Among the most important of these, albeit least studied, was Soong's attempt to assess and evaluate China's propaganda efforts. Part of Soong's job involved monitoring the American media and the manner in which China's cause was being presented to the American public. Soong believed that efforts to obtain additional aid from the United States and change the strategic thinking of the War Department depended upon effective Chinese propaganda. A lack of clarity and focus in the dissemination of Chinese propaganda could sabotage their efforts to influence American public opinion.

In retrospect, it seems clear that Soong overestimated the extent to which American policy in China could be influenced by Chinese propaganda efforts.

While Roosevelt sometimes seemed more concerned about image than substance, American policy in China was dictated by self-interest not Chinese pressure. Still, Soong was not entirely wrong in thinking that an improvement of Chinese propaganda might yield some dividends.

On June 26, 1942, after weeks of consultation with his aides in Washington and Chungking, T.V. Soong convened a meeting in Washington to discuss the Chinese propaganda effort. Minutes of the meeting were kept by Soong's aide, Victor Hu.[7] These minutes reveal that Soong was quite concerned about the shortcomings of China's propaganda machinery. Hu suggests that Soong identified at least six deficiencies in China's propaganda programs:

1. Lack of defined objectives
2. Lack of timely information
3. Lack of selectivity in releasing information
4. Lack of knowledge of American sensitivities
5. Lack of balance/tendency to sensationalize
6. Lack of truth/presentation of good news only[8]

According to Hu, Soong placed much of the blame for the shortcomings of Chinese propaganda in the United States on those who administered the Publicity Service in Chungking and advised them that unless certain changes were made, American reaction to the claims of the Chinese government would become increasingly skeptical and negative.[9] Soong expressed concern that there was a growing feeling among Americans that the Chinese were becoming "arrogant and uncooperative."[10] He was particularly concerned about the increased criticism of China being expressed by American journalists stationed in Chungking. While Soong believed that much of this criticism was "unfair," he suggested there was "a kernel of truth to it" and warned of the consequences of failing to close the gap between the statements of the Chinese government and the reports filed by American correspondents in China.[11]

Soong ordered his aide, Victor Hu, to prepare a memorandum to advise the Publicity Service as to how to improve Chinese propaganda efforts. Two primary goals were defined:

(1) Our goal being to obtain as much American assistance as possible, we must systematically present our military situation in such a light as to convince the American government and the American people that such assistance is of the utmost importance not only to China but also to the United States. Statements on one day that the military situation is all right and on the next that it is desperate can only confuse the American public.
(2) Our goal being to obtain the confidence and goodwill of the American people, we must present our difficulties in a way which will stimulate the interest and approval of the Americans so as to induce them to cooperate with us wherever their assistance may be desirable.[12]

Having defined the goals of Chinese propaganda efforts, Hu and Soong then discussed the methodology of achieving these goals. They advised underlings in the Publicity Bureau and Foreign Ministry in Chungking that although a reservoir of good will toward China existed in the United States, it could not be taken for granted. The American public would have to be cultivated. Chinese propagandists would have to be more sensitive to changing trends:

> In the United States, perhaps more than in any other country, public opinion, though friendly, may at different times have a different reaction to the same presentation of the facts.... We must be watchful of such fluctuations in American public opinion and adjust the technique of our propaganda to them.[13]

To more accurately monitor American public opinion and cultivate American sympathy, Soong argued in favor of establishing a central propaganda apparatus in Chungking that would be responsible to only two individuals, Chiang Kai-shek and himself.[14] Such an umbrella agency would be advised by Chinese and American journalists familiar with the political landscape in the United States. All Chinese governmental agencies would use this agency as a propaganda clearinghouse.

The kind of propaganda ministry Soong envisaged would have six primary functions:

1. To collect the news
2. To select the news to be released
3. To release the news
4. To provide materials for Chinese diplomats
5. To monitor the state of world opinion
6. To evaluate the efficacy of propaganda[15]

Unfortunately for Soong, his proposal had many opponents in Chungking and Chiang Kai-shek refused to act upon it.[16] The generalissimo's rule was based on balancing competing interests within the Kuomintang. When Ch'en Li-fu, Ch'en Kuo-fu, and other powerful figures within the party balked at making Soong into a *de facto* propaganda czar, Chiang decided not to implement Soong's proposal.

In September 1942, Soong was called to Chungking to consult with Chiang. He returned to Chungking just as his sister, Madame Chiang, was preparing to leave for the United States. Soong remained in China until the beginning of February 1943. His activities in Chungking seem to have been limited to briefing Chiang and attending to personal business. According to Chou En-lai, the communist representative to Chiang's government, Soong was "cut out" of economic matters and his function as foreign minister was "reportorial" not policy making.[17] Soong seems to have understood these limitations and spent most of his time in Chungking on Bank of China matters.

During the course of Soong's winter sojourn in Chungking, Churchill and Roosevelt met at Casablanca.[18] News of this summit meeting met with a mixed reaction in the Chinese capital. In public statements, Chinese leaders praised the conference. Privately, they fumed that Generalissimo Chiang was not invited to participate or send a representative to the conference.[19] Although the generalissimo could not have attended the conference because of the situation in China, Soong or some other subordinate could have been sent in the generalissimo's place.

Failure to consult the Chinese prior to convening the Casablanca Conference precipitated a mini-crisis in Sino-American relations. Chinese reaction was angry and immediate. Yee Ming, head of the Chinese News Service, an arm of the Publicity Bureau, told Chinese and American journalists in Chungking that the Casablanca Conference was "just another proof that it [the war] is an Anglo-American war with the idea of Anglo-American psychology and western superiority predominating."[20] Privately, Yee Ming had even harsher things to say, accusing Roosevelt of being "an opportunist" without a single advisor who "understands the Chinese."[21]

Yee Ming's inflammatory rhetoric was not unique. Others in Chungking joined in his protest. Soong was summoned to the generalissimo's villa and told to prepare to return to the United States where he was to personally present the government's concern about lack of satisfactory consultation to Roosevelt and his aides.[22] Soong left China early in February 1943 and was back at his desk in Washington by the end of the month.

Soong and his sister, Madame Chiang, were now both actively walking and working the corridors of power in Washington. While Madame Chiang was the more visible of the pair, her brother was resuming his weekly chats with administrative and congressional leaders. Frequently they lobbied the same individuals. Thus, on February 23, Madame Chiang met with Stimson. Four days later, Soong met with the secretary of war. Madame Chiang's talk with Stimson was described by the secretary as amiable and non-specific.[23] They talked of China and America, not about supplies or diplomacy. Soong's conversation with Stimson on February 27 was more specific and included detailed exchanges about Stilwell's problems in Chungking, the airlift over "the hump," and the matter of Chinese participation in Allied war councils.[24]

It was sometimes difficult for members of the administration to understand the sensitivity of the Chinese to matters of etiquette and face. Aware that something was amiss, Roosevelt sought the advice of Pearl Buck who submitted a lengthy memorandum on China and the Chinese leadership to the president in March 1943. In her memo, Mrs. Buck tried to explain the seeming over-reaction of Chinese officials to diplomatic slights of any kind by stressing the inexperience of Chiang and the Soongs:

> They are new to power and insecure and they feel compelled to hedge themselves about with a good deal of the trappings of royalty merely because they don't how much or how little their power really is. The King and Queen of England can

come and go with far more freedom and democratic behavior than the Soongs in China.[25]

Buck advised Roosevelt that one way of assuring the Chinese of his concern and support would be to visit China. If this was not possible, he might think of meeting with Chiang.[26]

As Soong made his rounds, he became concerned that the Chinese were being left out of Allied war councils because of British preferences and a growing perception among American officials that the Chinese were not cooperating with General Stilwell. He reported this to Generalissimo Chiang Kai-shek. In a lengthy cable sent to Chungking on March 21, 1943, Soong told Chiang that Churchill "characteristically" omitted China when speaking about the Allies. "This is not a mere slip," Soong advised the generalissimo, but a part of a British propaganda position that "China is not willing to fight or able to fight."[27] Soong urged Chiang to combat this view by cooperating with Stilwell as he planned for an offensive in Burma and forcing the British to commit to the campaign in Burma as well.[28]

Soong also raised the issue of British views on China with Roosevelt early in May just prior to the arrival of Churchill in the United States on the eve of the Washington Conference. The president admitted to Soong that the British were "lukewarm" about the upcoming offensive in Burma and not yet prepared to commit their forces to this campaign.[29] Soong then asked Roosevelt how the British could justify their criticism of China's lack of fighting spirit when they were not willing to make a stand. The president answered sympathetically. "I must talk to the British about the Burma operation," he said, "they do not appear to be seriously preparing for it."[30] Roosevelt also arranged for Soong to take the matter up with Churchill soon after he arrived in Washington.

As Soong understood only too well, the British were not much interested in waging war in the CBI. They were far more concerned with the war in Europe. With Allied forces having just successfully wrapped up their operations in North Africa and preparing to launch an invasion of Italy, diverting resources to China was very low on Churchill's agenda. Furthermore, the British did not wish to strengthen the position of Chiang's government because this might cause problems in the post-war era when Chinese demands for the end of European economic colonialism were sure to clash with British efforts to maintain the vestiges of their empire, including Hong Kong and the treaty ports along the south China coast.

Soong met Prime Minister Churchill at the White House on May 13, 1943. Harry Hopkins, Soong's chief ally in the White House, joined Soong and Churchill soon after their meeting started. According to Soong's minutes of the May 13 meeting, Churchill acknowledged that Roosevelt had raised the question of China and the proposed campaign in Burma at a luncheon just prior to their meeting.³¹ Having said this, Churchill went on to argue that the logistical problems of supplying American, British, and Chinese forces in Southeast Asia were such that the campaign might have to be postponed.³² "Am I to understand from what you said," Soong asked Churchill, "that you propose to abandon this plan which you and the President promised to implement at Casablanca?"³³ Churchill answered, "Nothing had been decided yet" and proposed that Soong should be invited to the next meeting of the Pacific War Council at which time the matter might be resolved.³⁴ At this point, the meeting was adjourned.

Upon returning to his office from the meeting with Churchill and Hopkins, Soong dictated a note to Hopkins expressing his frustration with Churchill. He reminded Hopkins that the Casablanca Conference had been convened without consultation with China and without the presence of a Chinese representative. This should not be allowed to happen again. "When the war against Japan is discussed in the future," Soong suggested to Hopkins, "I trust I may be called in to participate so that the Generalissimo may be continuously consulted."³⁵ Although Soong did not mention the Washington Conference directly, his message could hardly have been lost on Hopkins.

Reporting back to Chiang Kai-shek on his meeting with Churchill, Soong was even more blunt than he had been with Hopkins:

> Churchill's remarks yesterday and the attitude he adopts to his obligations undermines all confidence in the United Nations conception and makes future agreements impossible.³⁶

Chiang responded by cabling the State Department and President Roosevelt that to avoid the misunderstandings that resulted from the absence of a Chinese presence at the Casablanca Conference, Soong and Madame Chiang should serve as China's representatives when matters of concern to China were being discussed in Allied war councils.³⁷

T.V. Soong was an active participant in the discussions at the Washington Conference pertinent to China. He focused his attention and energy on overcoming British antipathy to the proposed Burma campaign and increased aid to China by advancing the position of his government and questioning the motives behind the reluctance of the British to honor the promises made at Casablanca. Soong did not hesitate to confront Churchill in stating China's case. Indeed, he seemed to enjoy doing so. Thus, at a meeting of the Pacific War Council on May 20, Soong suggested that the desperate situation his government faced was, in large measure, the result of the failure of British commanders to adequately prepare a defense of Burma.³⁸ Supporting the effort to recover the Burma road was the "least" that the British government could do to reestablish its credibility in the eyes of the Chinese.³⁹

Churchill did not accept Soong's arguments, but he found himself caught in the middle of Chiang's efforts to extract more aid from his American allies and Roosevelt's efforts to demonstrate good faith and placate the generalissimo. The prime minister did not share the view of the president that the Chinese might give up the war effort and make a separate peace with Japan, but he could not bring the president to see the fallacy of this position. What Churchill did come to understand was just how effective Chinese propaganda had been in making the possible collapse of China a political liability no American president could afford.

The ghost of Casablanca haunted the Washington Conference. This worked to the advantage of Soong who was able to extract concrete promises from Roosevelt and Churchill of more assistance.[40] In this effort, Soong was aided and abetted by General Claire Chennault, who had been called back to Washington by President Roosevelt along with General Joseph Stilwell. Like Soong, Chennault was another personal emissary of Chiang Kai-shek, albeit one who wore an American uniform.[41] Chennault's efforts to sell the president on an aerial offensive in China against the wishes of his superior, General Stilwell, bore the approval of Generalissimo Chiang. By lending support to Chennault, Roosevelt would be indicating his support of Chiang, a fact that was not lost on the president after his discussions with Soong and Chennault.

From the Chinese point of view, the Washington Conference was a reasonable success. Roosevelt had been persuaded to support General Chennault against General Stilwell and Churchill had been reluctantly forced to reiterate British support for the campaign to recapture Burma and reopen the Burma Road. From Soong's point of view, the conference had also been fruitful. He sat at the side of Churchill and Roosevelt and would hopefully do so in the future when the Allied leaders met to discuss the war in Asia. His stock in the Kuomintang leadership was on the rise.

With the Washington Conference out of the way, Soong prepared for the next meeting of the Pacific War Council, which was to be held in London in August, and a possible summit between Roosevelt, Churchill, and Stalin, which Chinese intelligence sources believed would take place soon after the August meetings in London. Prior to departing for England, Soong sought out Roosevelt's counsel and with the help of Soong's friend Harry Hopkins, such a meeting was arranged for July 16, 1943.

According to Soong's recollection of this meeting, President Roosevelt briefed him on how to deal with the prime minister. Roosevelt told Soong that Churchill "thinks as one huge indigestible mass" and often tried to overwhelm his friends and adversaries by the energy and force of his rhetoric.[42] He advised Soong:

> You must be cocky in your talk with Churchill; you must talk with the greatest confidence in the Chinese people and the future of China. The British must be shocked into taking notice of China. I want to put China into the sun even before she has the economic power.[43]

Roosevelt also suggested to Soong that British reluctance to recognize China as an equal partner in the war against the Axis nations was, in some measure, a response to the anti-imperialist stance of Generalissimo Chiang and the Kuomintang.[44] The British were sensitive to the problems of nationalism and hostile to those who called for an end to colonial domination in the post-war era. Churchill, the president told Soong, was particularly sensitive about Chinese support of the independence movement in India, which he considered an unnecessary interference in British affairs. He urged Soong to avoid talking about the future status of the Empire in his talks with the British.[45]

Armed with the insights gained from his meeting with Roosevelt, Soong departed for London shortly after their meeting on July 16. He arrived in London at the end of the month, a few days before the Pacific War Council was to convene on August 4. He spent these few days meeting with Wellington Koo, China's ambassador in London, and officials at the Foreign Office, including Foreign Minister Anthony Eden. His discussions with Koo and Eden led Soong to conclude that the British were still unenthusiastic about assisting China because they seemed to feel that the war against Japan could be won outside of China and without China's help.[46] His job would be to persuade Churchill that this was not the case.

The meeting of the Pacific War Council, Churchill presiding, was called to order at 3:00 P.M. on August 4. T.V. Soong was the first speaker on the agenda. In his opening remarks, Soong stated that Chinese military forces were ready for the Burma campaign and that these troops, trained in India under Stilwell's tutelage, were under the command of Chiang's "best general," Ch'en Cheng. All that remained before commencing the campaign in Burma was to secure a promise from "His Majesty's Government" that the British would commit the naval forces necessary for their part of the operation.[47]

Churchill spoke next, delivering a discourse on the progress of the war in Europe and Africa and then addressing matters in the CBI theater. The question in the CBI was "how to overwhelm Japan." There were several alternatives, including seeking the help of the Soviet Union, bombing Japan from bases in China, launching a westward attack on Japan from the Aleutian Islands, and increasing air power in China to enable the Chinese army to initiate a counteroffensive.[48] Mention of recapture of Burma was noticeably missing from Churchill's list.

Soong was surprised that Churchill had omitted mention of Burma and asked the prime minister whether this indicated that he meant to bow out of such an operation.[49] Churchill responded by suggesting to Soong that, according to British intelligence, it would take at least fifteen months to put the Burma Road back into operation after recapturing northern Burma from the Japanese. "It would be a better strategy," he told Soong, "to attack the enemy not where he was strong but where he was weak."⁵⁰ This eliminated virtually any operation in Burma.

No resolution of Anglo-Chinese differences resulted from the meeting of the Pacific War Council and none seemed likely until the next Allied summit meeting scheduled to take place in Quebec at the end of August. That being the case, Soong cut his visit to England short so that he could make a quick visit to Chungking to brief Chiang Kai-shek before returning to North America for the conference.

The Chinese had not been formally invited to participate in the upcoming Quebec Conference and this angered the Chinese government. Speaking for himself and Generalissimo Chiang, Soong sent an angry memorandum to Secretary of State Hull:

> The Chinese Government can no longer hide from its people ... and from the army the fact that China is not a party to either the consultations or the decisions for the conduct of Allied war operations and Allied peace plans.⁵¹

Soong reminded Hull that the Chinese had made repeated inquiries about obtaining permanent places on inter–Allied agencies, but to little or no avail. Even when the Chinese government was called upon to present China's position, "we give testimony like witnesses," Soong told Hull, "and don't have much participation in the final decisions."⁵²

"Despite noble words and rhetoric to the contrary," the concept of the Big Four was not being lived up to, according to Soong, causing Chiang and the Chinese government to lose face.⁵³ And this was not the only problem stemming from the lack of proper consultation. Given the fact that Generalissimo Chiang was the Supreme Commander of allied forces in China, failure to consult his government on matters of vital interest to China had resulted in unnecessary misunderstandings, which weakened his position and strained relations with the United States. Such problems could be remedied by expanding existing joint agencies to include Chinese representatives and creating an inter–Allied machinery with Chinese participation to formulate and coordinate policy in the CBI.⁵⁴

Soong returned to the United States on the eve of the Quebec Conference, but was not invited to participate in the conference. Two days after the other Allies opened their meeting in Quebec on August 17, 1943, Soong met with Stanley Hornbeck, assistant secretary of state for Far Eastern affairs, and vented his anger over being left out of the Quebec meeting, a fact Soong attributed to the British.⁵⁵ Hornbeck, who was not a confidant of Soong and had once described the foreign minister as the "lone ranger" of Chinese diplomacy, found himself in sympathy with Soong and was particularly taken by Soong's distinction between the way in which Roosevelt and Churchill conducted business.⁵⁶ Roosevelt, according to Soong, began his discussions with consideration of general principles and then moved on to discuss concrete possibilities. Churchill, on the other hand, was "matter-of-fact, unemotional, and constantly had in mind the question of *quid pro quo*."[57] He lacked the president's vision and was no friend of China.[58]

Soong did not get to meet with Roosevelt until after the Quebec Conference. When they did meet on August 30, the president suggested to Soong that his absence from the conference was the result of Churchill's insistence that China not be treated on the same basis as the United States, Great Britain, and the Soviet Union because "China had no stable government."[59] Roosevelt assured Soong that he rejected this idea:

> I said to him [Churchill]—Chiang may die—just as you or me—and still there will be a China. Split she may into north and south, and still it will be China. Split into Communist and Kuomintang, China will still be China.... You say yourself, I told him, China will be industrialized in 25 years; you fear communism in Europe. China will be the bulwark against communism in Asia. Well—Churchill found nothing to say to all that.[60]

Roosevelt's soothing balm and kind words did not assuage Soong's dismay. Meeting with Hopkins on September 5, the foreign minister made it clear that the Chinese demanded to be included in allied war councils:

> We do not want to discuss details of operations in other theaters, but we *insist* on fullest participation in every stage of deliberation and decision as regards our own and adjacent theaters.[61]

Hopkins agreed that China should be represented on the Combined Chiefs of Staff and the Munitions Board and expressed sympathy with Soong's statement that China could not become a great power "by default."[62]

Soong and Hopkins met again on September 15. Although the primary topic of their conversation was the Stilwell debacle, they also talked about China's place among the anti–Axis Allies. Once again Soong accused the Allies, including Roosevelt, of taking China for granted and suggested, "It was for the Roosevelt administration to invite us in."[63] Hopkins agreed that good relations with China were a cardinal principle of American foreign policy, but could make no promises to Soong except to suggest that a meeting between Chiang and Roosevelt was imminent and that Soong would be a critical figure at such a conference. "You must be there," Hopkins told Soong, when the president and the generalissimo meet.[64] "Surely I would be there with the generalissimo," Soong responded, "when he meets F.D.R."[65]

Before a meeting between Generalissimo Chiang and President Roosevelt was finalized, Hopkins and Soong agreed that an agenda which would lead to good results must be set. Hopkins asked Soong for his suggestions as to who in the State Department would be a good person to prepare the agenda. Soong suggested Dean Acheson, but Hopkins suggested that Acheson knew "little about China."[66] A few other names were discussed but no one was settled upon. The conversation then turned to the venue for the meeting.

Once again, no specific place was agreed upon. What was agreed upon was the fact, as Hopkins put it, that a meeting between Chiang and Roosevelt would be good for Sino-American relations and very popular in the United States.[67]

Soong met Roosevelt again September 16. As had been the case in his chat with Hopkins the day before, Roosevelt and Soong spent most of their time talking about Chiang's desire to have Stilwell replaced by a more acceptable representative. The president made no promises to remove Stilwell, but did tell Soong that he was asking Admiral Lord Mountbatten, who had been appointed commander-in-chief of allied forces in Southeast Asia at the Quebec Conference, to report to him on the "Stilwell situation" when he visited China in October.[68] FDR also hinted that this matter might be resolved at his meeting with Chiang, assuming the details of such a meeting could be worked out.[69]

On September 22, Soong met with Cordell Hull and Stanley Hornbeck to inform them of his chat with the president. Early on in the conversation, Soong told Hull and Hornbeck that he was going to accompany Mountbatten to Chungking where he hoped to brief Chiang on the events that had transpired since Soong was last in the Chinese capital and prepare him for a possible meeting with Roosevelt.[70]

Soong had a similar conversation with Henry Stimson on September 30. According to Soong's recollection of this meeting, he told Secretary Stimson that he placed great hope in the results that might be forthcoming from a Chiang-Roosevelt summit.[71] Stimson's diary entry for that day says nothing about the summit and notes only that Soong was going to Chungking to "consult" with Generalissimo Chiang.[72] Stimson did observe, however, that Soong was in a particularly introspective and quiet mood:

> He was as mild as milk.... He told me he was always working for us and how, whatever ways we scrapped, the Chinese never lost their confidence in me and so on and so on.[73]

Soong left the United States at the beginning of October. Soon after his return to Chungking, he became embroiled in a row with the generalissimo, which resulted in his being temporarily banished from Chiang's inner circle. Some rumor-mongers in Chungking suggested the falling out between Chiang and Soong was over a family matter. According to this view, Chiang resented Soong's independence and his propensity to make decisions without consulting Chungking. Shortly after Soong's return to China, it was alleged that the generalissimo gave him a particularly venomous lecture about his insubordination. Rather than endure such humiliation, as he had done in the past, Soong snapped and criticized Chiang in equally venomous tone, thus leading to his being banished from the generalissimo's inner circle.[74]

Others suggest that the differences between Chiang and Soong were policy-oriented. According to this view, the mood in Chungking was becoming increasingly conservative and anti–American and anti–British. As a member of the liberal wing of the Kuomintang leadership, Soong was seen as too sympathetic to the other Allies. With the conservative faction of the Kuomintang joined by Madame Chiang and H.H. Kung urging Chiang to replace Soong as his chief foreign policy advisor and to take a harder line with Churchill and Roosevelt, Soong found himself in a minority of two in the inner councils of the family with Madame Sun Yat-sen as his only ally.[75] Accordingly, Soong temporarily retreated to the seclusion of his villa, as he had done on other occasions in the past, to wait out the generalissimo's fury and the inevitable call back into Chiang's good graces.

Ironically, the man best able to advise Generalissimo Chiang at Cairo was not to be invited to accompany him to the conference. Not only was Soong forced to remain in Chungking while the generalissimo went off to Cairo, he was not even involved in the planning of the conference agenda or the preparation of Chiang for the summit. Although he was later "rehabilitated," Soong's absence from Cairo would have a significant effect on the outcome of the conference.

4

Chiang and Roosevelt Plan a Summit

By the time T.V. Soong returned to Chungking in October, plans for a meeting between Chiang Kai-shek and Roosevelt were well under way. The purpose of such a meeting, from the American point of view, was to bolster Chinese morale and soothe the ego of Generalissimo Chiang Kai-shek. Even if the meeting resulted in nothing important, "it would be even better than all the lend-lease materials the United States could get into China," as one State Department China hand advised the president.[1] The Chinese had greater expectations. They expected to gain a commitment of additional military and economic assistance when Chiang and the president met face-to-face.[2]

Even as Chiang and Roosevelt were discussing plans for a late autumn summit, Sino-American relations were becoming more strained. In July and August, a series of articles critical of the Kuomintang regime appeared in important American magazines and newspapers, chief among them a blunt critique of Chiang's government written by Hanson Baldwin, which was originally published in the *New York Times* and reprinted in *Reader's Digest* in August 1943. Much of the diplomatic correspondence between Washington and Chungking in July, August, and September focused on such articles and reflected growing anti–American sentiment among the generalissimo's inner circle of advisors, family, and friends.[3]

Baldwin's essay, "Too Much Wishful Thinking About China," was particularly offensive to the Chinese because it not only criticized the performance of Chinese military forces, but also questioned the validity of Chinese nationalism. "China," Baldwin argued, "was not a nation in our sense of the term but a geographer's expression."[4] According to Baldwin, Chiang Kai-shek was not the democratically elected leader of a modern nation-state, but, rather, a warlord, albeit a somewhat enlightened one, who ruled only a small part of what the geographers called China.[5]

The Chinese press reacted strongly to the Baldwin article and other critical analyses of the situation in China. *Ta Kung Pao*, a leading daily newspaper in Chungking, called Baldwin's essay an "insult to China and her people."[6]

Hsin Hua Jih Pao, the newspaper published by the Communist Party, a daily not noted for its support of the Kuomintang, labeled Baldwin's comments "purposeful slander."[7]

From the vantage point of the United States embassy in Chungking, whether justified or not, such criticism of the Chinese government was having an adverse effect on Sino-American relations.[8] "The more justifiable the criticism may be," said one senior diplomat in Chungking, "the more likely is resentment to be increased."[9] Chinese sensitivity was so great that even slight criticism often led to an abusive and defensive response, with the good faith of the United States often being called into question by Chinese rebuttals.

Until the summer of 1943, there had been relatively little criticism of the Kuomintang regime in the American print media. To the contrary, Chinese propaganda circulated widely in the United States, resulting in a situation in which many Americans could see little wrong with the government of Chiang Kai-shek. But, as T.V. Soong had feared, this situation could not last forever. Chinese journalists could be censored; western journalists could not. Eventually, they would report on the underside of Kuomintang rule and, as Soong had advised the generalissimo, the Chinese government needed to be prepared to respond to this criticism in a positive manner.[10]

Had criticism of Chiang Kai-shek's regime been limited to the press, Kuomintang authorities might not have been too alarmed, but such criticism was also beginning to be voiced by American political leaders. In a speech to the Senate on September 30, 1943, Henry Cabot Lodge called for a more realistic appraisal of America's allies:

> We must not perpetuate any more of these false notions. We invite ultimate cynicism, disillusionment and even hatred of our allies if we do so…
> It would be better for China and for us if a true picture were given to the American people. When Oliver Cromwell had his portrait painted, he said to the artist, "Paint me as I am, the wart and all."[11]

When Ambassador Clarence Gauss returned to China in September 1943 after a long holiday in the United States, he found Chinese leaders more upset about critics in the United States Congress than criticism in the American press. If they were troubled by Baldwin's article, they were even more upset by Senator Lodge's speech.[12] On the other hand, Gauss found that such criticism was having a salutary effect on the generalissimo. "It is reliably reported," the ambassador informed the secretary of state, "that Chiang Kai-shek has issued orders to commanders of Central Government troops in some areas to carry out at least one attack a month against the Japanese" in response to critics such as Baldwin and Lodge.[13]

Chiang and his subordinates had conducted a passive defense of their territory after 1939, husbanding their resources and hoping for American intervention and assistance before reactivating the war against Japan. America's entry into the war against Japan did not bring the rewards that the Chinese had expected and the generalissimo responded by maintaining the policy of avoiding confrontations with the Japanese. Chinese propagandists tried to mask this policy of passive resistance by painting a picture of the heroic resistance of Chinese forces and selling it in the American press. At first, they were quite successful, but as American and other European correspondents came to China in increasingly larger numbers, it was hard to hide the truth from western audiences.

The bad press China was receiving in the United States and the often vitriolic response of Chinese leaders to such attacks made the upcoming Sino-American summit even more important. Roosevelt, by now increasingly aware of the psychological implications of such a summit, dispatched another personal emissary, Major-General Patrick Hurley, to Chungking in mid–October for the purpose of ascertaining first hand the generalissimo's state of mind and to assess the situation in the CBI.[14]

Hurley left for Chungking on October 14, 1943. While he was en route to China, a journey that was to take him three weeks with stopovers in Cairo and New Delhi, plans for the Cairo Conference were being firmed up. On October 27, Roosevelt informed the generalissimo that he proposed to meet with him and Churchill sometime between November 20 and 25 at a location in the Middle East, possibly Alexandria:

> I will bring a small staff with me including our highest-ranking Army, Navy, and Air officers. I should think the conference would last about three days. I know you will not want to be away from China long, but it is far better for me to get away now than later.
>
> I am looking forward to seeing you because I am sure there are many things that can only be satisfactorily settled if we can meet face to face. Please keep this very confidential.[15]

Roosevelt sent Chiang another message on October 30, inviting the generalissimo to meet him and Churchill "in the vicinity of Cairo" on or about November 26.[16] Chiang replied to Roosevelt on November 2, accepting the president's invitation and assuring him that "everything will be kept strictly secret here."[17] The generalissimo also sent Roosevelt a letter, carried by General Brehon Somervell from Chungking to Washington, asking whether it was "desirable" for him to meet with the president and Mr. Churchill together or whether it was more profitable for him to meet with the president alone.[18]

On November 4, Roosevelt called Secretary of War Stimson to the White House and informed him, for the first time, that he intended to meet with Chiang Kai-shek in the near future. According to Stimson's recollection of the discussion, the president gave the impression that "he was going to make this journey mainly to realize the psychological benefits which would come from such a meeting rather than the solution of any concrete special problems."[19]

The president and the secretary also discussed T.V. Soong's fall from the good graces of the generalissimo and how his absence from Cairo might affect the upcoming summit.[20] Stimson told Roosevelt that General Somervell had described Soong as "the nigger in the woodpile in Chungking" and that Mesdames Chiang and Kung were plotting "actively against their brother."[21] The fact that Soong would not accompany Chiang Kai-shek to Cairo could, Stimson suggested, have a positive result since it would force the generalissimo to rely more on General Stilwell in preparing for the upcoming conference and encourage him to make peace with Stilwell.[22] Roosevelt acknowledged that this was already happening, telling Stimson that General Somervell had been able to get Chiang and Stilwell "kissing each other instead of fighting."[23]

Stimson and Roosevelt were right about the rapprochement between Chiang and Stilwell. Indeed, the day after FDR and Stimson first discussed the Sino-American summit, November 5, General Stilwell was called to the Chiangs' villa in Chungking to "help them with plans for the conference and to put things right with the powers."[24] The following day, November 6, Stilwell was called back to the villa for what he called a "love feast" with Generalissimo and Madame Chiang.[25] "It was milk and honey," Stilwell noted of this meeting in his diary.[26] "Peanut is happy now that we are pals again and wants me to draft proposals for the conference."[27]

On November 8, Roosevelt sent a message to Chiang Kai-shek clarifying details about the meeting in Cairo. He told the generalissimo that he expected to arrive in Cairo by November 21 and that he would be leaving Egypt for a meeting with Stalin and Churchill in Persia on November 26 or 27.[28] He asked Chiang to try to arrange to be in Cairo by November 22nd and promised to arrange good accommodations for Chiang and his party in the vicinity of Cairo.[29] Roosevelt asked the generalissimo to RSVP as quickly as possible as he would be leaving the United States for North Africa "in two or three days."[30]

Chiang responded to Roosevelt on November 9:

> Madame Chiang down with flu and dysentery. Funeral of late President Lin Sen scheduled for 17th. Provided Madame Chiang has recovered, I intend to leave here early on the 18th. Otherwise, I must delay my departure.[31]

Although Chiang preferred to meet with Roosevelt before the president's meeting with Stalin, he refused to go to Cairo without his wife.[32] In the event that she was not able to make the long and arduous trip to Cairo before the end of November, their meeting with Roosevelt would have to be put off until after the meetings between Churchill, Roosevelt, and Stalin.[33]

"I am terribly sorry to learn of Madame Chiang's illness," Roosevelt cabled the generalissimo on November 10, "and sincerely hope she will be fully recovered in time for our conference."[34] Roosevelt also indicated his agreement with Chiang that it would be best if the two of them could meet before Roosevelt met Stalin. That would allow the president to raise certain delicate matters with Marshal Stalin, such as how the Soviets might help the Chinese war effort, after having had the opportunity to discuss these issues with Chinese leaders.[35]

As cables finalizing arrangements for the Cairo summit were passing back and forth from Washington to Chungking to Washington, Roosevelt's personal envoy, General Patrick Hurley, arrived in Chungking. In his first meeting with the generalissimo, which took place on November 9, Hurley asked Chiang three questions:

1. Would he be willing to meet with Stalin?
2. Would he cooperate with the Soviets should they declare war against Japan?
3. Did he approve of the new "Pacific policy" suggested by General MacArthur and supported by the Joint Chiefs of Staff?[36]

According to Hurley's notes of this conversation and his report to Roosevelt, the generalissimo was unwilling to meet with the Soviet leader because he "would not be able to meet with Stalin in the state of friendliness such a conference would require."[37] On the other hand, Chiang indicated that he would cooperate with the U.S.S.R. in the war against Japan "in a military way."[38] Chiang also indicated he approved of the new island hopping strategy and expressed the hope that this would facilitate a landing of American forces in China as "a prelude to an all out attack on Japan."[39]

Hurley and Chiang had a second meeting on the morning of November 12 at which time he and the generalissimo discussed Roosevelt's ideas about colonialism and the post-war world.[40] At lunchtime, Madame H. H. Kung and General Stilwell were invited to join Hurley and Chiang and the conversation turned to the upcoming meeting between the president and the generalissimo. According to Stilwell's recollection of the conversation, Hurley and Madame Kung urged Chiang to bring him to Cairo.[41] This account is corroborated by Hurley, who reported to Roosevelt that the idea of bringing Stilwell to Cairo was discussed again at dinner on November 12, with Madame Chiang joining her sister and Hurley in pressing the generalissimo to include Stilwell in his delegation to Cairo.[42]

By the time Hurley left Chungking on November 14, Stilwell and Chiang had reached a temporary rapprochement and Stilwell was invited to join the small delegation that would accompany Generalissimo and Madame Chiang to Cairo. He was also to play an important role in helping Chiang prepare for the conference and was one of the only people in Chungking, aside from the Chiangs, to be informed of details about the meeting with Roosevelt and Churchill.

Although Chiang Kai-shek and Roosevelt had been arranging their summit for months, the generalissimo shared none of the details about the conference with his subordinates save for Madame Chiang and General Stilwell.[43] This secrecy, most unusual for Chungking, limited Chiang's ability to prepare for his conversations with Churchill and Roosevelt. Those upon whom Chiang normally relied for information, e.g., T.V. Soong and H.H. Kung, were entirely removed from the preparations, the end result being that Chiang left for Cairo without the benefit of briefing books or position papers except for one that Stilwell prepared on the military situation in Burma.[44]

Stilwell's proposals for the Cairo conference were contained in a lengthy memorandum he submitted to the generalissimo on November 11, 1943. In this memo, Stilwell suggested that Chiang ask Roosevelt for a commitment to equip and train 90 divisions of the Chinese army in three phases.[45] In return for this assistance, he suggested that the generalissimo promise full Chinese cooperation in the effort to recapture Burma, after which a major operation would be launched to seize Canton and the Hongkong area.[46] To facilitate these offensives, Roosevelt was to be asked to commit to increasing the Hump lift to at least 10,000 tons per month.[47]

Stilwell's memorandum did not deal with political considerations except to confirm that Chiang was "right" to expect that "an all-out effort will be made by the Allies to reopen communications through Burma using land, air, and naval forces."[48] This was a specific reference to the reluctance of Churchill and his government to commit to satisfactory participation in the proposed campaign in Burma. Stilwell and Chiang shared few common political views, but one they did share was the view that the British were only half-heartedly committed to the war in the CBI theater.[49]

Armed with Stilwell's proposal and accompanied by fourteen associates, Generalissimo and Madame Chiang Kai-shek left Chungking bound for Cairo on November 18, 1943. Stilwell and John Paton Davies, an American diplomat in China attached to Stilwell's staff as his chief political advisor, had left for Cairo three days earlier. At the time of their departure, no member of Chiang's entourage, with the exception of his wife, knew where they were going.[50] It was only when the Chinese delegation arrived in Agra, the first of two overnight stopovers en route to Egypt, that the generalissimo's subordinates were informed of their ultimate destination and the purpose of their mission.[51]

Chiang's entourage included twelve military officers, his wife, Hollington Tong, and Wang Ch'ung-hui, a former foreign minister who acted as a replacement for T.V. Soong, the current foreign minister who had fallen from the generalissimo's good graces. Wang was an experienced diplomat who had been educated at the University of California and at Yale, but his diplomatic experience had been limited to European assignments and he lacked contacts within the Roosevelt administration.[52] Indeed, it was for this reason that Chiang had replaced Wang as foreign minister with T. V. Soong in 1941, after Wang had served almost four years in that post.[53]

Wang Ch'ung-hui was a loyal member of Chiang Kai-shek's entourage, a man who would not try to upstage the generalissimo at Cairo.[54] On the other hand, he was also not likely to contribute much to the deliberations at Cairo because he had no influence with any members of the delegation accompanying Roosevelt nor was he likely to remonstrate with Chiang if circumstances demanded that pressure be put on the generalissimo. Stilwell, not one known for mincing words, described Wang as one of Chiang's "stooges."[55]

Except for Hollington Tong, Madame Chiang, and Wang Ch'ung-hui, the only other high ranking member of Chiang's entourage to have the experience of travel abroad and the ability to speak and understand English was General Shang Chen, the director of the Foreign Affairs Bureau of the Military Affairs Commission.[56] Like Wang, Shang Chen had joined the Kuomintang shortly after the 1911 Revolution and had been associated with Dr. Sun Yat-sen. Shang had also been associated with Chiang in the mid–1920's when he was planning the Northern Expedition (*Peifa*).[57] From that time onward, Shang Chen was a loyal subordinate of the generalissimo and held important posts in the Kuomintang hierarchy.[58] Like Wang Ch'ung-hui, he was reliable. Like Wang, Stilwell considered him another of the generalissimo's "stooges."[59]

Another of the generalissimo's compatriots on the trip to Cairo was General Chou Chih-jou. Like Chiang, Chou was more parochial than men like Shang Chen, Wang Ch'ung-hui, and Hollington Tong. He spoke little English, although he had visited the United States briefly in 1933 to study military aviation.[60] After graduating from the Paoting Military Academy in 1922, General Chou joined Sun Yat-sen's revolutionary army in Canton and served under Chiang Kai-shek on the faculty of the Whampoa Military Academy from 1924 to 1926.[61] Like Shang Chen, Chou participated in the Northern Expedition and subsequent efforts of the generalissimo to bring the warlords of north China under the control of the Kuomintang regime.[62] After the Japanese invaded China in 1937, Chou was made the director of the Aeronautical Affairs Commission in which capacity he would become closely associated with Madame Chiang and General Chennault.[63] Stilwell sometimes referred to him as the third of the "three stooges."[64]

The first stop of Chiang's entourage en route to Cairo was Agra. They stayed overnight in this Indian city on November 19. While in Agra, Chiang met General Carton de Wiart, Churchill's newly appointed special representative to the generalissimo, who was invited to accompany Chiang and his party to Cairo. De Wiart had been dispatched to China late in October, but since there was no residence ready for him in Chungking, he had been forced to wait in India for several weeks and arranged to introduce himself to Generalissimo and Madame Chiang when he found out they would overnight in Agra.[65]

General de Wiart's mission was to improve Anglo-Chinese relations and to provide Churchill with a personal "pipe-line" into the generalissimo's headquarters.⁶⁶ In his memoir, Carton de Wiart relates that prior to his departure for China, he had been warned that Chiang had a "violent temper" and that the generalissimo's staff was terrified of him.⁶⁷ When de Wiart finally met Chiang in Agra, he was surprised to find a man quite different from his reputation:

> [Chiang] was a small man with a great deal of simple dignity without any form of show, most unusual in dictators, who need an ornate facade to help build them up to their worshipping public.⁶⁸

Of all of those who were attached to Chiang Kai-shek's government during the war as special representatives of Allied leaders, Carton de Wiart was the most positively disposed toward the generalissimo and he was the only one of Churchill's subordinates to be sympathetic to the plight of the Kuomintang regime in Chungking. Whereas many of de Wiart's peers found Chiang to be uncompromising and egocentric, his attitude toward the generalissimo was very different. "I found him most reasonable on many occasions when I had to approach him," de Wiart noted in his memoir, "and sometimes when the reason for my approach was distasteful to us both."⁶⁹

General de Wiart's initial encounter with Chiang in Agra left him with a positive opinion of China's leader. Two years later, after his tour of duty was over in Chungking, he felt much the same way:

> I have never seen a man with such self-control; in spite of continual crises and difficulties, which swept over him, he never showed an outward sign of feeling. As a man, he was head and shoulders above any other man in China, a fact admitted even by the Communists.⁷⁰

On November 20, Chiang Kai-shek's entourage, with General de Wiart in tow, flew from Agra to Karachi where they spent the night. General Stilwell, Chiang's advance-man, had already left Karachi for Cairo with John Paton Davies. En route from Karachi to Cairo, Stilwell asked Davies to draft political proposals for the conference. "I was astonished to discover," Davies would later state in his memoirs, "that the General [Stilwell] had no prepared statement or plan ready for the conference," a fact he attributed to Stilwell's preoccupation with other matters and his strained relationship with the generalissimo.⁷¹ Davies hastily drew up a list of proposals on a sheet of Shatt-al-Arab Hotel stationary and gave it to Stilwell's aide-de-camp, General Frank Merrill. Together, they edited Davies' handwritten draft and handed a condensed version of one page to Stilwell when they arrived in Cairo.⁷²

As Chiang Kai-shek and his subordinates headed toward Cairo, President Roosevelt was also en route to the summit. According to the "Log of the President's Trip to North Africa and the Middle East," Roosevelt boarded the USS *Iowa* on the morning of November 12, 1943, where he joined the Joint Chiefs of Staff (JCS) and several dozen other members of the American delegation.[73] The president remained in his cabin until after lunch, met briefly with the Joint Chiefs of Staff, and came up on deck after 3:30 P.M. to enjoy the view, much to the chagrin of his security men who were almost paranoid that Roosevelt might be seen by enemy spies before the *Iowa* left coastal waters.[74] That evening the president and the JCS watched a movie.[75]

On the second day out of port, November 14, a gunnery exhibition was arranged for Roosevelt and the JCS. During the show, a torpedo was mistakenly released from one of the destroyers accompanying the *Iowa* and passed quite close to the president's flagship. An alarm was sounded, Roosevelt was rushed to cover, and the captain of the *Iowa* took evasive measures. Fortunately, no damage was done and no one was hurt, but the JCS were quite shaken up and Admiral King proposed that the destroyer's captain be immediately relieved of command when it was learned that the torpedo had been fired from one of the *Iowa*'s escorts and not a German submarine.[76] The president told King to "forget it" and seems to have enjoyed the excitement.[77] Harry Hopkins quipped that the torpedo must have been launched by "some damned Republican."[78]

Concern about Roosevelt's safety and maintaining secrecy about the site of the conference with Churchill and Chiang preoccupied the president's secret service escorts and the JCS. In his memoir, Admiral Leahy comments about the efforts that were made to keep the summit a secret so that the Germans would be completely "unaware of the prize target within their range."[79] This was no easy matter given the propensity of the Anglo-American press to seek out information about all political matters. The Chinese press could be muzzled by censors in Chungking. It was more difficult to censor the press in London and Washington.

The trip from Virginia to North Africa was a long one and the crossing was rough. The *Iowa*, surrounded by four destroyers, pursued a zigzag course, which cut down on her maximum speed of 25 knots. The crossing took almost seven days, leaving ample time for the president and his advisors to prepare for the conference. Indeed, they met on a daily basis to discuss various military and political matters, which would come up during the talks in Cairo and the Teheran summit with Stalin that was to follow the meeting in Egypt.

On November 15, Roosevelt met with the JCS for a long meeting during which a variety of issues relating to the European theater were discussed, including the possibility of General Marshall assuming command of the cross–Channel invasion.[80] On November 16, there was another long meeting at which the president and the JCS discussed the future of French overseas colonies and the upcoming discussions with Generalissimo Chiang and "Red Joe" Stalin.[81]

On November 17, a report was relayed to the Iowa from Cairo that news of the Cairo conference may have been leaked by the press, alarming the president's security men and his advisors. In his *History of the Second World War*,

Churchill reveals that some of the president's aides wished to move the conference from Cairo to Khartoum because of their concern that the Germans might launch an air strike against Cairo from Greece or Rhodes.[82] Roosevelt had nothing to do with this request, according to the prime minister, because the president was "indifferent" about his personal safety.[83]

Churchill dismissed the idea of moving the site of the conference to Khartoum since that city in the Sudan could not accommodate the parties coming to the summit, but he did look into the possibility of changing the venue of the meeting to Malta. Ultimately, Churchill dismissed the idea of using Malta as an alternative to Cairo because the island was equally vulnerable to a German air attack and lacked the defenses the British could mount in the vicinity of Cairo.[84] The prime minister informed the president of his conclusion and Roosevelt agreed that the summit would remain in Cairo.[85]

Roosevelt's "Log" lists no schedule of meetings for November 18. On November 19, the president did meet with the Joint Chiefs from 2:00 to 5:10 P.M. at which time they discussed the agenda of the upcoming summit, including matters relating to China and the CBI theater.[86] Unlike Chiang Kai-shek, who did not discuss the agenda for the conference with his aides prior to or en route to Cairo, Roosevelt had ample opportunity to do this while on board the *Iowa* en route to North Africa.[87]

The *Iowa* passed through the Straits of Gibraltar on the evening of November 19. The next morning, Roosevelt's party reached Oran, with the president out on deck smoking a cigarette, his profile clearly visible and, perhaps, identifiable to observers.[88] When the president disembarked from the *Iowa*, he was greeted by his sons Franklin Jr. and John, and General Eisenhower, Harry Hopkins, Admiral Leahy, and "Pa" Watson for a mid-morning flight to Tunis.[89] Upon arrival in Tunis at 2:20 P.M., the presidential party proceeded to Eisenhower's villa where the general and the president shared dinner and a lengthy post-dinner conversation.[90]

The following day, November 21, FDR and Eisenhower packed a picnic lunch and left for a tour of the battlefields, returning to Eisenhower's villa at 3:45 P.M.[91] That evening the president dined with his sons; Admiral Leahy; Dr. Ross McIntyre, the president's personal physician; General Watson, the president's secretary; and Harry Hopkins. After dinner, the presidential party departed for the Tunis airport and an overnight flight to Cairo.[92] General Marshall and other members of the JCS contingent had already flown from Tunis to Cairo.[93]

As Chiang Kai-shek and his entourage approached Cairo from the east and Roosevelt and his party were making their way westward across the Atlantic, Prime Minister Churchill, the host of the conference, was also en route to Cairo. The prime minister left England on November 12, accompanied by his daughter Sarah; General Hastings Ismay, his military aide; Admiral Andrew Cunningham, First Sea Lord; and John Winant, the American ambassador to the Court of Saint James. When he left England, Churchill was ill, suffering from a bad cold and a reaction to recent inoculations against typhoid and malaria.[94] For several days, he remained confined to his cabin, but he was able to go ashore to speak with French officials in Algiers when his party arrived there on November 17. The British entourage left Algiers after a port call of only several hours. Their next stop was Malta.

Churchill and his subordinates arrived in Malta on November 17 and there he had the opportunity to meet with General Eisenhower and General Alexander, both of whom were decorated by Churchill for their role in the North African campaign.[95] Because of his continued illness, the prime minister remained in Malta for the next two days. Although he was bedridden, Churchill "continued to conduct business without cessation."[96] It was while he was in Malta that the prime minister received Roosevelt's cable requesting a possible change of venue for the conference with Chiang.

Churchill's flagship, the *Renown*, left Malta at midnight on November 19 bound for Alexandria. En route to Alexandria, he and his aides discussed the situation in Europe and the Mediterranean and the upcoming meeting with Stalin.[97] There is no indication that the situation in China received much of the prime minister's attention, but soon after Churchill arrived in Egypt on November 21, the China tangle was to dominate his agenda, much to his chagrin.[98]

Given the situation of the Anglo-American Allies in November 1943, Churchill had little interest in wasting time on Chiang Kai-shek and the China tangle. With Stalin pressuring the Allies for a cross–Channel invasion and the situation in Italy far from resolved, the last thing the prime minister wished to do was to engage in a debate over the CBI with Roosevelt. Churchill was far more skeptical about the capabilities of the generalissimo than Roosevelt. He expected little from the Chinese and wished to give them little help in return. Furthermore, Churchill was concerned about protecting British imperial interests and resented Chiang's meddling in the affairs of the Empire.[99] Despite these misgivings, Churchill had agreed to meet Chiang in Cairo and discuss the future of the CBI theater to humor Roosevelt and move the agenda along to more important issues.

As daylight dawned over Cairo on the morning of November 21, 1943, Chiang Kai-shek, Winston Churchill, and Franklin D. Roosevelt were fast approaching that city and their rendezvous in the shadow of the pyramids and under the eyes of the sphinx. For the next six days, these three heads of state conducted private diplomacy at the highest level. Although no earth shattering decisions were reached at the conference, what happened at Cairo would have an important impact on Sino-American relations with implications which influenced the course of events even after the Second World War was over.

5
November 21–22, 1943: The Cast Assembles

Chiang Kai-shek and his entourage arrived in Cairo on the morning of November 21, several hours before Churchill and a day before Roosevelt. The generalissimo's travel plans had been so well-kept a secret that when he arrived in Cairo, no one was on hand at the airport to greet him.[1] General Chennault, who had a hunch that the Chiangs might be arriving, drove out to the airport and was just getting out of his car when the Chinese delegates deplaned.[2] Had Chennault not gone to the airport, the generalissimo and his party would have been left waiting on the tarmac with no transportation to their quarters and no easy way to reach their hosts.

General Stilwell, Chiang's advance man in Cairo, had no idea what time the generalissimo was due into Cairo and at the time Chiang and his entourage touched down, he was meeting with his aides, John Paton Davies and General Frank Merrill, to go over a position paper they had drawn up at his request en route to Cairo.[3] Stilwell's biographer, Barbara Tuchman, suggests that Madame and Generalissimo Chiang Kai-shek were livid about the absence of a proper greeting party, a slight they attributed to British hostility to the Chinese and Stilwell's failure to prepare for their arrival.[4]

Chennault was able to alert Stilwell that Chiang had arrived and arranged to have him and his entourage transferred to their villa on the outskirts of Cairo, adjacent to the pyramids. A call was also placed to Sir Miles Lampson, former British minister to China, who, in the absence of Churchill, immediately proceeded to pay a courtesy call on the Chiangs. When he arrived at their villa, he presented his calling card to one of the Chinese attendants who immediately informed the generalissimo that "Lord Killearn" wished to see him. Not realizing that Lampson had been knighted and not recognizing his new name, Chiang refused to receive this visitor. Undaunted, Lampson walked into the garden of Chiang's villa where he was immediately recognized by the generalissimo.[5]

Chiang and Lampson greeted each other cordially, but in the absence of Madame Chiang, who was still ill with the flu and had taken to bed immediately after arriving at their villa, or one of the generalissimo's other translators, the conversation between Chiang and Lampson was limited to repeated "how are you's."[6] Sensing that something was amiss, one of Chiang's secretaries went to the Mena House Hotel and asked Hollington Tong to come to the generalissimo's villa as quickly as possible. Tong arrived in time to salvage what was becoming a comic situation and was then ordered to stay with the generalissimo for the duration of the conference to avoid another such embarrassing encounter.[7] In his memoirs, Tong reveals that for the next five days, Chiang kept dropping into his room to make sure that he was there so that there would be no repeat of the Lord Killearn incident.[8]

Winston Churchill arrived in Cairo shortly after noon on November 21. According to Alan Brooke's notes, the prime minister was ill and "in a very excitable mood."[9] The news that Chiang and his party had already arrived did little to improve Churchill's mood. Churchill had never been enthusiastic about inviting the generalissimo to Cairo and the early arrival of the Chinese delegation threatened to "throw the conference out of gear," as the prime minister noted after the war.[10] Churchill, who wished to take to his bed, was forced to postpone his rest in order to greet Chiang properly and make amends for the absence of an official greeting at the airport.[11]

Churchill first suggested paying a courtesy call on Generalissimo and Madame Chiang at their villa, but the generalissimo insisted that as Churchill's guest, he should pay a call on his host and arrangements were hastily made for Churchill to receive Chiang.[12] Soon after Churchill reached his villa, Chiang and one of his military aides and translators arrived. Madame Chiang was ill and did not accompany her husband to this first meeting between the prime minister and the generalissimo. The only other person present was Lord Mountbatten.[13]

According to Mountbatten's recollection of the meeting, Churchill thanked the generalissimo for coming and promised to return the courtesy the next day.[14] After Churchill's greeting was translated for Chiang, the generalissimo asked Churchill when he would visit with him and Madame Chiang. "Tell his Excellency," Churchill said, "that when the sun is at its zenith I will come."[15] Chiang's translator was nervous and mistranslated the prime minister's response.[16] The generalissimo, unaware that Churchill was not an early riser, suggested that he would expect him at 10:00 A.M. the next morning. Upon hearing this from the translator, Churchill exclaimed, "I never get up as early as that!"[17] After some further confusion, the prime minister was able to explain to Chiang's translator what he meant and a date was made for the afternoon of November 22.[18]

The first encounter between Churchill and Chiang bordered on being a comic opera, but the misunderstanding between the two men was not solely due to language problems. Although the prime minister and the generalissimo tried to observe proper protocol in their first face-to-face encounter, they shared a mutual suspicion of each other, which was not easily masked by diplomatic niceties. As if this mutual hostility was not enough, Churchill's fever and distemper did not help matters. He was in no mood to be diplomatic or prolong the conversation.

Mountbatten observed the conversation between Chiang and Churchill with some amusement. He would later note that this encounter was useful because it exposed Churchill to the firsthand experience of "how impossible the Chinese are to deal with."[19] Mountbatten was in a position to know about the difficulties of dealing with the generalissimo and his staff. As a consequence of his appointment as Supreme Commander of Allied Forces in Southeast Asia in September 1943 and his visit to Chungking in October, Mountbatten was already initiated into the byzantine maze of Kuomintang politics.[20]

At about the time that Chiang Kai-shek left Churchill's villa, General Marshall and his party arrived in Cairo. En route they flew over the battlefields of Libya and Egypt. Upon arrival, Marshall was transferred to a small villa near the Mena House Hotel, the main venue of the conference, where he was met by Alexander Kirk, United States Ambassador to Egypt; Charles Winant, United States Ambassador to England, who had just arrived with Churchill; and Averell Harriman, Assistant Secretary of State.[21]

Admiral Ernest King and General Henry A. Arnold, the other members of United States Joint Chiefs of Staff, arrived in Cairo in the early evening and were transferred to the villa, which they were to share with General Marshall for the next five days. Accommodations for the JCS were hardly elegant. The Marshall villa had eight beds and only two baths, a fact that posed some problems, according to General Arnold.[22]

While the generalissimo, the prime minister, and the JCS were settling in, General Stilwell was called to Chiang's villa to consult with General Shang Chen and the generalissimo.[23] They met for several hours before dinner and again for a shorter chat after dinner.[24] As Stilwell noted in his diary later that night, the generalissimo and his associates were quite anxious about the opening of the conference and were particularly concerned about making a good impression on the president and the prime minister. After reassuring Chiang that all was in order, Stilwell left the generalissimo's villa.[25]

After leaving Chiang, Stilwell went to Marshall's villa where he and Marshall discussed the situation in the CBI. According to Stilwell's diary, Marshall suggested the possibility of removing him from China in order to give him a field command.[26] Marshall confided to Stilwell that Roosevelt had been under regular pressure from Chungking to replace him and even though Stilwell and the generalissimo were on a second honeymoon, the president remained concerned that Stilwell might not be the best man for the job in China.[27] Marshall was not ready to make a decision and Stilwell was ambivalent. They agreed to let the matter rest.[28]

As Marshall and Stilwell called it quits for the night, Churchill, Alan

Brooke, and Ismay were burning the midnight oil at the prime minister's villa. Alan Brooke recalled that the "P.M. kept us up till after 1:00 A.M." and continued to be in an excitable mood.[29] Churchill was particularly upset by his encounter with Chiang and even more so by the fact that he and Roosevelt would have little opportunity to thrash out a united front which they could present to Stalin in Teheran before leaving for Iran because of the presence of the Chinese and the president's preoccupation with placating Chiang.[30]

Churchill and Brooke were not alone in expressing their dismay at finding the Chinese established in Cairo before Anglo-American talks could be launched. Ismay was also frustrated that the "cart had been put before the horse," but he placed the blame on the American Joint Chiefs of Staff who "far from being upset by the premature arrival of the Chinese delegation, seemed positively pleased to have a chaperone."[31] At 10:40 P.M., as Marshall was chatting with Stilwell and Churchill was meeting with Brooke and Ismay, Roosevelt, Leahy, and Hopkins left Tunis for Cairo, arriving in Cairo at 9:35 A.M. on the morning of November 22 after a brief detour south to allow the president and his entourage to follow the course of the Nile to the delta.[32] Roosevelt was immediately transferred to the residence of Ambassador Kirk, also in the Mena district, which was to be his home for the duration of the conference.[33]

Unlike the accommodations provided for Marshall, Arnold, and King, Roosevelt's villa, which he shared with Leahy and Hopkins, was spacious and beautifully furnished. Adjacent to the villa, which was one mile from the Mena House Hotel and "just a good spit" away from the pyramids, was a lovely flower garden where the president spent much of his leisure time and entertained guests.[34] Refreshments for the president, his personal entourage, and his guests were provided by his personal chef and members of the service staff of the White House who accompanied FDR to Cairo.[35]

Roosevelt arrived at Kirk's villa at 10:30 A.M. and had no appointments until the afternoon. While the president rested, the prime minister caught up on his sleep, and the generalissimo prepared to host the prime minister, staff meetings commenced. The British Chiefs of Staff (BCOS) held their first formal session of the conference at 11:00 A.M. while the American Joint Chiefs of Staff (JCS) started their first formal session at approximately the same time.

General Brooke presided over the meeting of the BCOS, which included General Ismay, Field Marshal John Dill, Air Chief Marshall Portal, and Admiral Andrew Cunningham. The minutes of this meeting suggest that although the British were most concerned about settling differences with their American counterparts over questions pertaining to the Mediterranean and the European theater, they recognized that "in light of the generalissimo's arrival, it would be necessary to consider SEAC operations early in the conference."[36]

Field Marshal Dill, who represented the BCOS in Washington, informed his colleagues that the "Americans had considerable forces in Southeast Asia and expected to be consulted about the SEAC theater."[37] Alan Brooke responded that the British "should not have to seek U.S. consent" before commencing any operation in Southeast Asia and expressed more concern about the fact that the Americans would likely press for the diversion of forces from the Mediterranean to support Stilwell's proposed offensive in Burma as a means of placating Chiang Kai-shek.[38] This was likely to come up when the BCOS met with the JCS later that afternoon.

At the meeting of the JCS, the Burma campaign was the major topic on the agenda. That being the case, General Stilwell and General Wheeler, the engineer in charge of planning the construction of a new Burma road and moving supplies through India into Burma, were invited to join the JCS in order to prepare a position paper which could be advanced when the Combined British and Americans Chiefs of Staff (CCOS) met.[39]

Shortly after the BCOS and the JCS adjourned their meetings for lunch, Prime Minister Churchill paid his courtesy call on Generalissimo and Madame Chiang at their villa. This was Churchill's first real opportunity to gauge the measure of the generalissimo, the man the Americans thought of as "one of the dominant forces in the world."[40] Churchill recalls that his first impression of Chiang was that he was "a calm, reserved, and efficient personality" who was at the "apex of his power."[41] Madame Chiang seems to have made a greater impression on the prime minister who described her as "a most remarkable and charming personality."[42]

During the course of his visit with the Chiangs, Churchill apologized to Madame Chiang for failing to meet with her when the two of them were in Washington in March 1943, an inadvertent slight.[43] He told her that he hoped that "no undue formalities" would stand in the path of their meeting again in the future.[44] If Churchill meant to make amends with Madame Chiang and her husband, he was not entirely successful. In a report made to Wellington Koo shortly after the Cairo summit, Wang Shih-chieh, a member of the Chinese delegation at Cairo, told Koo that the first meetings between Chiang and Churchill did not go well and it was only after Roosevelt arrived that a cordial tone was established for the discussions.[45]

As Churchill was ending his courtesy call on the Chiangs, the CCOS held their first session of the conference at the Mena House Hotel at 3:00 P.M. General Brooke presided over the meeting.[46] As the meeting started, Ismay announced that Roosevelt was hosting a reception for Generalissimo and Madame Chiang at 5:00 P.M. Since several of those present at the CCOS meeting were invited to attend the tea at Roosevelt's villa, it was agreed that the meeting would adjourn before 4:45 P.M.[47]

At the outset of the meeting, Marshall read a memorandum from Stilwell which outlined Chiang Kai-shek's views on future operations in the China theater and suggested that the CCOS study this document, copies of which were circulated, so that it could be discussed the following day when Chiang and his staff would be invited to join Churchill, Roosevelt, and their CCOS for the first formal session of the conference.[48] Marshall also raised the issue of Chinese participation in CCOS meetings on an ongoing basis when matters relating to the CBI were discussed. This, he suggested, "might facilitate good faith and mutual understanding."[49] Marshall suggested that the same kind of invitation be extended to the Soviets when matters of concern to them were brought up.[50]

Marshall's proposal to expand the CCOS to a four-power body did not sit well with the British, who had little use for the Chinese, and even his colleague, Admiral King, objected to the idea because it would greatly complicate matters. King pointed out that it would be impossible for the Chinese and Russian delegates to sit at the same table since they were not engaging the same enemy and had hostile relations.[51] He also suggested that Soviet participation in discussions concerning the war against Japan could cause a problem because of their neutrality in this conflict.[52]

After some additional discussion, it was agreed that the Chinese be invited to send representatives to meetings of the CCOS when matters of immediate concern to China were to be discussed, but that they not be granted a permanent place on the CCOS.[53] The same courtesy was to be extended to the Russians.[54] At this point, Alan Brooke moved the agenda to a discussion of strategy in the CBI and China's role in the war against Japan.[55] The CCOS meeting was adjourned shortly before 5:00 P.M.

As the CCOS were concluding their meeting, the generalissimo, his wife, and the prime minister went to Roosevelt's villa where the president hosted a tea in honor of the Chiangs.[56] Members of the CCOS were also invited so that they could meet the Chiangs before the formal sessions of the conference commenced. Madame Chiang was well known to some of the people who assembled at the president's villa, but her husband was not. Roosevelt's tea provided the CCOS with an opportunity to take the measure of China's supreme leader.

General Marshall, who like other members of the CCOS knew Chiang only through the reports of Stilwell, was somewhat surprised by meeting Chiang in the flesh and described the generalissimo as "more like a traditional Chinese scholar than a ruthless military and political leader controlling the destinies of millions of his countrymen."[57] Chiang's "ascetic look" and "impassive" demeanor was not what Marshall expected.[58]

If Marshall found Chiang to be "unobtrusive and colorless," he found his wife to be animated and more decisive than her husband.[59] Marshall described her as "stunningly dressed with charm compounded of femininity and forcefulness."[60] He would later note that she kept a watchful eye on the proceedings, clarifying and interpreting her husband's views in a manner that no ordinary translator could manage.⁶¹ Others participants at the conference, such as Carton de Wiart, echoed Marshall's view that Madame Chiang was much more than an attractive companion to the generalissimo and stressed that she put her obvious cleverness to good use in assisting her husband.⁶²

Although the majority of those present at the Cairo conference were impressed by the "missimo," not everyone was enthralled by Madame Chiang. Ismay, who was also present at the president's reception for the Chiangs, would later suggest that, "in spite of her acute mind, she knew less about waging war than her husband who knew little enough!"⁶³ Alan Brooke accused Madame Chiang of gatecrashing and using her feminine charm to distract the proceedings, but admitted that she was "the leading spirit of the two [Chiangs]."⁶⁴

The problem, according to Ismay and Brooke, was that when dealing with the Chinese, they were never sure whether to address their remarks to the generalissimo or his wife. Since Madame Chiang was the constant companion of the generalissimo and frequently served as his translator even when an official translator was present, she could not be ignored and when they chose to do so, Madame Chiang would interrupt the deliberations to correct the official translator. "Excuse me gentlemen," she would say, "I do not think the interpreter has conveyed the full meaning to the Generalissimo."⁶⁵

Neither Churchill nor Roosevelt relied on a single aide or confidant in the same manner as Chiang relied on his wife and this proved to be troublesome, particularly to the BCOS, who had not had the opportunity that their American counterparts had to meet and speak with Madame Chiang prior to coming to Cairo. Whereas Marshall and his colleagues had come to appreciate her ability and cleverness, their British counterparts seemed to be more preoccupied by her charms and wiles, as the following observation from Brooke's notes suggests:

> Although not good-looking, she certainly has a good figure, which she knew how to display at its best. Gifted with great charm and gracefulness, every small movement of hers arrested and pleased the eyes. For example, at one critical moment her closely clinging black dress ... displayed a slit which exposed one of the most shapely of legs. This caused a rustle amongst some of those attending the gathering.⁶⁶

After Roosevelt's reception, Generalissimo and Madame Chiang returned to their villa for dinner, while Churchill and Roosevelt shared dinner at the president's villa along with Harry Hopkins, Lord Mountbatten, and Admiral Leahy.⁶⁷ Stilwell was called to the Chiangs' villa for consultation with Madame Chiang about the preliminary meeting between Chiang, Churchill, and Roosevelt scheduled for later that evening at Mena House. Madame Chiang was particularly concerned that her husband make a good impression on the president and the prime minister and the generalissimo, with whom Stilwell also met, seemed concerned about this session.[68] Stilwell reassured Madame Chiang and her husband that all was in order and told them that his memorandum on the situation in China had already been distributed to the CCOS earlier in the day.[69]

That Madame Chiang should have been concerned about appearances and impressions was quite natural. Although she was a cosmopolitan and well-traveled person, her husband was not. He was not familiar with the strange ways of the "barbarians" and was uncomfortable in strange surroundings. In Chungking, none dare challenge Chiang. In Cairo, he would be merely one among equals, a supplicant for more aid and assistance. Without the presence of T.V. Soong, it would be Madame Chiang's responsibility to help her husband make a favorable impression and to win concessions that would enhance his position in China after returning from Cairo. This would be difficult given the ambivalence of the British and the sometimes-wavering support of the Americans.

According to Stilwell, Madame Chiang and her husband were quite nervous about the preliminary meeting of the generalissimo, the president, and the prime minister, which was scheduled for 9:00 P.M. at Mena House. All of the major players would be there: Roosevelt, Hopkins, Leahy, King, Arnold, Somervell, Chennault, and Wedemeyer; Churchill, Brooke, Ismay, Dill, Mountbatten, Carton de Wiart; and a bevy of their underlings.[70] It was important, Madame Chiang told Stilwell, that nothing go wrong.[71]

Although no minutes were kept of the preliminary meeting between Chiang, Churchill, and Roosevelt, based on the notes of many of those in attendance, it would appear that much of the meeting was given to introductions and a discussion of the agenda for the plenary sessions, which were to begin the following day. This being the case, except for some cursory remarks and pleasantries, the generalissimo, the president, and the prime minister said little, leaving it up to their aides to detail the upcoming schedule of events and define the major agenda issues. In this capacity, Stilwell spoke for Chiang and the Chinese delegation.

In his post-war memoirs, General Arnold recalls that whereas there was a respectful and easygoing relationship between the president, the prime minister and their subordinates, the relationship between Chiang, Stilwell, and the Chinese generals illustrated none of the camaraderie that was exhibited between Churchill and the BCOS or Roosevelt and the JCS.[72] This was noticeable as early as this first preliminary session. Alan Brooke noted the "ghostly silence" of the Chinese who had little to contribute to these initial proceedings or any of the later deliberations and blamed much of this on Stilwell whom Brooke described as "nothing but a hopeless crank with no vision."[73] If Stilwell was Chiang's best spokesman, little could be expected from the Chinese.[74]

The preliminary meeting adjourned at 11:10 P.M. and the participants returned to their villas.[75] Stilwell accompanied Generalissimo and Madame Chiang back to their villa where he and the generalissimo's aides assessed the day's activities and discussed the agenda for November 23. In his diary, Stilwell described Chiang's aides as being agitated and somewhat upset about the generalissimo's first encounters with Churchill and fearful of what lay in store when the formal proceedings commenced.[76] Since there was little he could do to assuage their fears, Stilwell returned to his accommodation and went to sleep.[77] By this time all lights were out in the Mena district.

Although few issues of substance were discussed or resolved while the cast of characters was assembling in Cairo between November 21 and 22, the tone of the conference was being set. The early arrival of Chiang Kai-shek and the Chinese delegation, Churchill's ill health and temper, and the somewhat tardy arrival of President Roosevelt that left the prime minister solely responsible for greeting his Chinese guests, contributed to a climate of tension and frustration, which would continue for the remainder of the conference.

According to Alan Brooke, Churchill's black mood and bad temper were exacerbated by the early arrival of the Chinese, but the real cause of his frustration was deeper. It was the recognition that he was no longer the predominant partner in the Anglo-American alliance, which really upset him.[78] Had Churchill planned the Cairo conference, the Chinese would not have been invited, but it was Roosevelt who planned the conference and Churchill was forced to accept the Chinese presence against his will and better judgment.[79]

Churchill did not react well to playing second fiddle to Roosevelt. As Alan Brooke noted on the way to Cairo, the prime minister seemed to be responding to his subordinate role by articulating strategic proposals "which in his heart he knew were unsound, purely to spite the Americans."[80] Churchill had sometimes behaved in this manner in the past, but in this instance, Brooke feared that the prime minister might not be "easy to swing back on the right line."[81]

If Churchill was agitated about the arrangements and agenda for the Cairo conference, Generalissimo and Madame Chiang were no less apprehensive about what to expect at the conference. Unlike Churchill and Roosevelt, who shared common bonds of friendship and language, the generalissimo and his wife were outsiders. Although Madame Chiang's command of English was excellent, her husband knew nothing of the language and neither one of them were on really intimate terms with the president or the prime minister. Clearly, they were at a disadvantage and this contributed to their preoccupation with matters of protocol and face.

From the Chinese perspective, the events of November 21 and 22 did not bode particularly well. The lack of a proper greeting party to receive them at the Cairo airport was an ill omen. The almost comic-opera call that Chiang paid on Churchill at his villa later on the day of their arrival seemed another ill omen and did little to assuage their concern over how they would

November 21–22, 1943 69

Prime Minister Churchill greets President Roosevelt a day after the president's arrival at the Cairo Conference, November 23, 1943. Courtesy of the Franklin D. Roosevelt Library and Museum, Hyde Park, New York.

be received and treated when the formal sessions of the conference commenced.

Roosevelt's arrival in Cairo on the morning of November 22 and the reception he hosted for the Chiangs later that afternoon may have helped to allay some of their fears, but the generalissimo and his wife remained anxious. Given their uneasy relationship with General Stilwell, who was their main advisor at Cairo, and the absence of the experienced and urbane T.V. Soong, who remained in his bureaucratic exile in Chungking, Generalissimo and Madame Chiang had only each other to lean on. This put an unusual burden on Madame Chiang whose nerves were already frayed without such additional responsibilities.

The initial mood at the Chiangs' villa, as described by Stilwell and Hollington Tong, was fraught with tension.[82] Chiang's subordinates and servants seemed to be well aware of the high level of anxiety of their master and mistress.[83] Whereas Roosevelt seemed serene and self-confident and Churchill seemed feisty and combative, Generalissimo and Madame Chiang seemed restless as they prepared for the formal opening of the conference on November 23.

6

November 23, 1943: The Play Begins

As the sun rose over the pyramids in the Mena district on the morning of November 23, the cast of characters at the Cairo conference prepared for a busy day. The first plenary session of the conference was scheduled for 11:00 A.M. at Roosevelt's villa. In anticipation of this occasion, the BCOS were meeting at 9:45 A.M. at the Mena House Hotel, the JCS were meeting elsewhere in the hotel at the same moment, Chiang Kai-shek was meeting with Stilwell and his staff at the Chinese villa, Churchill was enjoying a leisurely breakfast at his villa, and Roosevelt was entertaining a steady stream of visitors at his villa.

Although the BCOS would have preferred to discuss future operations in Europe and the Mediterranean, their morning agenda for November 23 was dominated by discussion of the SEAC and CBI theaters just as it had been the day before. Admiral Cunningham reported that because of the involvement of American naval forces in the Pacific, the Royal Navy would be pressed to provide naval cover for the offensive in Burma, which was to be proposed by Lord Mountbatten and General Stilwell at the plenary session at 11:00 A.M.[1] Field Marshal Dill warned his colleagues that the Americans had strong feelings about British commitment in the CBI and suggested that Churchill's decision on the matter of providing naval support would be considered a litmus test of British sincerity by Roosevelt and Chiang Kai-shek.[2] He also reminded them that the Americans expected to be consulted before SEAC policy was decided.[3]

Alan Brooke argued against giving the Americans power to veto planned activities in Southeast Asia.[4] Like Churchill, Brooke never quite accepted the fact that the British were now junior partners in the war effort and he resented the pressures put on his government to divert resources from the war in Europe in favor of a highly questionable offensive in Burma, which seemed designed more to placate Generalissimo Chiang Kai-shek than to offer a realistic chance to defeat the Japanese in Southeast Asia and open the door to China.[5] Still, even Brooke recognized that the British had no choice but to go along with a Burma campaign in some form. England's role, he told his colleagues, was to be the voice of sanity at the upcoming plenary sessions, scrutinizing the plans that the Chinese and Americans were prepared to present and raising the hard questions that the Americans and Chinese might not wish to have asked.[6]

If Alan Brooke and the BCOS were concerned about the proposals their American and Chinese counterparts were to present at the plenary session, Marshall and the JCS were no less concerned about the attitude of the British toward Chiang Kai-shek and the CBI theater. Meeting in another wing of the Mena House Hotel at the very same moment that Brooke was conducting the BCOS session, Marshall and his colleagues voiced their suspicion that the British might try to scuttle the offensive in Burma by refusing to make a firm commitment of naval forces necessary for such an operation.[7]

Should Churchill refuse to agree to a timetable for committing British naval forces in the Indian Ocean in support of an offensive in Burma, as Marshall thought likely, relations would be strained between the Chinese and their Anglo-American allies and Stilwell's efforts to get Chiang Kai-shek to commit Chinese forces in Burma would be jeopardized.[8] It was imperative, the JCS agreed, that pressure be put on their British counterparts to "give careful and considerate attention to Chiang's demands."[9]

While the BCOS and JCS were meeting at the Mena House Hotel, Stilwell was meeting with Generalissimo and Madame Chiang at their villa, briefing them and other members of the Chinese delegation on the memorandum he had prepared for discussion at the plenary session and preparing them for Mountbatten's presentation, which was also to be made at the first plenary at 11:00 A.M.[10] As had been the case the night before, Stilwell found Chiang and his wife to be quite nervous and on edge.[11] Their subordinates seemed even more apprehensive.[12]

If suspicion and apprehension characterized the meetings of the BCOS, the JCS, and the Chinese delegation, calm reigned supreme at Churchill's villa where the prime minister's daughter, Sarah, breakfasted with her father and a few aides. Having had a good night's sleep, Churchill was feeling better, his fever was down, and his mood more cheerful.[13] Indeed, he was even up early enough to stop over at Roosevelt's villa for a chat with the president prior to the first plenary session.[14]

By the time Churchill arrived at the villa, Roosevelt had already met with half a dozen people, including Lord Mountbatten, Generalissimo and Madame Chiang, Generals Wedemeyer and Wheeler, and Andre Vyshinsky, Stalin's representative at the Cairo conference.[15] The president was in fine form, enjoying his role as the center of attention and host for the first plenary session of the summit. His guests remarked on his unusually good humor.[16] His aides remarked on his optimism.[17]

The plenary session began, as scheduled, at 11:00 A.M. As the presiding officer, Roosevelt welcomed Generalissimo and Madame Chiang to the council of the Allies and expressed the hope that the Cairo summit would bear fruit for many years to come.[18] Before moving to the formal agenda, Roosevelt went on to assure his Chinese guests that "there was unanimous agreement that every effort should be made to send more equipment to China, with a view to accelerating the process by which we could launch an offensive against the heart of Japan itself."[19] Though nothing was said at the time to contradict the president, Ismay later recalled that Roosevelt had been warned against making any such promises in advance of the deliberations, but "great men have a tendency to brush aside practical considerations they find inconvenient and to make concessions to expediency."[20]

Having welcomed the Chinese delegation and engaged in a bit of rhetorical hyperbole in the process, much to the dismay of the British, the president invited Lord Mountbatten, Supreme Commander of Allied Forces in Southeast Asia, to present a general survey of proposed activities in Southeast Asia. Mountbatten obliged Roosevelt by outlining his goals for 1944, concentrating on proposals for a tri-partite offensive in Burma.

Mountbatten's proposal called for the launching of a campaign in Burma in January 1944, at which time British units based in India would move east toward Burma with an eye toward capturing key positions in the northern part of that country.[21] This, Mountbatten told his audience, would not be easy because of the difficulty of the terrain and the problem of supplying British forces. Unlike the Japanese in Burma, who were at the end of an excellent line of communication and had vast resources, British forces would have to depend on air supply for their operations.[22] Such airdrops would be the responsibility of the United States Army Air Force.[23]

According to Mountbatten's plan, as British forces moved east into Burma, a Chinese army [Ledo Group], trained by Stilwell in India, would join them while a second Chinese army [Yunnan Force] would move west into Burma from China.[24] It was hoped that these operations would surprise the Japanese because of the boldness of the advance through what was assumed to be impassable country and the novel methods of supply that would be employed to support the venture, namely parachute drops.[25]

At this point, Mountbatten paused to ask Chiang Kai-shek whether the proposal was agreeable.[26] The generalissimo responded by asking Mountbatten to illustrate the campaign on a map.[27] After this was done, Chiang asked a series of very pointed questions about the logistics of supply and naval and air cover. Would the Allies be able to increase monthly tonnage over the Hump and, if so, by how much? How many additional aircraft would the Allies make available to facilitate the offensive? How large a naval task force would the Allies assemble in the Bay of Bengal?[28]

Mountbatten told Chiang that the airlift over the Hump would be expanded to 10,000 tons per month by April 1944, up some 3000 tons from the average monthly tonnage for 1943.[29] To accomplish this, at least twenty-five additional "first-line aircrafts" would be provided by the allies, with the United States Army Air Force providing the majority of these planes.[30] When Chiang expressed some skepticism that these goals could be realized, Mountbatten assured him that there was "every prospect of the demand being met."[31] Mountbatten left it to Churchill to respond to the generalissimo's query about naval cover.[32]

Churchill promised a "formidable British fleet" would be assembled in the Indian Ocean "in due course."[33] This fleet would be "more powerful than any detachment the Japanese could make from their main fleet in the Pacific."[34] Chiang expressed pleasure that the British would commit their naval forces, but he pressed Churchill to state when these forces would be ready for action. "As I have said in Chungking," the generalissimo told the prime minister, "the success of operations in Burma depended not only on the strength of Allied naval forces in the Indian Ocean, but on the simultaneous coordination of naval action with land operations."[35]

Churchill's response to Chiang's query was that naval operations could not necessarily be coordinated with land operations in Burma because the main British fleet base was almost 3000 miles away from Burma.[36] The situation in Southeast Asia, Churchill told Chiang, was not like Sicily "where it was possible for the fleet to work in close support of armies."[37] Such linkage would be impossible in Burma.[38] Furthermore, it would not be necessary to victory because the Allies would "have a qualitative as well as quantitative supremacy over the enemy" on the ground with more than 320,000 men at their disposal in Burma.[39]

Chiang was not satisfied with Churchill's response. Without an absolute naval superiority in the Indian Ocean, it was his belief, he told the prime minister, that the Japanese would be able to reinforce their garrisons in Burma, thus negating whatever numerical advantage the Allies enjoyed at the start of the campaign.[40] Churchill agreed that every effort should be made to prevent the Japanese from bringing reinforcements through the Straits of Sunda and Malacca, but he told the generalissimo that he could not guarantee that the Royal Navy could totally prevent such resupply efforts.[41]

At this point, Chiang reiterated his conviction that victory in Burma depended upon the launching of simultaneous land and naval operations in Burma.[42] Burma was the "key to the whole campaign in Asia."[43] Once they were forced out of Burma, Japanese bases in China and Manchuria would become untenable.[44] That, Chiang told Churchill, was why the Japanese would fight tenaciously to retain their hold on Burma and why the Royal Navy must be ready before any land operations were commenced.[45]

Churchill disagreed with Chiang's estimate of the situation. In the prime minister's view, the success of land operations in Burma did not hinge entirely on simultaneous land and sea action. Since the Royal Navy would not be able to send a full strength task force into the Bay of Bengal until the late spring or early summer of 1944, he urged Chiang and Roosevelt to go ahead with the campaign as originally conceived by Mountbatten and Stilwell.[46] It was unlikely, according to the prime minister, that the Japanese would send a show of force into the Bay of Bengal before the Royal Navy task force was assembled in May or June.[47]

Because Churchill was well aware of the importance the Chinese attached to operations in Southeast Asia and Roosevelt's concern that the Chinese be placated, he suggested that Anglo-Chinese differences might be reconciled if he and the generalissimo had "further talks" about the Burma campaign.[48] Roosevelt, who sensed that the plenary session had reached an impasse, was only too happy to accept Churchill's proposal for one-on-one talks with Chiang. He adjourned the meeting shortly before 1:00 P.M., expressing the hope that Generalissimo Chiang Kai-shek would take the opportunity of meeting with British and American representatives and engage in "frank discussions" with them.[49]

The discussion of the proposed campaign in Burma at the first plenary session was polite on the surface, but beneath the facade of cordiality, tempers were fraying. Alan Brooke was livid that Chiang seemed to make the whole Burma campaign contingent upon the readiness of British naval forces in the Indian Ocean.[50] In a diary entry made on November 23, he noted that the generalissimo had "no grasp of war in its larger aspects."[51] He also noted that Madame Chiang, who understood even less about war than her husband, was advising him to press his unrealistic demands on Roosevelt in the hope that the president would force Churchill to make concessions to the Chinese.[52]

Alan Brooke was not the only British officer to leave the plenary session with misgivings. Mountbatten also left the session with mixed feelings, but his anger was directed at Brooke not Chiang.[53] Although the generalissimo's linkage of naval and land operations in Burma might complicate the proposed campaign in Burma, it was Brooke's adamant opposition to diverting resources to Southeast Asia and the pressure he was putting on Churchill to support this view which really threatened the viability of the Burma campaign.[54]

Had it not been for the fact that the Americans liked Mountbatten, the BCOS might have tried to abort his proposed Burma offensive before it could be presented at Cairo. But this was not to be the case because the BCOS were well aware, thanks to Dill, of the fact that "Mountbatten had made a great impression on the Americans" who would not permit them to block discussion of the campaign in Southeast Asia.[55] Furthermore, the BCOS also understood that Chiang Kai-shek would ultimately endorse Mountbatten's proposal and demand the British do likewise.[56] Unless Churchill could be persuaded to confront Roosevelt, who seemed equally adamant in his support of a campaign in Southeast Asia as Brooke and the BCOS were opposed to such a venture, the campaign would go forward.

Mountbatten was somewhat of an outcast among Churchill's military advisors. Some, like Ismay, privately dismissed him as a lightweight who held high position only because of his membership in Royal Family.[57] Others, including Alan Brooke, were agitated by his ego and his grandstanding.[58] Whereas the Americans seemed to find Mountbatten a dashing figure in his admiral's uniform, the BCOS found him to lack fundamental understanding of the realities of the war. Mountbatten may have cut a fine figure, but fine figures did not win wars.

Mountbatten understood that he had more support from the Americans and Chinese than he did from his peers in the BCOS. He also understood that the key to getting the go-ahead for some kind of campaign in Burma was to secure Chiang Kai-shek's unqualified support for such a venture. If the generalissimo's reservations could be overcome, his approval of the Burma campaign would trigger Roosevelt's approval as well and Churchill would have no choice but to go along, despite the opposition of Brooke and the other BCOS.

Shortly after the first plenary session adjourned, while Churchill and Roosevelt were lunching at the president's villa, Mountbatten paid a call on Generalissimo and Madame Chiang at their villa. The purpose of the call was to overcome Chiang's opposition to participating in the Burma offensive. To do so, Mountbatten brought detailed maps and technical charts, which he went over for a second time with the Chiangs. Mountbatten hoped to prove that the goals proposed by the South East Asia Command (SEAC) were reasonable and that the success of the campaign in Burma was contingent on Chinese participation and support.[59]

According to Mountbatten's recollection of the conversation, Chiang approved of the idea of an offensive in Burma but felt that the plan that the SEAC was suggesting was too modest.[60] What the Chinese wanted was a bolder venture, which would include the capture of Rangoon and Lashio and the reopening of the land route from Burma to China.[61] Mountbatten tried to tell the generalissimo that such a plan "was not possible" and gave "exact reasons" why it could not succeed.[62] This did not seem to phase Chiang. "Never mind," he said to Mountbatten, "we will carry it out all the same."[63]

While Mountbatten was meeting with Generalissimo and Madame Chiang, members of the JCS were meeting with their Chinese counterparts in order to brief them prior to their first meeting with the CCOS, which was scheduled for 2:30 P.M. at the Mena House Hotel. A second purpose of this meeting was to solicit comments and recommendations from the Chinese generals. According to Arnold and Leahy, the Chinese generals seemed well informed and committed to some kind of an offensive in Burma, but they had little to say beyond this.[64] Leahy recalls that they said "they had not had enough time to make a careful study of the proposed plan" and thus could not make any specific recommendations.[65] Arnold observed that the relative silence of the Chinese generals was due to other reasons, namely their fear of making any decisions independently of the generalissimo.[66]

Mountbatten left Chiang's villa shortly after 2:00 P.M., at which time the generalissimo called Stilwell to tell him that he would be coming to the CCOS meeting to comment on Mountbatten's proposal.[67] Minutes later, Stilwell received a second call from the generalissimo who told him that he would not be coming to the CCOS meeting.[68] Within minutes after receiving this second call, Chiang called Stilwell a third time to say that he had changed his mind again and would come to the CCOS meeting.[69] Just as he was leaving for the Mena House Hotel, Stilwell received a final call from the generalissimo who had changed his mind again and told Stilwell not to make any specific proposals regarding Chinese participation in the Burma campaign when the meeting convened.[70]

As Stilwell noted in his diary, the generalissimo was clearly upset about rumors that his aides had performed badly and confused as to how to best rectify the situation. Stilwell likened Chiang's vacillation over whether he should present China's case at the CCOS meeting to thinking aloud on the telephone. Although he was annoyed at Chiang's barrage of calls, Stilwell was not surprised that the generalissimo decided not to attend the CCOS meeting. Chiang had opted to consult privately with Roosevelt where he was likely to get a more enthusiastic response than from the CCOS.[71]

Stilwell had barely enough time to get to the Mena House Hotel before the CCOS meeting was opened by Alan Brooke at 2:30 P.M. Since he was not in a position to speak in specific terms on behalf of the generalissimo, it was agreed that the CCOS would discuss Stilwell's memorandum, "The Role of China in the Defeat of Japan," which had been presented to the CCOS on November 22 and which had not been discussed at the first plenary session because of the prolonged discussion of Mountbatten's proposal.[72]

Stilwell's memorandum outlined an eight-phase plan of attack against Japan. During the first phase, the Chinese would assist the SEAC in invading northern Burma. In phase two, Chinese and Allied forces would open a new land route from Burma to China. During phase three, additional Chinese military units would be airlifted to India for retraining and eventual redeployment against Japanese bases in China. In phase four, the United States Army Air Force and the Chinese Air Force would commence intensive bombing of Japan from Chinese bases. During phase five, Chinese forces would capture Canton and Hong Kong; this campaign would last from November 1944 to May 1945. Phase six would involve Allied air and naval forces in a campaign to close the Straits of Formosa and the South China Sea to the Japanese, beginning in the autumn of 1944. Having neutralized the Straits of Formosa, the seventh phase of the plan, an invasion of Formosa would commence. The last phase of the plan called for an attack on Shanghai in November 1945.[73]

Reaction to Stilwell's memorandum was lukewarm. Alan Brooke and the BCOS felt that many of Stilwell's proposals, particularly points five through eight, were unrealistic and Admiral Leahy agreed with Brooke's assessment, arguing that attacks on Japanese positions in Canton, Hong Kong, Shanghai, and Formosa were well beyond the logistical capabilities of the Allies.[74] Marshall agreed with his colleagues, but suggested that the first four points of Stilwell's plan, which called for the recapture of Burma and the opening of a new Burma road could be achieved and urged approval of these operations.[75] Since this part of Stilwell's plan coincided nicely with Mountbatten's ideas and would have the approval of Chiang, Marshall urged approval of points one through four.[76]

Marshall's comments precipitated a renewed discussion of Chiang Kai-shek's willingness to commit his land forces to the campaign in Burma if the British could not guarantee deployment of the Royal Navy in the Bay of Bengal prior to the launching of the offensive in Burma in January 1944. Stilwell suggested that the generalissimo might be satisfied if "we could guarantee naval security in the Pacific."[77] Mountbatten offered a somewhat different observation, pointing out that although the generalissimo was not interested in the "specifics of naval forces," he was most concerned about "synchronizing land and naval operations" and might be loath to commit his forces without British guarantees.[78]

The CCOS hoped that the Chinese generals, who were expected to join the deliberations shortly, would be able to clarify the generalissimo's position. Thus, when Chiang's subordinates arrived, Brooke invited them to comment on Mountbatten's proposal and Stilwell's plan, urging them to "raise questions and put forward suggestions."[79] If Brooke and the other members of the CCOS expected to be enlightened, they were to be sorely disappointed.

Speaking on behalf of General Shang Chen and the other Chinese officers, Chu Shih-ming stated that the Chinese representatives had not had adequate time to study these plans and would prefer to discuss them the next day.[80] After a few moments of silence, Mountbatten suggested that since the Chinese generals were not ready to make substantive comments, perhaps they might discuss their contingency plans for deployment of the Yunnan Force in the opening phases of the Burma campaign, should such an offensive receive the generalissimo's blessings.[81] Once again, there was silence.[82] Finally, Stilwell responded to Mountbatten's query, outlining in detail how the Yunnan Force might be deployed. During the course of Stilwell's remarks, Brooke peppered him with additional questions.[83]

Since the Chinese generals had nothing further to contribute, Brooke proposed that the CCOS meeting be adjourned until 2:30 P.M. the next day, at which time the Chinese would make some kind of presentation.[84] After the session ended, Brooke turned to Marshall and said "That was a ghastly waste of time!"[85] "You're telling me!" replied Marshall.[86] Marshall's response only served to aggravate Brooke more. "Considering that it was thanks to him [Marshall] and the American outlook that we had to suffer this depressing interlude," Brooke noted in his diary, "I felt he might have expressed his regret otherwise."[87]

Alan Brooke was not the only member of the CCOS to be disturbed about the session. Although the official records of the meeting reveal no acrimony, the private papers of the participants suggest that it was a very stormy session. Whereas Brooke and the other members of the BCOS were stunned and annoyed at the silence of the Chinese, the American officers present at this session were equally upset by the behavior of their British counterparts. Stilwell noted that Brooke was so nasty and insulting that Admiral King almost climbed over the table to punch him.[88] Marshall and Arnold confirm Stilwell's observation about the mood of the meeting, although they do not seem to have shared Stilwell's wish that King had socked Brooke![89]

Although Stilwell found Alan Brooke to be "an arrogant bastard," his real frustration was not with Brooke but, as usual, with the generalissimo and his subordinates. The Chinese generals gave a "terrible performance," according to Stilwell, forcing him to bail them out.[90] As Brooke fired questions at the Chinese, Stilwell was forced to "bat them back," knowing full well that they were afraid to ask or answer any questions without the generalissimo's express approval.[91] If this embarrassing situation was to be avoided the next day, Stilwell had to consult with Chiang and his subordinates before the day was done to help them to get their questions and answers ready.

Stilwell was able to get an audience with the generalissimo and his staff at 6:00 P.M.[92] He briefed them until 8:40 P.M., at which time he returned to his quarters. Generals Wedemeyer and Merrill were there as well.[93] Trying to be diplomatic, which was not easy for him, Stilwell urged the generalissimo to present his position clearly or, at least, to allow Shang Chen and the other Chinese generals to do so for him.[94] Although Chiang had to excuse himself to prepare for dinner at Roosevelt's villa later that evening, Stilwell, Wedemeyer, and Merrill had ample time to complete their briefing of the generalissimo's subordinates.[95]

Generalissimo and Madame Chiang Kai-shek dined with President Roosevelt at his villa at 8:00 P.M.[96] The only other person present was Harry Hopkins.[97] After dinner, they talked late into the night. According to the generalissimo's diary, a wide range of issues were discussed, including plans for the occupation and reconstruction of Japan, plans for the disposal of territories occupied by Japan, and plans for the post-war reconstruction of China.[98]

Roosevelt, who often preferred to talk as opposed to listening, allowed the generalissimo to do most of the talking.[99] This was his opportunity to get Chiang's views on a wide variety of matters unfiltered through the lenses of the State Department, the War Department, or his special emissaries. Indeed, this was one of the primary reasons the president had pushed so hard for the Cairo conference. This fact was not lost on the generalissimo who proved more responsive and less reserved than at any other point during his stay in Cairo.

Chiang told Roosevelt that when the war was over, the Allies must rid Japan of the militarists who had led their country down the road to Pearl Harbor, but he offered no suggestions as to what kind of government should be established in Tokyo after the war.[100] When asked by the president whether the Chinese expected to play a major role in the occupation of Japan, the generalissimo replied that China would have her own reconstruction problems to solve and would be happy to have the United States in charge of the occupation so long as the Chinese secured the return of all territories seized by the Japanese warlords between 1931 and 1941.[101]

Generalissimo and Madame Chiang were more concerned by the immediate military and political problems in China than they were by the broader post-war geopolitical issues and they made this clear to Roosevelt.[102] China's most pressing need, they told the president, was to obtain adequate supplies of munitions and provisions for the Chinese army, without which the army would not be able to carry the fight to the Japanese.[103] While the critics of his government had accused the generalissimo of hoarding supplies for eventual use against the Chinese communists when the war against Japan ended, Chiang assured Roosevelt that this was not the case.[104] All available manpower and material were being devoted to the war effort.[105]

Chiang did not deny that he was very much concerned about the Chinese communists. "They must be kept under government surveillance," he told the president.[106] When Roosevelt suggested that American intelligence indicated that the communists were honoring their commitment to the United Front against Japanese aggression, the generalissimo suggested that this might not be the case.[107] But even if the communists were honoring their agreements with the Kuomintang for the moment, what of the future? "Communism and imperialism," Chiang told Roosevelt, "were the two central problems of our time."[108]

The generalissimo suggested that he was also concerned with Stalin and the Soviet government. "I profoundly mistrust Soviet intentions," he said to the president, and he suggested that Roosevelt keep "a close watch" over Soviet deeds and activities.[109] The generalissimo, who was aware that Roosevelt would soon be meeting with Stalin, wished to make it clear to the president that he felt that vague promises of Soviet intervention in the war against Japan at some uncertain future date should not be used as an argument to limit supplies to the CBI theater or abort the plans outlined in the proposals of Mountbatten and Stilwell as some, particularly the British, were suggesting.[110]

Generalissimo and Madame Chiang left the president's villa shortly after 11:00 P.M.[111] From their point of view, the evening had been a successful one.[112] Roosevelt shared this assessment of the meeting, telling his son Elliott, "I learned more from my conversation with the Chiangs than I did from more than four hours with the Combined Chiefs."[113] The generalissimo knew what he wanted, Roosevelt told his son, and knew he could not get it all, but Roosevelt suggested, "but we'll work something out."[114]

Roosevelt also told his son that despite the disclaimers of the generalissimo and his wife, he believed that many of Chiang's best forces were not being committed to the war against Japan but were being deployed instead against the communists in the northwest of China.[115] He suggested that this might account for Chiang's efforts to obstruct Stilwell's program of training Chinese troops in India because Stilwell would not tolerate the hoarding of these troops and their supplies for a post-war civil war.[116]

With the departure of Generalissimo and Madame Chiang from Roosevelt's villa, day one of the formal proceedings at Cairo came to an end. It had been a day characterized by acrimony and anxiety with no specific agreements reached nor understandings achieved. The differences between the British and Chinese had yet to be compromised or resolved and the friction between Chiang and Churchill was beginning to affect the cordiality of Anglo-American relations.

Churchill, Alan Brooke, and other members of the British delegation at Cairo clearly resented the presence of the Chinese and the time wasted in discussing matters relating to the CBI theater. They placed responsibility for this unnecessary diversion of time squarely on Roosevelt and his subordinates. Ironically, Roosevelt, Marshall, and other members of the American delegation felt that it was the British who were wasting time by refusing to commit to a program of action in Southeast Asia. If only Churchill would give the green light for Mountbatten's proposed offensive in Burma, other more pressing matters could be discussed and attended to.

Generalissimo and Madame Chiang were also perturbed by day one of the conference. Although they were received with great courtesy and some pomp by Roosevelt and Churchill, it was clear to them that they were unwanted guests, at least insofar as the British were concerned, and they were convinced that the British meant to scuttle any significant campaign in Burma and China. Their response was to link commitment of Chinese land forces to simultaneous commitment of British naval forces and rally the Americans to their side, hoping that Churchill would succumb to Roosevelt's pressure. They believed they had made a positive impression on the president, but it remained to be seen how things would work out on day two of the conference.[117]

7

November 24, 1943: The Plot Unfolds

The first day of the conference had been fraught with difficulties. Chiang Kai-shek, who had come to Cairo with very mixed feelings about British policy in the CBI, had little reason to feel better after his observation of Churchill and Alan Brooke at the plenary session on November 23. Churchill and Brooke, who had come to Cairo with very jaded views of the generalissimo's government and the centrality of its role in the war against Japan, had little reason to change their opinions, given what they observed of Chiang and his entourage at the plenary session and the first meeting of the CCOS. Realizing that frayed tempers and bruised egos threatened to abort an agreement on the course of action in the CBI and SEAC theaters for 1944, President Roosevelt hoped for some progress on November 24.

Roosevelt expressed his consternation over the apparent lack of progress in the talks to his son Elliott, who arrived in Cairo early on the morning of November 24, 1943.[1] According to his son, the president believed that the British were reluctant to mount a serious offensive in Burma and were using the matter of naval force in the Indian Ocean to torpedo plans for an extensive engagement of Japanese forces in the jungles of Southeast Asia.[2] Should no agreement be reached on an offensive in Burma, this would have a devastating effect on Chinese morale, according to Roosevelt, and the failure to open a new land route from Burma to China could jeopardize Chiang's ability to continue the war against Japan.[3]

"The job in China can be boiled down to one essential," Roosevelt told his son, "China must be kept in the war tying up Japanese soldiers."[4] This required increasing the flow of supplies to China, whether by increasing the airlift over the Hump or completing the Ledo Road from Burma to China.[5] The president went on to tell his son that the situation in China was very grave. While General MacArthur and others in the Pacific thought that their theater was a forgotten one, it was China that was really the forgotten theater. "Compared to the CBI," Roosevelt said to his son, "the Pacific is at Times Square and Forty Second Street!"[6]

Elliott Roosevelt recalls that his father was not totally naive about Chiang Kai-shek and his regime and realized that the generalissimo's government was not devoting all of its resources to the war against Japan.[7] Although the president knew that the generalissimo was diverting supplies and manpower to the northwest to guard against the Chinese communists, he still believed that the Chinese military was playing a vital role in bottling up almost one million Japanese troops in China. Should the Chinese give up the battle, these troops could be sent to the Pacific where they would pose a much greater hazard to the Allies.[8]

Shortly after his conversation with his son, Elliott, Roosevelt met with Averell Harriman.[9] The purpose of this meeting was to brief the president for his upcoming meeting with Stalin, but according to Harriman, considerable time was devoted to discussing Stalin's views on the situation in China and the possibility that the Soviets would join the United States in the war against Japan after the defeat of Germany.[10]

Harriman had submitted a memorandum on Sino-Soviet relations to the president on November 23.[11] In this memo, Harriman suggested that contrary to Chiang Kai-shek's belief, Stalin desired peace with China after the war and recognized that the generalissimo was the only leader in China capable of creating a stable government after the war.[12] Harriman also suggested that while Stalin recognized Chiang's position as China's pre-eminent leader, he hoped that the generalissimo could reach an accommodation with the Chinese communists, which would lead to "democratic and social reforms in China" in the post-war era.[13]

Whether or not Roosevelt read Harriman's memorandum is unclear, but even if he did not, the ambassador reiterated the main points in this memo when he briefed the president on November 24. He also took up the matter of Soviet participation in the war against Japan, an issue not discussed in his memorandum.[14] On this point, Harriman reconfirmed what Cordell Hull had learned at the Moscow Foreign Ministers Conference in October, namely that Stalin had tentatively agreed to declare war on Japan when the war in Europe was over.[15] Harriman suggested that Roosevelt might confirm this fact for himself when he and Churchill met with Stalin at Teheran following the conclusion of the deliberations in Cairo.[16]

The intervention of the Soviet Union in the war against Japan would have important consequences for the Allies. Should this happen, as Harriman thought likely, the importance of the Burma campaign proposed by Chiang and Stilwell would be subject to question. Indeed, in a conversation with Claire Chennault on the morning of November 23, Harriman was surprised to find that Chennault, long an advocate of increased efforts in the CBI, seemed to now favor the Europe first strategy long advocated by Marshall and the JCS.[17] According to Harriman, Chennault even went so far as to suggest that in light of the possibility of Soviet intervention, the proposed Burma campaign was "senseless."[18]

Chennault's seeming conversion to the Europe-first strategy may well have been self-serving. If the plans proposed by Mountbatten and Stilwell were approved at Cairo, there would undoubtedly be a marked shift in the flow of supplies from Chennault's 14th Army Air Force to the forces under Stilwell's command, thus necessitating a reduction of Chennault's activities in China. Still, regardless of Chennault's motives, the introduction of the possibility of Soviet intervention in the war against Japan added a new element to the discussions at Cairo.

Before meeting with the president, Harriman also briefed the JCS at their morning session at the Mena House. He told them that the Soviets would join the United States and the United Kingdom in the war against Japan as soon as the Germans had been defeated.[19] Until then, however, the Russians wished to avoid a premature break with Japan, which might have an adverse effect, such as the Japanese seizure or closing of the port of Vladivostok.[20]

Harriman urged the JCS to raise the matter of Soviet participation in the war against Japan when they met with their Russian counterparts at Teheran.[21] Harriman told the JCS that Churchill and Roosevelt need not be shy in pointing out "the advantages that the Soviets would receive from such participation" and stressed that in dealing with the Russians, candor was often the best policy.[22] According to Harriman, the Soviets were blunt and appreciated bluntness from others.[23]

How much of an impact Harriman's remarks had on the JCS is unclear, although almost all of them were wary of the generalissimo's regime and its capabilities. Their support of proposed operations in Burma was, in large measure, recognition of the larger geopolitical views of their commander-in-chief, the president, who still seemed convinced of the military and political rewards to be reaped in soothing Chiang Kai-shek's ego and placating the Chinese.

As Harriman was briefing the JCS, Alan Brooke opened the morning session of the BCOS elsewhere in the Mena House Hotel. Although the minutes of this meeting suggest that matters relating to the European theater and the upcoming Operation Overlord dominated the agenda, the BCOS did discuss two matters relating to China and the SEAC theater, those being Mountbatten's proposed plan of action for 1944 and a request from Generalissimo Chiang and his staff that the Chinese be seated as permanent members of the CCOS.[24]

The Chinese had proposed that the Combined Chiefs of Staff, which included only British and American officers, be transformed into a United Chiefs of Staff (UCS), which would also include Chinese and Soviet representatives. This proposal would be on the agenda of the second plenary session at 11:00 A.M. and the afternoon meeting of the CCOS at 2:30 P.M. Although neither the American chiefs nor their British counterparts were enthusiastic about the idea, it was viewed by the Chinese as a sign of good faith and was placed on the agenda at the urging of President Roosevelt.[25]

None of the British chiefs wished to see the CCOS expanded into a UCS. Speaking for his colleagues, Field Marshal Dill, who was as close and sympathetic to the American side as any British officer, argued that the proposal to create a UCS was "not a practical solution."[26] Only the United Kingdom and the United States were involved in all war theaters, he pointed out, and a special bond existed between the two powers.[27] Furthermore, given the strained relations between the Chinese and Soviet governments and the fact that Chiang and Stalin were fighting different enemies and were not partners in the war effort, the addition of Chinese and/or Russian representatives to the CCOS could only complicate matters.[28]

Dill suggested that the Chinese and Soviets could be invited to join the CCOS as needed.[29] When matters pertaining to China and the SEAC theater were discussed, Chinese representatives could be invited to join their Anglo-American counterparts. When matters pertaining to Russia and the war against Germany were discussed, Soviet officers could be invited to join the CCOS.[30] Dill was relatively sure that Marshall and the Americans would support such an idea and it was agreed that the BCOS would advance this position when the matter came up.[31]

The second plenary session of the conference opened at 11:00 A.M. at Roosevelt's villa with the president presiding over the meeting.[32] Since the meeting was to be devoted to an assessment of the situation in Europe, plans for Operation Overland, and, if time permitted, the expansion of the CCOS, the Chinese were not invited to participate and there was no substantive discussion of matters relating to the CBI or SEAC theaters.[33] Because discussions of Operation Overlord took more time than anticipated, the matter of the UCS proposal was not discussed. The plenary session adjourned at 12:40 P.M.[34]

While the plenary session was going on, General Stilwell was preparing to brief Generalissimo and Madame Chiang prior to their luncheon meeting with General Marshall, which was scheduled to begin at the conclusion of the plenary session.[35] Because Stilwell had, of necessity, become Chiang's chief lieutenant at the conference, he was moved from his original billet into quarters adjacent to the generalissimo's villa, a move which placed him on call on a twenty-four hour basis and gave him easier access to the Chiangs.[36] Upon completing preparation of a briefing book for the generalissimo and his wife in his new venue, Stilwell proceeded to the Chiangs' villa.[37]

Stilwell arrived at the Chiangs' villa just before noon. When he arrived, he found that the generalissimo was closeted with his staff while his wife was still in bed.[38] Stilwell asked one of the servants to wake Madame Chiang so that he could discuss strategy with her before General Marshall's arrival.[39] After a short wait, Madame Chiang received Stilwell and the two of them discussed a number of questions, including a proposal that Stilwell had drawn up at the generalissimo's urging, requesting the dispatch of more American troops to China.[40]

Marshall arrived at the generalissimo's villa just before 1:00 P.M.[41] The purpose of his visit was to hear Chiang's objections to the proposals that Mountbatten had made the day before and to persuade the generalissimo to give the "green light" to Mountbatten's plan.[42] According to Stilwell's recollection, Marshall "talked a streak" at lunch, but the generalissimo remained skeptical of the Mountbatten plan and British commitment to an effective campaign in Burma.[43]

Chiang was direct with Marshall, telling the general that Mountbatten's proposal would result in Chinese forces suffering the brunt of casualties in Burma while the British risked little because of their reluctance to launch a simultaneous amphibious operation in Burma and their unwillingness to commit sufficient manpower and airpower to the SEAC theater.[44] The generalissimo made it clear to Marshall that unless the British agreed to substantially increase their commitment to the proposed Burma offensive, he would not commit his Yunnan forces to the fray nor would he allow the Ledo force, recently trained by Stilwell in India, to participate in the offensive.[45]

Marshall tried to reassure Chiang that Mountbatten's plan was only the first phase of the effort to retake Burma and would be "less costly" than the generalissimo believed.[46] According to Stilwell, Marshall's assurances were not sufficient and it was agreed that the matter would be taken up again at the CCOS session that afternoon.[47] Marshall invited Chiang to participate in this discussion and the generalissimo agreed to do so.[48] Later, Chiang decided not to attend the CCOS meeting and ordered Stilwell to go in his place and "tell them his views."[49] Marshall was still talking to Chiang when the CCOS meeting commenced at 2:30 P.M.[50]

By the time that Marshall arrived at the CCOS session, his colleagues had unanimously rejected Chiang's proposal to invite Chinese representatives to sit on the CCOS on a permanent basis.[51] As soon as he was seated, Marshall was immediately asked by Alan Brooke to inform the group of the generalissimo's latest view of Mountbatten's proposal.[52] Marshall reported that Chiang disapproved of the plan because he felt that Mountbatten's proposal, as presently constituted, would place the burden of responsibility and losses on the Chinese and offered no guarantee of victory.[53] Marshall told his colleagues that the generalissimo had suggested that several conditions would have to be met before he approved of the campaign. First, the British would have to commit to launching an amphibious operation, preferably in the Andaman Islands, simultaneously with the land campaign in Burma.[54] Second, British forces would have to agree to the occupation of Mandalay, which represented a substantive increase in the scope of Mountbatten's original plan.[55]

Marshall's comments shocked Alan Brooke and the other British chiefs.

Although they remained calm, it is clear that they were very angry. Writing in his diary at the end of the day, Brooke noted that Chiang "had suddenly decided that unless several impossible conditions could be fulfilled, he refused to play his part in the operations."[56] In Brooke's opinion, the generalissimo was holding the conference hostage to unrealistic demands and his Anglophobic prejudice was blinding his judgment.[57]

Sensing the anger and frustration of his British colleagues, Marshall tried to make them understand that Chiang's "extreme interest" in the details of just how the British would participate in the campaign in Burma was a matter which needed to be addressed because the generalissimo would use this as a litmus test of Churchill's commitment to the CBI.[58] He urged the British to present some plan for increasing their naval presence in the vicinity of Burma as a token offering to the Chinese.[59] He also suggested that Mountbatten should be sent to consult and negotiate with Chiang as soon as possible.[60]

Mountbatten was not opposed to explaining his proposal to Chiang yet again, but he expressed concern that the generalissimo listened but did not seem to hear what others told him.[61] In particular, Mountbatten was frustrated by the fact that Chiang did not comprehend that his proposal was only the first part of a complicated and long campaign to wrest Burma from the Japanese.[62] Brooke seconded Mountbatten's comments, telling his colleagues, "in taking the first step, we are committing to the recapture of all Burma."[63]

Once again, Marshall tried to explain that the conditions Chiang demanded reflected his fear that Chinese forces would be left to carry out their advance without adequate support from the other Allies.[64] Once he understood that this would not be the case, the generalissimo would come-round.[65] Hopefully, Mountbatten could reassure Chiang and his entourage before the next plenary session.[66] As Marshall was concluding his remarks, the Chinese generals arrived at Mena House accompanied by Stilwell and Chennault.

After the Chinese officers were seated, Alan Brooke asked them if they felt they had adequate time to consider Mountbatten's proposal and what they thought of it.[67] General Shang Chen, speaking for his colleagues, indicated that they had examined the plan and had some comments to offer "in a spirit of helpfulness," but before offering these comments, the Chinese generals wished to ask some questions.[68] Brooke invited them to do so.[69]

General Shang put a series of questions to the CCOS. Specifically, he asked how many British units would be deployed in Burma, what was their battlefield experience, and what kind of special training and equipment they had.[70] Mountbatten answered each of these questions while Brooke and the other British chiefs looked on.[71] They remained silent as Mountbatten painstakingly gave General Shang more details about the deployment of British forces than he or the other Chinese officers might have wanted to know, but, as Alan Brooke's notes reveal, he and his peers were quite upset by the questions posed by General Shang.

In a diary entry made later that day, Brooke described the return of the Chinese generals as "a lamentable fiasco" and commented that they wasted an hour of time asking "the most futile questions."[72] According to Brooke, the kind of questions raised by General Shang were trivial and could have been answered outside of the confines of the meeting of the CCOS had the Chinese merely consulted lower ranking British staff officers.[73] "It was evident," Brooke noted, "that they understood nothing about strategy or higher tactics and were quite unfit to discuss these questions."[74]

Brooke might have even been more upset had he realized that the questions that Shang Chen raised at the afternoon session of the CCOS were actually prepared for the Chinese generals earlier in the day by General Stilwell.[75] As it was, at least according to Stilwell, the British were quite "agitated" that the Chinese would dare to question the capability of their forces.[76] If they had known that the Americans also wanted to know the answers to these questions, they might really have been agitated.[77]

After Mountbatten answered his questions, General Shang commented on Mountbatten's proposal. "Chiang Kai-shek instructs me to emphasize synchronization of naval action and land operations," he told his audience, and he would be "most disappointed" if he did not know what commitments the British would make before he left Cairo.[78] Having said this, Shang went on to point out the generalissimo felt that the present plan for action in Burma in 1944 did not go far enough and was too limited. A bolder plan of action was needed.[79]

General Shang also stated that Chiang Kai-shek was concerned that plans for a land operation in Burma would drain resources from China. Whatever the needs of the land operation that might ultimately be approved in Cairo, Shang told his peers that the generalissimo was insistent that the airlift to China not drop below 10,000 tons per month.[80] Though this might be thought to hinder land operations in Burma, Chiang wanted the allies to remember that operations in China and Burma were closely linked and that the pressure exerted on Japanese forces from China "must be maintained."[81] Shang's comments linking approval of land operations in Burma with a promise that there would be no reduction in supplies flown into China stunned his audience. Even the seemingly ever-patient Mountbatten could not restrain himself from responding to Shang's recapitulation of the generalissimo's views. "It was illogical," Mountbatten told Shang, "to call for a more extensive land operation in Burma while demanding no reduction in the 10,000 tons to China."[82] This was especially so given the fact that the 10,000 ton figure was a target yet to be reached.[83] "The Chinese must make up their minds," he said to Shang, "what they wanted, 10,000 tons a month to China or the land operation in Burma."[84]

General Marshall seconded Mountbatten's statement, telling General Shang that if the Chinese wanted to open a new road from Burma to China, they must fight to do so.[85] He reminded the Chinese delegates that unless this land route was opened there could be no increase in supplies to China because the Allies could not provide additional aircraft for the Hump lift because of more important commitments elsewhere.[86]

General Shang and the other Chinese delegates seem to have been surprised by the harsh tone of Mountbatten's comments and Marshall's remarks. Having just said that the generalissimo would approve of no plan of action in Burma that would result in a reduction of the supply effort in China, General Shang promised to take up the matter with Chiang. "I am not in a position," he told his colleagues, "to give a decision regarding any reduction in Hump tonnage, but I will report your views to the generalissimo."[87]

As if to insure that the General Shang relayed the correct message to Chiang, Mountbatten reminded him that plans for the operation in Burma, including the question of supplies, had been discussed with the generalissimo and that Chiang had promised to regard necessary diversion of supplies "sympathetically."[88] Alan Brooke went even further, telling Shang that the reopening of the Burma Road could not be accomplished unless the generalissimo agreed to a reduction of the air lift into China and to the use of what supplies reached China to feed and fuel the efforts of Chinese forces in Burma.[89]

Since the Chinese generals were not in a position to make any decisions on any matter of substance without the express approval of Chiang Kai-shek, it was agreed that the CCOS meeting would adjourn and that General Shang would inform the generalissimo of what had just been discussed.[90] It was also agreed that General Shang would arrange a meeting between Chiang and Mountbatten so that he could discuss the supply problem with the generalissimo and get him to understand that there would have to be sacrifices on all sides if there was to be any campaign in Burma.[91]

The frustration exemplified by the tone of the CCOS meeting indicated that the atmosphere of the conference was turning increasingly sour. "All had so many different ideas about what to do and how to do it," General Arnold noted of the conference and its atmosphere, "that it was most difficult to come to any logical conclusion."[92] The British criticized the Chinese as unrealistic while the Chinese said the British were unwilling to fight.[93] The Americans, according to Arnold, were coming to believe that the conference might prove fruitless, at least in so far as resolving the China tangle.[94]

The next scheduled event after the conclusion of the CCOS meeting was a cocktail party hosted by Generalissimo and Madame Chiang Kai-shek.[95] Interestingly, neither Roosevelt nor Churchill chose to attend this event, with the president sending his son Elliott in his place while Churchill designated his daughter Sarah to represent him. According to Elliott Roosevelt, his father was too busy receiving "a stream of guests" to attend the party at the Chiangs' villa.[96] Churchill chose not to attend because he was likewise preoccupied and would be entertaining Generalissimo and Madame Chiang later that evening for dinner.[97]

Except for the absence of Churchill and Roosevelt, everybody from the three delegations was there. As Elliott Roosevelt told his father later that evening, "the room was filled with braid and brass."[98] According to the president's son, Madame Chiang worked the crowd like a real performer, concentrating her attention on him and the prime minister's daughter, while the generalissimo mingled more casually with the other guests.[99] She was an "expert flatterer," he told the president, and used her charm to seduce her listeners, particularly the men at the party.[100]

Elliott Roosevelt joked with his father that not having the opportunity to lavish her attentions on the president, Madame Chiang devoted her energy to entertaining him, discussing the future economic development of China with great enthusiasm and soliciting his views on the future of Sino-American relations.[101] "During the conversation," Elliott told his father, "she leaned forward, looking at me brightly, agreeing with everything I said, while resting her hand firmly on my knee."[102] When the president's son managed to slip away from Madame Chiang, she turned her attention to Sarah Churchill.[103]

It is interesting to note that Elliott Roosevelt's comments about Madame Chiang mirrored those of Alan Brooke and Churchill. All of them were taken by her feminine charm, but were disturbed by her public role at the conference. As the sole female participant in the substantive deliberations at Cairo, she made her male counterparts uneasy. While they treated her with respect, it seems clear that they were uneasy about her role at the conference and uncertain about how much she influenced the generalissimo.

Later that evening when Elliott Roosevelt reported on the cocktail party to the president, his father asked him about his impression of the Chiangs. Elliott was candid. He had come to no conclusion about the generalissimo, but felt that Madame Chiang was a person of whom to be wary.[104] According to his recollection of the conversation, the president agreed with him and suggested that Madame Chiang was little more than an opportunist.[105] Still, the president said, with all of their faults, "we've got to depend on the Chiangs."[106] Unfortunately, there was no other leader in China to take the generalissimo's place and, as Roosevelt realized only too well, he was quite dependent on his wife.[107]

While his son was at the cocktail party hosted by Generalissimo and Madame Chiang, Roosevelt took an hour out of his afternoon schedule to drive out to visit the Sphinx with General Arnold.[108] En route, the president asked Arnold for his views about the situation in China and plans for the campaign in Burma.[109] In particular, Roosevelt was interested to know whether the Army Air Force would be able to meet Chiang's demands for a minimum supply operation of 10,000 tons per month while, at the same time, providing additional supplies for the offensive in Burma.[110]

Arnold advised Roosevelt that he could not satisfy Chiang's requests for supplies in the short term without jeopardizing the offensive in Burma.[111] In the long term, however, this would not be a problem. Arnold assured the president that the time was coming when he "would be able to get more tonnage into China by air than the Chinese would be able to haul away from the airdromes on the roads available in and around Kunming."[112] At this point, Roosevelt and Arnold reached the Sphinx and the conversation ended.[113] After a few minutes, they drove back to the president's villa and went their separate ways.[114]

Roosevelt had his last appointment of the afternoon at 5:30 P.M. and then returned to his bedroom for a rest before dinner.[115] He dined with Ambassador Harriman, Hopkins, Leahy, McIntyre, and "Pa" Watson at 8:30 P.M., chatting and playing cards with his companions until after midnight, at which time his guests left.[116] Shortly after they departed, his son Elliott returned from a night on the town in Cairo and he and his father talked late into the night.[117]

During their post-midnight chat, Roosevelt expressed his concern that the friction between British and Chinese representatives was spilling over and straining Anglo-American relations.[118] The president told his son that the British had no faith that the Chinese army could be whipped into fighting shape and had adopted a strategy in Burma of going small and slow as opposed to "our strategy of going as fast and as big as we could."[119] Roosevelt commented that he felt that Churchill and his colleagues were angered by what they perceived as American pressure to support Chiang Kai-shek and were responding to this by putting up road blocks with regard to finalizing plans for Operation Overlord almost as if to spite their American allies.[120]

Roosevelt was also critical of Chiang Kai-shek. Although the president had not been present at the CCOS meeting at which the Chinese announced that the generalissimo could not support the campaign in Burma without assurances that there would be no reduction in supplies flown into China, a new precondition, he was informed of the acrimonious discussion of this question by Admiral Leahy at dinner.[121] Roosevelt commented to his son that the Chinese were not making matters any easier by placing new demands on the table each time the Burma campaign was discussed.[122] The president also suggested that, having observed the activities of the Chinese delegation at close hand for two days, he was beginning to appreciate the difficulties that General Stilwell faced in China.[123]

While Roosevelt dined with his aides, Prime Minister Churchill hosted a dinner for Generalissimo and Madame Chiang Kai-shek at his villa. According to Chinese accounts of the dinner party, the generalissimo and the prime minister discussed plans for Mountbatten's offensive in Burma at length.[124] Churchill is said to have given Chiang details of proposed deployments of units of the Royal Navy in the Bay of Bengal and a timetable for completion of this buildup.[125] The prime minister assured the generalissimo that all British forces would be in place by May 1944 and promised to provide more detail before the end of the conference.[126]

There is no indication that Churchill's assurances were sufficient to get Chiang to agree to commit his forces to the offensive in Burma, at least not that evening. Although the prime minister's willingness to provide details on the deployment of British forces was a step in the right direction from the point of view of the Chinese, they still had reservations about the operation and wanted to obtain additional information before making their final decision to join their allies in a new Burma campaign.

The second day of the conference came to an end with more questions open than answered. Despite the cordial tone of the dinner party at Churchill's villa, Anglo-Chinese differences were far from resolved and the frustration of the BCOS with Generalissimo Chiang Kai-shek and his entourage now seemed to be infecting the JCS. The generalissimo's intransigence was beginning to anger Marshall, King, and other members of the Joint Chiefs, who were beginning to share the skepticism of their British colleagues about the capabilities of Chinese forces and the ability of the Chinese government to wage a real war against Japan.

Marshall and his colleagues were caught in somewhat of a bind. On the one hand, they were well aware of Roosevelt's view of the importance of China's role in the war and his support of the generalissimo's regime. On the other hand, they could see at first hand the difficulties of dealing with Chiang and his aides and balked at honoring the preconditions he laid down as seemingly absolute prerequisites for Chinese participation in the proposed Burma campaign. Furthermore, they were not necessarily sure that Chinese efforts beyond the status quo in the CBI were vital to winning the war against Japan given the possibility that the Soviet Union would join the Allies in that effort when the war against Hitler was won. Ironically, President Roosevelt was beginning to have some of the same misgivings about his Chinese allies, although he was not yet ready to renounce his conception of Chiang Kai-shek's China as a great world power and an invaluable ally. Roosevelt still believed that agreement on a course of action in the CBI and SEAC theaters could be reached before he and Churchill went to meet Stalin in Teheran, but his confidence that the Cairo conference would prove to be a watershed in forging a closer alliance between China, the United Kingdom, and the United States was somewhat shaken.

The first two days of the conference had produced no substantial agreement on matters relating to the CBI and SEAC theaters among the three Allies. With only two more days left in Cairo to reconcile differences before the participants went their separate ways, it was imperative that some breakthrough be made on day three of the conference.

8

November 25, 1943: The Second Act Begins

The third day of the conference was Thanksgiving Day. While President Roosevelt planned to have a gala Thanksgiving celebration that evening for the generalissimo and the prime minister, it was business as usual during the day. With major differences between the Chinese and their Anglo-American allies still unresolved, there was no time for leisure and relaxation. Roosevelt and Churchill were scheduled to leave for Teheran on November 27 and Generalissimo and Madame Chiang were expecting to return to China that same day. If agreement were to be reached on the future course of action in the CBI and SEAC theaters, it would have to be reached by November 26. The clock was running out.

The primary obstacle to reaching an agreement on future operations in Burma and China was Chiang Kai-shek's continuing suspicion of British motives. Although Churchill had gone to some lengths to assure the generalissimo that the British were indeed committed to the proposed campaign in Burma at the dinner party he hosted for the Chiangs on November 24, they remained skeptical of his sincerity. Churchill recognized this and on the morning of November 25, he paid a call on Generalissimo and Madame Chiang at their villa accompanied by Anthony Eden, the British Foreign Secretary.[1]

As Eden told V.K. Wellington Koo, China's ambassador to the Court of St. James, after the Cairo conference, Churchill spent much of this morning session treating the Chiangs to a lecture on grand Allied strategy, including his analysis of the military and political situations in Africa, Italy, and the Near East.[2] According to Eden, the purpose of this lecture, which was translated for the generalissimo by Madame Chiang, was to place operations in Southeast Asia and China in the broadest possible framework so that Chiang might better understand Britain's responsibilities and difficulties.[3]

It is doubtful that Churchill's remarks had much of an impact on the Chiangs. In his diary, Eden notes that Generalissimo and Madame Chiang listened politely to the prime minister's remarks, but made no comments which would have indicated that they sympathized with his position. Rather, they seemed concerned about obtaining more details about the specifics of British naval and military commitments in the CBI and SEAC theaters.[4]

Although no understanding was reached at the morning meeting between Churchill and Chiang, Eden found the generalissimo to be very different from what he had expected. He described Chiang quite favorably in his diary:

> I was much impressed by Chiang. He is smaller and slighter than I expected, very well made, with small and beautifully shaped hands and feet. He would be difficult to place in any category and does not look like a warrior. He has a constant smile, but his eyes don't smile so readily and they fix you with a penetrating unswerving look, in marked contrast to Uncle Joe's habit of looking at one's navel. His strength is that of a steel blade.[5]

Eden had an equally positive impression of Madame Chiang. Contrary to what he had been told about the "missimo," he found Madame Chiang to be an impressive woman:

> Madame surprised me. She was friendly, a trifle queenly perhaps. Obviously used to getting her own way, but an earnest interpreter and neither as sprightly nor as touchy as I had been led to expect.[6]

Eden liked Chiang and his wife and noted in his diary that he would "like to get to know them better."[7] He expressed these same views to Wellington Koo some weeks after the Cairo conference, leading Koo to remark that Foreign Secretary Eden was one of the only members of Churchill's entourage to have any positive feelings about China's leaders.[8] Koo attributed Eden's unique view of the Chiangs to his being more open-minded than his colleagues and mused at how different things might be if more of Churchill's advisors shared such views.[9]

While Churchill, Eden, and the Chiangs were discussing grand strategy, Roosevelt met with Harriman and Lord Cadogan, Eden's assistant at the Foreign Office, to discuss the agenda for his upcoming meeting with Stalin.[10] Following their departure, the president attended to the mail, which had arrived from Washington by diplomatic pouch that morning.[11] After finishing this, Roosevelt joined Churchill and the Chiangs for a photo session in the garden of his villa.[12]

The photo session was attended by more than seventy journalists representing the press of the three Allies. These journalists were permitted to take photos from a barricaded area, but were not permitted to ask questions of or interview the participants in the conference.[13] If Foreign Secretary Eden found this session to be a "desperate waste of time," the journalists found this photo opportunity to be an agony of frustration.[14] They had been in Cairo for more than two days and had been kept away from the conferees by British and American military police assigned to secure the conference.[15]

Members of the press who accompanied the generalissimo, the president, and the prime minister to Cairo expected to be able to interview the Big Three and/or their aides and expressed great displeasure over their inability to do so. Speaking for the American press contingent, Cyrus Sulzberger of the *New York Times* presented the following note to Harry Hopkins:

> We wish to express the strongest dissatisfaction with the manner in which we are being treated during the present important conference. We demand that we be taken further into the confidence of the authorities on an off-the-record basis and be given some idea of what everything is about in order to prepare our advance material.[16]

Sulzberger and his colleagues were particularly interested in interviewing Chiang, Churchill, and Roosevelt and in assuring access to Stalin and his aides during the Teheran conference. Sensing the seriousness of the situation, Hopkins agreed to meet with Sulzberger and other representatives of the press, but there was not much he was able to tell them when he met with them the next day.[17] His boss, the president, did not want to have reporters snooping about, especially in light of the unresolved differences between the Allies.[18]

The photographs, which were taken at the noontime session, particularly the famous shot of the Big Three plus Madame Chiang, in which Chiang and Roosevelt are smiling at each other while Madame Chiang and Churchill seem engrossed in meaningful dialogue, were designed to illustrate the harmony among the Allies. There was to be no hint of discord. As Stanley Hornbeck noted shortly after the conclusion of the conferences at Cairo and Teheran, the press may have understood that "all was not as rosy between the conferees [Chiang, Churchill, and Roosevelt] as might have been thought," but the president was not about to have the press present the achievements of the conference in an unfavorable light.[19]

Following the photo session at Roosevelt's villa, Churchill and Eden lunched privately at the prime minister's villa while Roosevelt and the Chiangs went their separate ways.[20] According to Eden, Churchill spent much of the lunch hour telling him about the difficulties of dealing with Roosevelt. Churchill described the president as "a charming country gentleman who was not given to business-like procedures."[21] The prime minister suggested to Eden that he [Churchill] had to "play the role of the courtier" in dealing with Roosevelt and had to seize opportunities to influence the president's thinking "as and when they arose."[22]

Eden expressed amazement at Churchill's patience with Roosevelt.[23] In reading Eden's memoirs, one gets the feeling that the foreign minister thought that the president was as much, if not more, of an obstacle to achieving progress at the conference than the generalissimo and his wife. After the war, Eden said that the Cairo conference was "the most difficult I ever attended."[24] According to Eden, the difficulties the British encountered in Cairo could be attributed to two factors. First, British fortunes in the Far East were at

Chiang Kai-shek, Franklin D. Roosevelt, and Winston Churchill pose for cameras at the Cairo Conference, November 25, 1943. The smiles of the three leaders belie the unresolved differences beteween them and the acrimony between Chiang and Churchill. Courtesy of the Franklin D. Roosevelt Library and Museum, Hyde Park, New York.

their lowest ebb and the contribution that England could make in this area was slight.[25] Second, Roosevelt's "obsession" with the merits of Generalissimo Chiang and his government represented a distortion of reality and clouded his judgment, thus straining relations between the president and the prime minister.[26]

Eden was not alone among the British in questioning the logic and rationality of American policy in China. Years after the conference, Field Marshal Alan Brooke also raised this question as he prepared to write his memoirs. In a letter to Riley Sunderland, one of America's most prominent military historians and co-author of the official United States Army history of World War II, Brooke asked General Sunderland how he would explain the seemingly irrational views of General George Marshall with regard to China when in all other matters, Marshall seemed a model of reason.[27] Sunderland's reply to Brooke reinforces the judgment of Eden:

> What the JCS thought did not matter since they had been ordered to support China. Since Mr. Roosevelt ... held the views he did on China and Chiang, Marshall as his subordinate was obliged to act and speak accordingly in Anglo-

American exchanges, even as he sought to convince Mr. Roosevelt of the contrary.[28]

Sunderland went on to suggest that Roosevelt changed his opinion of Chiang Kai-shek and the situation in China after the Cairo conference, moving a good deal closer to the view of Marshall, but by then the harm had been done.[29]

Ironically, Roosevelt's view of the China tangle was changing even as the Cairo conference was still in session. Writing to his wife on November 25, the president told her about the difficulties he was experiencing with Chiang and Churchill. "I have been working hard, acting as a solvent between various people," he said, and indicated that he was not sure he could provide enough "lubrication" to bring the prickly generalissimo and the stubborn prime minister to mesh in gear.[30] Later that day, the president made the same point in a conversation with his son Elliott, but this time he seemed to pin more of the blame for the failure of the talks on Chiang than on Churchill.[31] Still, Roosevelt was not yet ready to give up on the generalissimo since there was no one else in Chungking who seemed able or willing to take his place.

After the picture-taking session at Roosevelt's villa, the next formal activity on the conference schedule was the meeting of the CCOS, which convened at 2:30 P.M. in the Mena House Hotel. The first item on the agenda of the CCOS meeting was Mountbatten's report on his efforts to gain Chiang's approval of the proposed campaign in Burma.[32] What Mountbatten had to tell his peers gave them little cause for optimism that the impasse between the generalissimo and his allies could be easily resolved.

Mountbatten met with Generalissimo Chiang, at the direction of the CCOS, on the evening of November 24, after Chiang's cocktail party and before the generalissimo's dinner with Churchill. Mountbatten told his associates that Chiang insisted that his "alternative plan" be carried out in Burma.[33] According to Mountbatten's recollection of the conversation, he tried in vain to persuade the generalissimo that this plan would require a commitment of supplies and aircraft that the Allies could not make.[34] Mountbatten told Chiang that "he must" support a more realistic plan, but the generalissimo remained adamant.[35]

Mountbatten had some other unpleasant news to report to the CCOS. The generalissimo was not only adamant that the Anglo-American proposal for the campaign in Burma was too modest and timid, he also refused to permit any diversion of supplies from China to support operations in Burma.[36] When Mountbatten told Chiang that the Allies could not deliver more than 8,900 tons per month to China during the first six months of the Burma campaign, the generalissimo insisted that 10,000 tons was the absolute minimum supply effort acceptable to him.[37] He intimated that if the CCOS could not make such a guarantee, he would take the matter up with Roosevelt.[38]

General Arnold, commanding officer of the United States Army Air Force, jumped in at this point and suggested that it would be difficult to guarantee that there would be no reduction in the supplies flown into China when the Burma offensive was launched.[39] It would be impossible, he added, to provide for the expanded campaign in Burma advocated by the generalissimo. Such a plan would require that several hundred additional supply planes be assigned to the Hump lift, an unthinkable commitment in light of plans for other operations in 1944.[40]

General Marshall, sensing the anger of his colleagues, suggested that he would take up Chiang's requests with President Roosevelt.[41] Mountbatten suggested that before any decision was reached on an operation in Burma, the CCOS must obtain Chiang Kai-shek's written consent to the plan.[42] The other members of the CCOS agreed with Mountbatten and voted to have him draw up a detailed formal proposal and submit it to the generalissimo for his immediate action.[43] At this point, the CCOS meeting adjourned.

Commenting on the lack of progress at the CCOS meeting, Alan Brooke noted in his diary that each day the Chinese seemed to up their demands. "Chiang Kai-shek is busy bargaining to obtain the maximum possible out of us," he said, and this was turning the conference into "a dismal show."[44] Brooke was not alone among the BCOS in this view of the situation. One of Mountbatten's aides indicated shortly after the end of the conference that Mountbatten had come to conclude that the generalissimo was a "twisty old divot" whose efforts to play the Anglo-American Allies off against each other threatened to sabotage any progress in 1944.[45]

Prior to the conference, Mountbatten had been much more positive in his opinion of Chiang Kai-shek, describing the generalissimo as a man who would "feed out of his [Mountbatten's] hands."[46] By the third day of the conference, the admiral had changed his opinion. Chiang fed out of nobody's hand. If anyone was providing the birdseed, it was the generalissimo, and even then there was little seed to pass around.[47]

General Marshall went to Roosevelt's villa after the CCOS meeting, picking up General Stilwell along the way.[48] General Stilwell had spent much of his day with Generalissimo and Madame Chiang, trying to get them to agree on plans for a campaign in Burma without success.[49] Even more than Mountbatten and Marshall, Stilwell was familiar with the difficulty of doing business with the Chiangs and it may have been for this reason that General Marshall wanted Stilwell with him when he briefed the president.

Marshall and Stilwell saw Roosevelt at 4:30 P.M., a half hour before the president was scheduled to host Generalissimo and Madame Chiang for tea.[50] Marshall told the president about the lack of progress at the CCOS meeting and Chiang's escalating demands.[51] He then asked Stilwell to inform the president of his discussions with the generalissimo.[52] Stilwell was only too happy to comply and gave the president the same "dope" he had given Marshall on the walk over to Roosevelt's villa.[53]

The crux of Stilwell's message to Roosevelt was that Chiang was still holding out for an expanded operation in Burma and assurances that the British would provide sufficient forces to guarantee that Chinese armies would not take the brunt of the casualties in such a campaign.[54] Stilwell also told the president that he had not yet been able to persuade the generalissimo to accept Mountbatten's more modest proposal because Chiang was still convinced that the Allies could provide the additional aircraft and supplies necessary for his vision of a proper offensive in Burma.[55]

Since Generalissimo and Madame Chiang were expected at any moment, Roosevelt had to cut the conversation with Marshall and Stilwell short. Before dismissing Marshall and Stilwell, the president indicated that he hoped to have the opportunity to continue his discussion with Stilwell sometime before the end of the conference.[56] At this point, the generals left Roosevelt's villa. Moments later, at 5:00 P.M., the Chiangs arrived.

Elliott Roosevelt indicates that his father had hastily arranged the tea for the generalissimo and his wife after learning that they would not be able to attend his Thanksgiving dinner party later that evening due to Madame Chiang's continuing bout with dysentery and the flu.[57] Since Roosevelt had unfinished business to take up with the generalissimo, who would not attend important political or social functions without his wife, this late afternoon meeting seemed an appropriate opportunity to chat with the Chiangs in the privacy of the garden of his villa.

Except for the presence of his son Elliott, Roosevelt met alone with Generalissimo and Madame Chiang.[58] As was often the case, Madame Chiang translated for her husband. According to the generalissimo's diary, a wide variety of issues were discussed at the tea, including Anglo-Chinese differences, Sino-American relations, and the economic and political future of China in the post-war era.[59] The conversation was a most cordial one, with the president listening to the Chiangs with "keen attention" and "great respect," according to Elliott Roosevelt's recollection of the occasion.[60]

As the president's son remembers the meeting, Madame Chiang did most of the talking, "as usual," but she was clearly speaking for her husband and with his approval.[61] Roosevelt understood this and often replied directly to the generalissimo after Madame Chiang raised a question. Thus, when Madame Chiang recited a litany of the difficulties her husband had in communicating with Prime Minister Churchill, the president looked directly at Chiang, sighed, and told him, "Churchill gives me a great deal of headache too."[62]

According to Chiang's description of his encounter with Roosevelt, the president seemed tired and pessimistic about the future.[63] He seemed especially worried about post-war relations between the peoples of the West and

Chiang Kai-shek, Franklin D. Roosevelt, and Madame Chiang Kai-shek in the garden of President Roosevelt's villa at the Cairo Conference, November 25, 1943. Courtesy of the Franklin D. Roosevelt Library and Museum, Hyde Park, New York.

the East and the problem of dismantling the colonial empires of England and France.[64] Chiang noted that Roosevelt voiced strong disapproval of British colonialism, an opinion shared by the generalissimo and his wife, who seized the opportunity to tell their host that the lack of progress at the Cairo conference in reaching an accord on future policy in Southeast Asia was, in part, the result of Churchill's determination to preserve Britain's empire intact after the war.[65]

Roosevelt did not respond to this suggestion and the conversation turned to other matters. According to the president's son, Madame Chiang launched into a long-winded discussion of her plans for increasing literacy in China when the war was over.[66] She also talked about the need for other improvements and reforms.[67] The president listened quietly to Madame Chiang's monologue, leading his son to question whether his father really believed what he heard. "I found myself wondering," Elliott Roosevelt noted in his diary, "if he [my father] was not perhaps reflecting that these reforms which Madame Chiang was describing would not have to wait on some other force than the Chiangs."[68]

Before Generalissimo and Madame Chiang left the president's villa, there was a brief discussion of the political situation in China. According to

Elliott Roosevelt, the generalissimo indicated to his father that he would attempt to improve relations with the Chinese communists upon his return from Cairo, as he had promised in an earlier conversation with the president.[69] Chiang's diary contains no mention of this, although it does suggest that the generalissimo and the president did discuss KMT-CCP relations.[70]

Interestingly, neither Elliott Roosevelt's nor Chiang Kai-shek's accounts of the tea suggest that there was any discussion of the impasse over plans for the campaign in Burma. It does not appear that the Chiangs lobbied the president for his support on this issue or that Roosevelt tried to use his influence and good offices to persuade the generalissimo to give his approval to Mountbatten's more conservative plan for an offensive in Southeast Asia. Considering the fact that Marshall and Stilwell had met with Roosevelt just before his meeting with the Chiangs to alert him to the lack of progress over this issue, it is somewhat surprising that he did not raise it with his guests.

Perhaps Roosevelt decided to avoid confronting the Chiangs on purpose. In his private meetings with the generalissimo and his wife, the president seems to have been more concerned with boosting their morale than in forcing them to confront reality. One reason that Roosevelt had pushed hard for the Cairo summit, despite British objections to the presence of the Chinese at any summit, was to give the Chinese leaders their place among the powers and the "face" they desired.[71] He may not have wished to jeopardize his good standing with the Chiangs by taking a hard line on policy with them, especially when he could have his subordinates take this stand in his place.

Generalissimo and Madame Chiang left Roosevelt's villa just after 6:00 P.M.[72] Following their departure, the president met briefly with some of his aides to go over plans for his trip to Teheran on November 27th and then he retired to his room for a rest before the Thanksgiving dinner party he was hosting for Churchill and the CCOS that evening.[73] Roosevelt dressed for dinner at 7:30 P.M. and was ready to greet his guests when they arrived at 8:00 P.M.[74]

The president's Thanksgiving gala was a lavish affair with all of the appropriate trimmings.[75] Churchill described the scene in the following terms:

> Two enormous turkeys were brought in with all ceremony. The President ... carved for all with masterly, indefatigable skill. As we were above twenty, this took a long time, and those who were helped first had finished before the President had cut anything for himself. As I watched the huge platefuls he distributed to the company I feared he might be left with nothing at all. But he calculated to a nicety, and I was relieved, when at last the two skeletons were removed, to see him set about his own share.[76]

When the dinner was finished, the president and his guests went into the living room, which had been used for the plenary sessions of the conference, and turned on the phonograph for a dance party. Since Sarah Churchill was the only woman present, she had more than her share of partners and several of the men danced with each other. Churchill relates that he shared a dance with General "Pa" Watson to the delight of the president and other onlookers.[77]

At 9:30 P.M., Harry Hopkins summoned General Stilwell to the president's villa for a continuation of his chat with Roosevelt.[78] When he arrived, Stilwell found the party in full swing and noted that the guests were quite inebriated.[79] Hopkins was so drunk that Stilwell spent the next half hour talking to Churchill. While a recording of "Whoopee" was repeatedly played on the phonograph at a very high volume, Churchill and Stilwell tried to talk about the unresolved problems of the day.[80]

Roosevelt's guests left by 10:30 P.M., at which time the president joined Stilwell.[81] The only others present were Harry Hopkins, Elliott Roosevelt, and the president's son-in-law, John Boetinger.[82] As Stilwell and Roosevelt sat side by side on a couch, the general talked about his problems in China.[83] First, Stilwell talked about the problem of inadequate supplies, urging Roosevelt to do what he could to increase the airlift over the Hump.[84] Next, Stilwell talked about British efforts to divert supplies from China to the SEAC theater.[85]

While Stilwell was talking about the supply problem, the president interrupted him to ask about the status of the Ledo Road.[86] Stilwell told the president that despite British reservations about the possibilities of opening up this new land route into China, completion of the Ledo Road was not beyond the realm of reality if there was a will to complete the project.[87] The problem, he intimated to Roosevelt, was that the Americans wanted to build a road to China while the British wanted to beat a path to Singapore.[88]

Stilwell and Roosevelt also talked about the general's progress in reshaping and training the Chinese army. The president was eager to know how many units had gone through the retraining program and their battlefield capabilities.[89] Stilwell informed Roosevelt that two divisions were already in the field, but he admitted that they were not fighting as well as they might.[90] Stilwell attributed their mediocre performance to "stage frights" and suggested that once these new units overcame these frights, they would prove as capable as any units in the British or American armies.[91]

Although the personality problems that had been a constant irritant in China were not discussed in as much detail as the issues of supplies and training, Stilwell did tell Roosevelt about his difficulties with Chiang and his minister of war, General Ho Ying-chin.[92] According to Elliott Roosevelt, his father liked Stilwell and was sympathetic to his problems in dealing with the generalissimo, but had no advice to offer the general in how to improve his relationship with Chiang except to suggest that he be careful to treat him courteously.[93]

A very different version of this discussion about how to deal with the generalissimo was told by one of Stilwell's subordinates, General Frank

Generalissimo Chiang and President Roosevelt in the garden at Roosevelt's villa at the Cairo Conference, November 25, 1943. British Foreign Minister Anthony Eden stands behind Chiang. Courtesy of the Franklin D. Roosevelt Library and Museum, Hyde Park, New York.

Dorn. According to Dorn, shortly after Stilwell returned form Cairo, he told him:

> The Big Boy [Roosevelt] is fed up with Chiang and his tantrums, and said so. In fact he told me in that Olympian manner of his: "If you can't get along with Chiang and can't replace him, get rid of him once and for all. You know what I mean. Put someone in we can manage."[94]

It is hardly likely that Roosevelt told Stilwell to replace Chiang or assassinate him as Dorn suggests in his book.[95] It is more likely that the president expressed his frustration with the generalissimo as a means of sympathizing with Stilwell's plight, a ploy Roosevelt often used with his guests.[96] In retelling the story of his conversations with Roosevelt to Dorn, Stilwell may have succumbed to a bit of hyperbole, which Dorn took too seriously.[97]

Stilwell, Hopkins, and Boetinger bid the president goodnight about 11:30 P.M., leaving Roosevelt alone with his son Elliott for another of their late night/early morning conversations.[98] According to the president's son, his father was very chatty and seemed particularly keen to discuss his views of Generalissimo Chiang and the situation in China.[99]

Roosevelt told his son that Chiang would have liked to convey the message that the Chinese communists were contributing little to the war effort against Japan so that he did not have to allow their representatives a role in determining war policy and planning for the post-war era.[100] "Again, we know differently," he said, adding that it was in response to American pressure that the generalissimo had agreed to the suspension of the hostilities against the Chinese Communist Party (CCP) and the formation of a democratic government after the war.[101]

The president went on to say that Chiang had agreed, in principle, to take the CCP into his government prior to elections at the end of the war if the United States was able to guarantee that the British would not be allowed to return to their privileged positions in Shanghai, Canton, and other treaty ports after the defeat of Japan.[102] Elliott Roosevelt asked his father whether he was prepared to make such a promise. "Not for nothing," he said, indicating that when the generalissimo demonstrated he was inclined to establish a truly democratic unity government, then the United States would support his position vis-à-vis the British.[103]

Roosevelt told his son that the generalissimo was "cheered" by his attitude toward the dismantling of colonial empires in the post-war era.[104] According to Elliott Roosevelt, his father suggested to Chiang that the British would have no choice but to grant independence to India and would probably do so peacefully.[105] Eventually, even Hong Kong might revert to Chinese control under certain conditions.[106]

Although Roosevelt and Chiang shared a common hostility toward colonialism and economic imperialism, the president wanted to use this issue to gain leverage with Chiang. He was not about to make commitments to the Chinese without getting a quid pro quo from them in return and he would not make concessions to Chiang without considering the impact these concessions would have on his relationship with Churchill. Despite his fascination with China and its future place in the family of nations, Roosevelt understood that Anglo-American unity could not be sacrificed in the process of courting Chiang Kai-shek.

American support of Chinese efforts to end treaty port privileges and extraterritorial rights, something that Generalissimo Chiang was most eager to obtain, was not to be easily given away by Roosevelt. This was his ultimate trump card in forcing the Chinese to make concessions of their own, beginning with the matter of agreeing to plans in the CBI and SEAC theaters during the new year, 1944. With only one day to go before the cast of characters departed Cairo on November 27, the generalissimo was under considerable pressure to demonstrate good faith and come to some agreement with British and American proposals for a campaign in Burma.

Contrary to the belief that President Roosevelt was under the spell of Generalissimo and Madame Chiang, he was much more realistic and pragmatic than the British or members of his own entourage believed. On the one hand, he was experiencing some of the same difficulties in dealing with the Chinese that Alan Brooke, Churchill, Ismay, Marshall, Mountbatten, and Stilwell had encountered. On the other hand, he was not so optimistic about Soviet promises to enter the war against Japan in the near term as to be willing to risk alienating Chiang Kai-shek and his associates by dealing with them with sledgehammer-like bluntness.

China served the function of a punching bag in the war against Japan. Although there was little chance that the Chinese could achieve a definitive victory over Japan in China, this was not necessary. As long as the Japanese could not bring the Chinese government to its knees, almost one million Japanese men would be tied down in China. Keeping China in the war by providing minimal amounts of supplies and puffing up the egos of China's leaders was a cheap strategy requiring few American combat troops and equally few casualties.

9

November 26–27, 1943: End of the Second Act

November 26 would be the last day that Generalissimo Chiang, Prime Minister Churchill, and President Roosevelt were together in Cairo. Since little progress toward arriving at a consensus over policies in the CBI and SEAC theaters had been made on November 25, it was imperative that the three leaders reach some understanding on November 26, if only for the purpose of preparing a communiqué for the press to disseminate to the world, which would give the illusion that the Allies were united on a course of action for 1944.

Beyond sustaining the image of cooperation among the Allies, it was also important, at least insofar as Roosevelt was concerned, that Generalissimo Chiang and his entourage leave Cairo with something tangible to bring back to Chungking. As the conferees were preparing to depart from Cairo, it still seemed evident to Roosevelt that the final assault against Japan would be launched from bases in China. Keeping China in the war as an enthusiastic ally remained essential. This being the case, it was not sufficient to merely plump up Chiang's ego; he had to be sent home with ammunition to solidify his position in the Kuomintang hierarchy and reinforce his popularity with the Chinese people.

Sending Generalissimo Chiang home with an agreement on plans for 1944 that he could accept and that would enhance his image in China was easier said than done. The generalissimo's idea of what was appropriate in Burma remained far removed from the realities of the resources that the CCOS felt the Allies could provide for such a campaign. Even the president realized this. His job on this last day of the conference would be to help Mountbatten and the CCOS craft a proposal to which Chiang could commit himself and use his good offices with the generalissimo to persuade him to put his seal of approval on the document.

One of Roosevelt's first appointments on this last day of the conference was a mid-morning session with Mountbatten.[1] The previous afternoon at the CCOS meeting, Mountbatten had been charged with drawing up a written proposal fixing details for the offensive in Burma, which was to be presented to Chiang for his written approval before he left Cairo.[2] It was this plan that Mountbatten outlined to the president on the morning of November 26th.[3]

After the exchange of some preliminary pleasantries, Mountbatten provided the president with a litany of his difficulties in getting the generalissimo to agree on a course of action in Burma.[4] He then went on to outline the essence of a proposal he hoped to present to Chiang.[5] The proposal contained few surprises, but Mountbatten was concerned that it might be regarded as controversial by the generalissimo because it rejected his demands for an expanded operation in Burma. On the other hand, Mountbatten hoped to overcome Chiang's opposition to this point by including a more detailed statement of British commitments to the campaign and a timetable for such commitments.[6]

Although neither Mountbatten nor Roosevelt kept a record of their conversation, Mountbatten later told John Paton Davies that he had informed the president that Chiang was driving him "absolutely mad."[7] According to Davies, Mountbatten also told him that the president was sympathetic to his plight, regaling Mountbatten with some choice stories of his own difficulties in dealing with the generalissimo and suggesting he would do what he could to help.[8]

Mountbatten left Roosevelt just before 11:00 A.M. to meet with General Stilwell.[9] A few minutes later, Madame Chiang was received by the president.[10] Although there is no transcript of their conversation, Roosevelt wrote a note to H. H. Kung later that day in which he indicated that he and Madame Chiang discussed the serious economic problems faced by her husband's government and what the United States could do to provide economic assistance to China.[11] There is nothing in Roosevelt's letter to suggest that he and Madame Chiang talked about reconciling Anglo-Chinese differences over the proposed course of action in Burma.[12]

While Roosevelt was meeting with Madame Chiang, Mountbatten was sharing his frustration over the failure to get Chiang Kai-shek to agree on a plan of action for 1944 with General Stilwell. "Mountbatten is fed up with Peanut," Stilwell noted in his diary, but "who is not?"[13] Stilwell indicates that Mountbatten wanted him to press the generalissimo to come to terms with reality.[14] That, he told Mountbatten, would not be easy.[15]

Mountbatten left Stilwell at 11:25 A.M., leaving Stilwell little time to get over to Chiang's villa for his 11:30 meeting with the generalissimo, his aides, and General Arnold.[16] Stilwell arrived somewhat late and found Chiang's aides "green with fright" because their boss had been kept waiting for three minutes.[17] "What a life for those boys," Stilwell noted in his diary, "scared pee-less all the time!"[18]

The purpose of the meeting with Chiang and his staff was to go over supply problems posed by the proposed Burma offensive. "Peanut went into his usual song and dance," Stilwell noted, and "wants Louis [Mountbatten] to keep his hands off the Air Transport Command."[19] General Arnold confirms Stilwell's observations. According to Arnold, Chiang wanted to divorce Mountbatten completely from China operations:

> Chiang K'ai-shek did not realize that without Burma, without India, without Mountbatten to stir up the Indian communications people, and without forcing the Japanese out of Burma, there wouldn't be any hump traffic.[20]

According to Arnold, all the generalissimo could see were his own requirements. Although Arnold was finally able to convince Chiang that the Army Air Force was doing all it could to increase the tonnage of supplies flown into China, he noted that the generalissimo would still not admit "any connection between the Hump operations and Mountbatten's Burma campaign."[21] Stilwell recalls that despite all of Arnold's efforts, the generalissimo still insisted that he must have his 10,000 tons per month and, at one point in the conversation, Chiang argued that Roosevelt had promised him 12,000 tons per month![22] Finally, the generalissimo indicated he might agree to accepting a temporary reduction in the tonnage flown into China.[23]

While Stilwell and Arnold were meeting with Chiang and Roosevelt was meeting with Madame Chiang, Anthony Eden lunched with Wang Chung-hui. In his diary, Eden noted that Wang, who had preceded T.V. Soong as China's foreign minister and was now serving as director of the Chinese National Defense Council, was most eager to talk about the future status of Tibet, Hong Kong, and the issues of extraterritoriality and treaty port privileges.[24] Wang told Eden that the Chinese hoped the British would recognize China's claim to Tibet when the war was over and show an equal willingness to negotiate on other issues.[25] After lunch with Wang, Eden had tea with the generalissimo where the same questions were again discussed.[26]

Eden made no commitments in his conversations with Wang and Chiang. He would later note that the British would have to take a firm stand on these issues when the war was over.[27] Although the foreign secretary was less abrasive than Churchill in dealing with the Chinese, he was no more interested than the prime minister in negotiating away British privileges in China or any place else in Asia.

The generalissimo, the president, and the prime minister lunched alone at their respective villas and worked with aides in the early afternoon drafting proposals for a communiqué, which was to be discussed and finalized when the Big Three met later that afternoon at 4:30 P.M. While they were laboring on this statement, the CCOS were meeting at the Mena House Hotel, trying one last time to break the deadlock surrounding plans for the campaign in Burma.

Alan Brooke opened the CCOS meeting at 2:30 P.M. The first item on the agenda was a discussion of the plan that Mountbatten had prepared at the request of the CCOS for Chiang's written approval.[28] The proposal contained six provisions:

1. Since the 535 additional planes requested by Chiang to facilitate an expanded offensive in Burma could not be provided, he was to be asked to agree to Mountbatten's original proposal.
2. Chiang's stipulation that the British launch an amphibious operation in the Andaman Islands in March 1944 was to be taken into consideration by the CCOS, but no firm commitment could be made until all amphibious operations proposed for 1944 were considered.
3. The British would assemble a fleet "adequate to cover an amphibious operation, Operation Buccaneer, and to obtain control of the Bay of Bengal" which would be in place by March 1944.
4. No more than 1100 tons of supplies/month would be diverted from China to Burma. Diversions in excess of this figure would occur in case of a "critical emergency" and only after obtaining Chiang's permission. All efforts would be made to guarantee minimum supply drop of 10,000 tons/month by the Spring of 1944.
5. Chiang to delegate command over Ledo Force to General Slim until Ledo Force reached Kamaing when command would be assumed by General Stilwell.
6. Action in Burma would stop during monsoon season and resume after the monsoon season (October 1944), but the precise distribution of supplies and designation of forces would have to be determined at a later date.[29]

The draft of Mountbatten's proposal met with no opposition from the other members of the CCOS.[30] After his presentation, Alan Brooke moved the agenda to a discussion of plans for Operation Overlord and associated activities in the Mediterranean. In the course of this discussion, Brooke and Admiral Andrew Cunningham, commanding officer of the Royal Navy, suggested that if the British received the go-ahead to invade and capture the island of Rhodes, Operation Buccaneer might have to be delayed or scrapped.[31] These comments set off a nasty exchange between Brooke, Leahy, and Marshall.

Leahy interrupted the discussion to state that he and the other members of the Joint Chiefs of Staff had been led to understand that British proposals for operations in the Mediterranean, including the capture of Rhodes, would not interfere with the carrying out of Operation Buccaneer.[32] Brooke responded by saying that this was not necessarily the case. He suggested that the Allies did not have the resources to carry out Overlord, Buccaneer, and the capture of Rhodes simultaneously and suggested that if Operation Buccaneer was sufficiently important, the Allies might have to consider postponing Operation Overlord.[33]

Marshall reacted angrily, lecturing Brooke on the importance of Operation Buccaneer, which he suggested was more critical than yet another operation in the Mediterranean.[34] Operation Buccaneer was crucial for two reasons:

1. Operation Buccaneer was of vital importance to the Pacific War.
2. Cancellation of Operation Buccaneer would have grave political consequences.[35]

Alan Brooke did not buy Marshall's argument. Responding to his American colleague, he suggested that going ahead with Operation Buccaneer would delay the final victory against Germany.[36] Postponing Operation Buccaneer would shorten the war against Germany. Since the defeat of Germany was the first priority of the Allies, Brooke urged Marshall and Leahy to view the matter from a "purely strategical aspect."[37]

Air Marshall Portal went even further than Brooke in arguing for the postponement or abandonment of Operation Buccaneer. The Soviets, he suggested, would press Churchill and Roosevelt for an early date for the launching of Operation Overlord when they met Stalin at Teheran.[38] If they meant to placate him, they would have to agree to defer amphibious operations in the Bay of Bengal so as to ensure there were enough landing craft in Europe.[39] Portal went on to argue that Operation Buccaneer was not vital to the land war in China and that if judged solely on its strategic merits, such an operation was unnecessary.[40]

At this point, Admiral King suggested that it was "unsound" to think that landing craft presently in the Bay of Bengal could be brought back to Europe in time for use in Operation Overlord.[41] He also took exception to Portal's argument that an amphibious attack on the Andaman Islands was not crucial to the success of operations in Burma and China. King argued that the campaign in Burma would not be complete without Operation Buccaneer.[42] He also suggested that delaying the ultimate defeat of Japan was no more acceptable than postponing Operation Overlord and prolonging the war against Germany.[43]

Marshall echoed King's assessment. According to Marshall, postponing Operation Buccaneer would not shorten the war against Germany.[44] He also told his British colleagues that the United States had gone far to meet British views and cater to their sensitivities. Now it was their turn to show some sensitivity to the position of the United States.[45] Bluntly put, this meant that Operation Buccaneer could not be postponed.[46]

The vehemence with which Marshall, Leahy, and King supported Operation Buccaneer may have taken their British counterparts somewhat by surprise. Alan Brooke and the other British Chiefs were under the impression, not necessarily incorrect, that the JCS did not share their president's enthusiasm with Chiang Kai-shek and may have calculated that the American chiefs were lukewarm in their support of Operation Buccaneer. What they did not realize was that Marshall, Leahy, and King were aware that Roosevelt had made promises to Chiang, which had to be fulfilled. Marshall and his colleagues understood that the generalissimo must have something to show for his trip to Cairo. This included Operation Buccaneer.[47]

Despite the "mother and father of a row" between the British and American Chiefs, as Alan Brooke described it in his diary, no agreement was reached on the date of Operation Buccaneer.[48] Speaking for his colleagues, Leahy made it clear that the JCS would not abandon Operation Buccaneer unless ordered to do so by President Roosevelt.[49] If Brooke and his colleagues wanted to scrap the plan, they would have to get Churchill to convince the president to change his mind. Until this happened, Operation Buccaneer was to remain a real option for 1944.[50] What Leahy did not tell Brooke was that the JCS would be happy to see the president change his mind. Their support of Operation Buccaneer was based on his prodding.

Reflecting on the acrimonious debate over Operation Buccaneer after the war, Leahy suggested that the British had never shared America's interest in China nor did they accept the argument that China was vital to the war effort.[51] Although Leahy may have believed the British were right, he never said so directly.[52] He also suggested that they did not share Roosevelt's concern over the casualties American forces would suffer in the Pacific should the Chinese drop out of the war.[53] This being the case, it was of less concern to Churchill than to Roosevelt that Chiang Kai-shek go back to Chungking with specific promises in hand.[54]

Marshall, too, had some post-war thoughts about the debate over Operation Buccaneer on November 26. His views were quite like those of Leahy. In an oral interview with his biographer, Forrest Pogue, long after the Cairo conference, Marshall suggested that the British were much more interested in defeating Germany than in the war against Japan, which they saw as largely an American show.[55] Given their Eurocentric view, they saw Operation Buccaneer as a waste of resources. While Marshall was hardly surprised at British priorities, he faulted them for not being more sensitive to American goals.[56]

Marshall also pointed to another problem, the essentially negative image of Chiang Kai-shek held by many British officers and diplomats.[57] Save for Eden and Carton de Wiart, none of Churchill's advisors had much use for the Kuomintang regime. Marshall was more sympathetic to the generalissimo than many of his British counterparts and some of his American subordinates, like Stilwell, who considered Chiang as an incompetent unworthy of much support. Marshall had a very different view:

> During the war Chiang had a terrible problem getting good men.... Chiang didn't have any competent people to put in for his incompetents.... He couldn't find out what the devil was going on. He was constantly sold down the river by his advisors.[58]

Some were quick to criticize the generalissimo, but as Marshall also pointed out, the British and Americans had their share of incompetents and made their share of mistakes too.[59]

At about 4:00 P.M., as the acrimonious discussion of Operation Buccaneer was winding to a close at the CCOS meeting, Generalissimo Chiang went over to Roosevelt's villa. The generalissimo was not expected until 4:30 when the three leaders were to hammer out a communiqué, but he was eager to have some time alone with the president before Churchill arrived.[60] Although the president had not planned this little tête-à-tête with Chiang, he received the generalissimo immediately, leaving the completion of his correspondence of the day for a later moment.[61]

With General Chu Shih-ming serving as his translator, Chiang informed Roosevelt of the continuing impasse over plans for 1944, blaming British unwillingness to commit to Operation Buccaneer for the failure to reach agreement.[62] The generalissimo also told the president that unless the British made more specific commitments to the campaign in Burma, he would have no choice but to withhold Chinese forces from further engagement in Southeast Asia.[63]

According to Chiang's recollection of this conversation, FDR indicated that he was also unhappy with the vacillation of the British, but this was not the only thing that the president saw as getting in the way of a positive conclusion to the conference.[64] If Chiang's account of this conversation is to be believed, Roosevelt stated that the crux of the problem was not disagreement over the logistics of an offensive in Burma, but, rather, the unwillingness of Churchill to recognize and treat China as one of the "Big Powers."[65]

Although the British had their reservations about taking the Chinese into the inner councils of the Allies, Roosevelt assured Chiang that before the conference ended, Churchill and Alan Brooke would consent to Operation Buccaneer and an expanded naval presence in the Bay of Bengal.[66] Thus, there would be simultaneous operations in northern and southern Burma in 1944, as the generalissimo had originally wished.[67]

Roosevelt had barely finished assuring Chiang that all would end well before the conferees departed from Cairo when Harriman, Churchill, Eden, and Madame Chiang arrived at the president's villa to flesh out a final communiqué that could be distributed to the press before the end of the conference.[68] Since little substantive progress had actually been made in resolving differences between the Allies and laying plans for 1944, there was not much that could be publically stated. Even if the Allies had come to terms on plans for 1944, they would not have wanted to reveal their plans in a detailed public document.

Framing the Cairo communiqué proved easier than resolving the differences still separating them because the text of the communiqué was purposefully vague, as the introductory paragraph reveals:

The several military missions have agreed upon future military operations against Japan. The Three Great Allies expressed their resolve to bring unrelenting pressure against their brutal enemies by sea, land, and air. The pressure is already rising.[69]

In fact, the Allies had not agreed on plans for future military operations against Japan nor was it clear that they would do so before the day was out. Furthermore, it was likely, at least in the minds of Churchill and Roosevelt that even if they came to terms before leaving Cairo, discussion with Stalin could alter plans made in Cairo. For these reasons, they made the introductory paragraph of the communiqué as innocuous as possible, hoping that there would be agreement on a future course of action in Burma when the day ended or, if not, giving the appearance that agreement had been reached.

Images were as important as realities when it came to China, particularly to Roosevelt, who worried that many of the American journalists covering the conference were aware that things were not working out as well as he would have liked.[70] The last thing that the president wanted was to have stories of discord between the Allies disseminated in the press. This may have been one of the reasons why the journalists covering the conference were kept at arm's length from the participants and why normally loquacious aides and staff members in Roosevelt's entourage seemed as silent as the Sphinx.

If the first paragraph of the Cairo communiqué was purposefully vague, the second paragraph was equally innocuous, or so it appeared on the surface:

> The Three Great Allies are fighting this war to restrain and punish the aggression of Japan. They covet no gain for themselves and have no thought of territorial expansion. It is their purpose that Japan shall be stripped of all the islands in the Pacific which she has seized or occupied since the beginning of the First World War in 1914, and that all the territories Japan has stolen from the Chinese, such as Manchuria, Formosa, and the Pescadores, shall be restored to the Republic of China. Japan will also be expelled from all other territories that she has taken by violence and greed. The aforesaid three great powers, mindful of the enslavement of the people of Korea, are determined that in due course, Korea shall be free and independent.[71]

The content of the second paragraph of the communiqué was particularly pleasing to Generalissimo Chiang Kai-shek because it stated publically and clearly for the first time what the Allies had discussed privately in previous deliberations: namely that China would regain control of territories occupied by the Japanese since 1895. This statement would play very well in Chungking from which the Chinese press would trumpet the word to the hinterlands of Free China and Japanese-occupied areas.

The inclusion of a statement about the post-war fate of Korea in the Cairo communiqué was an addendum, prepared by Hopkins at the president's request, which had not been discussed in detail at the conference except in a private conversation between Roosevelt and Chiang at dinner on the evening of November 23.[72] On that occasion, Roosevelt asked the generalissimo for his views on the post-war disposition of Japanese occupied areas, including Korea.[73] According to Elliott Roosevelt's account of this conversation, Chiang seemed little interested in the fate of Korea.[74] A reading of the generalissimo's diary entry for November 23 confirms his comments and suggests Chiang's primary concern was the repatriation of Japanese-occupied China.[75]

Except for Roosevelt's conversation with Chiang on November 23, there is no indication in the published records of the proceedings of the Cairo conference or the private papers and published memoirs of the principal participants in the conference that the question of Korea received any discussion or that the post-war consequences of the Cairo declaration as it pertained to Korea were recognized or even considered. Surely, Churchill was little interested in Korea and Chiang, whose interest in Korea should have been greater than the prime minister's, did not show much more concern about the fate of that neighboring state. The fact that the seemingly innocuous statement about the fate of Korea could pose problems when the war was over was lost on all of the signatories to the Cairo communiqué.[76]

In his study of American policy in Korea, Bruce Cumings suggests that Roosevelt's desire to include a statement about the future status of Korea in the Cairo Declaration had more to do with his desire to push the concept of trusteeship as a vehicle to dismantle colonial empires in the post-war era than with his appreciation of the strategic importance of the Korean peninsula.[77] Cumings also suggests that the president hoped to involve the Chinese and Soviets in a Korean trusteeship "condominium" which would insure stability in East Asia in the post-war period while guaranteeing that the Koreans were adequately prepared for independence.[78] Neither Chiang nor Churchill thought it necessary to oppose the president on incorporating these ideas into the Cairo Declaration.

The last paragraph of the Cairo communiqué was even more general and vague than the first two paragraphs:

> With these objects in view, the three Allies in harmony with those of the United Nations at war with Japan will continue to persevere in the serious and prolonged operations necessary to procure the unconditional surrender of Japan.[79]

There was nothing new in this statement. The idea of waging war until the unconditional surrenders of Germany and Japan had been articulated at the Casablanca conference in January 1943. At best, the reiteration of this idea would make the Allied position clear to the enemy and serve as a reminder to the citizens of the Allied nations as to the ultimate goals of the war.

Although the Cairo communiqué was drafted quickly and without much discussion, it was decided to postpone the announcement of the declaration until after Churchill and Roosevelt met with Stalin at Teheran, lest there be any need to alter the statement as a consequence of the Teheran conference.[80]

Until such time as the Cairo declaration was released to the press, all that was to be said to the journalists covering the conference was that the first phase of the deliberations was over.[81]

The drafting of the communiqué and the discussion of when to release it to the press took approximately an hour.[82] By 6:00 P.M., the president was back at work on his correspondence.[83] He shared an early dinner with a few members of his staff at 7:30 P.M. and went to bed at 10:00 P.M., anticipating a very early departure for Teheran the next morning.[84]

While the president returned to his correspondence, Generalissimo Chiang went back to his villa to brief his staff and General Stilwell on the deliberations of the day.[85] The generalissimo told his entourage that he had received verbal assurances from Roosevelt that the British would ultimately agree to Operation Buccaneer, but he suggested that a formal commitment had not yet been made to go ahead with this operation.[86] This being the case, Chiang asked Stilwell to remain in Cairo until Churchill and Roosevelt returned from Teheran to press the president and prime minister for final approval of the amphibious operation in the Andamans.[87]

Although the generalissimo's briefing of his subordinates indicated a generally positive attitude about the outcome of the conference, Chiang's private views were much more pessimistic, as the following excerpt from his diary suggests:

> My experiences at Cairo have convinced me that Britain will not make any sacrifice, however small, for the benefit of others. For all that the United States had done for her, Britain will not make the slightest concession to American opinion. What does she care whether China lives or dies?[88]

Chiang acknowledged that Roosevelt had assured him that the British would succumb to American pressure, but he remained skeptical that the president could force Churchill to honor the commitment to provide adequate resources for operations in Southeast Asia in 1944.[89]

After briefing his staff on the events of the day, Generalissimo Chiang shared a quiet dinner with his wife and went to bed at an early hour.[90] Like Roosevelt, the generalissimo planned to leave Cairo on the morning of November 27, but since he still had some unfinished business with General Stilwell, Chiang was not able to leave Cairo as early as the president.

The business that Chiang had to take up with General Stilwell was related to the proposal that Mountbatten had presented to the generalissimo at the instruction of the CCOS. After breakfast on the morning of November 27, Stilwell was called to Chiang's villa where the generalissimo told him that he was unwilling to put his signature to Mountbatten's plan until he received assurances that the British would agree to Operation Buccaneer and the supply question was resolved.[91] The generalissimo made it clear to Stilwell that the only deal that would be acceptable to him was a firm British commitment on the amphibious operation in the Andaman islands and an equally firm assurance that the Hump lift into China would not fall below 10,000 tons per month.[92]

Having given Stilwell his orders, Chiang announced that he was leaving Cairo.[93] Stilwell was not happy to be left behind cleaning up the generalissimo's mess. "War by committee is a bust," he noted later that day in his diary, "the executors are left out on a limb."[94] Stilwell would much rather have gone back to China than to "stick it out for Buccaneer and 10,000 tons," but he had no choice in the matter.[95] As Chiang's chief of staff at the Cairo conference, Stilwell recognized his responsibilities.

Stilwell also recognized the fact that the generalissimo was not solely to blame for the failure of the three leaders to finalize plans for 1944, a point he made to Mountbatten at lunch that afternoon after explaining Chiang's refusal to give final approval to the admiral's proposal for the campaign in Burma.[96] It is not likely that Mountbatten was soothed by Stilwell's rationalization of Chiang's thinking. After all of the work he had put into drafting, presenting, and revising his plan of battle for 1944, Mountbatten still lacked approval to implement the plan.

According to Stilwell, Mountbatten decided to make one last attempt to persuade the generalissimo to commit his forces to the offensive in Burma by catching Chiang and his entourage as they stopped in India en route to China to inspect Chinese units being trained under American supervision there.[97] Since Churchill did not need his services in Teheran, Mountbatten proposed to take the next available flight to Ramgarh where he would have more time to make things right with the generalissimo.[98] Stilwell did not have great confidence that Mountbatten could do much to change Chiang's mind, but told Mountbatten it was worth a try.[99] It was better than cooling his heels in Cairo.[100]

If Chiang Kai-shek left Cairo with regret over the failure of the Allies to reach final agreement on any substantive issue, Churchill seemed perfectly delighted to be done with the first phase of the Cairo conference and off to discuss more important matters in Teheran. The prime minister had never thought it was a good idea to invite Chiang Kai-shek and his entourage to Cairo. He had predicted it would be a waste of time and in his mind, it was:

> What we had apprehended from Chiang K'ai-shek's presence now in fact occurred. The talks of the British and American Staffs were sadly distracted by the Chinese story, which was lengthy, complicated, and minor.[101]

After the war, Churchill also suggested that if Chiang had to be invited to Cairo, it should have been after the Teheran conference when the Allies would have been in a better position to make plans for the CBI and SEAC theaters.[102] By inviting the generalissimo to Cairo before their meeting with Stalin, Churchill believed the president had put the proverbial cart before the horse. "Chinese business," said Churchill, "occupied first instead of last place at Cairo," greatly complicating the discussions that were to take place in Teheran.[103]

What Churchill particularly resented was the fact that so much time was wasted at the Cairo conference discussing Operation Buccaneer, thus depriving the Anglo-American Allies of the opportunity to discuss Operation Overlord and arrive at a common position on this cross–Channel offensive before they met with Stalin.[104] This was not only a waste of precious time, it also put a strain on Anglo-American relations. The JCS and the BCOS already differed on matters relating to the timing and scope of Operation Overlord; they did not need to exacerbate their differences in a meaningless debate over Operation Buccaneer.[105]

Although he was upset that Roosevelt had spent so much time and energy on the Chinese in Cairo, Churchill apparently believed that the president might come to his senses as a consequence of the discussion that would take place in Teheran. In particular, Churchill was concerned about the president's assurances to Chiang that Operation Buccaneer would be launched simultaneously with the land campaign in Burma. The prime minister had never approved of such an operation and still hoped to prevail upon Roosevelt to "retract his promise."[105] Perhaps Stalin would prove to be a helpful ally in this regard.

10

November 28–29, 1943: Interlude in Teheran, Part I

When Churchill and Roosevelt departed for Teheran on the morning of November 27, they left Generalissimo and Madame Chiang Kai-shek behind in Cairo, but they carried their Chinese baggage with them to Iran. Again and again, questions about operations in Southeast Asia and China found their way onto the formal and informal agendas of Churchill, Roosevelt, and Stalin in Teheran. Although the China tangle did not occupy center stage in Teheran, it lurked in the wings, influencing the course of events at the Teheran conference.

Roosevelt and his entourage arrived in Teheran at 3:00 P.M. on the afternoon of November 27.[1] The president's plane landed at a small Russian military air field five miles south of the city.[2] Security for Roosevelt's arrival was very tight. Except for a small number of armored cars driven by American military personnel, which transported Roosevelt and his aides to the American Legation, there was no greeting party at the airport nor did welcoming crowds line the president's route.[3]

Churchill arrived in Teheran about an hour after Roosevelt. His arrival, by contrast, had a carnival air and security was very lax.[4] Whereas Roosevelt's passage from the military airport to the American Legation was unannounced and swift, the prime minister's caravan took a route crowded with onlookers waving Allied flags.[5] People crowded Churchill's car, getting to within a few feet of the prime minister.[6] There was little or no security for the prime minister. As Churchill would later note, if there had been a plot to kill him, it might very well have been successful.[7] The prime minister arrived at the British Legation without incident, no thanks to those who planned his arrival.

Security was a very real concern in Teheran. Even more than Cairo, Teheran was said to be filled with enemy agents.[8] Indeed, before the president departed for Teheran, he was advised by both the British and the Russians that it might be best if he stayed at one of their legations in Teheran, which were adjoining, as opposed to the American Legation, which was about a half mile away.[9] Roosevelt initially refused invitations from Churchill and Stalin to be their guest because he felt he would have more privacy at the American minister's home.[10] He would soon change his mind.

Roosevelt was particularly eager to meet Marshal Stalin. As soon as the president settled in at the United States Legation, he sent an invitation to Stalin to join him for dinner.[11] Stalin declined Roosevelt's invitation, stating that he had only just arrived in Teheran himself and needed to rest before the formal opening of the conference on November 28.[12] In his place, M.A. Maximoff, the Russian Charge d'Affaire in Teheran, paid a courtesy call on the president.[13] After Maximoff's departure, Roosevelt met with Harriman, who briefed him on what to expect of Stalin. The president then dined with Harriman, Hopkins, Leahy, and a few other aides.[14] After the president had gone to bed, Harriman received a note from the Soviet foreign minister, V.M. Molotov, urging him to use his good offices with Roosevelt to persuade the president to move to the Russian Legation.[15] Molotov advised Harriman that Stalin was very much concerned about driving to and from the American Legation because of the presence of German agents in Teheran who might well assassinate him or the prime minister.[16] Harriman conveyed this message to Roosevelt shortly after the president took his breakfast on the morning of November 28. After some discussion, Roosevelt agreed to accept Stalin's invitation and moved to the Russian compound later that afternoon.[17]

While Harriman and Roosevelt were talking about moving the president to the Soviet Legation, the BCOS were meeting at the British Legation.[18] The first item on their agenda was a discussion of the conclusions reached at the last meeting of the CCOS in Cairo on November 26 and the still as yet unresolved question of Operation Buccaneer.[19] Alan Brooke informed his colleagues that Roosevelt had "apparently promised" Chiang Kai-shek that Operation Buccaneer would take place and that the American Chiefs of Staff "had no latitude on this issue."[20] If this amphibious operation were to be cancelled, Churchill would have to prevail on Roosevelt to do so.[21]

It was decided to send Ismay to see Churchill immediately to ask the prime minister whether he was prepared to give his assent to Operation Buccaneer or if he wished to take this matter up "afresh" with Roosevelt.[22] Ismay went up to Churchill's bedroom, where the prime minister was nursing a nasty cold and a sore throat, to discuss the matter with him.[23] He returned in short order to tell his colleagues that Churchill was not ready to agree to Operation Buccaneer and would continue to press the president to drop his support of this program.[24]

In his diary entry for November 28, Alan Brooke lamented the fact that Churchill would not go along with Operation Buccaneer.[25] Although he and the other members of the BCOS did not think this operation was necessary, they were tired of arguing with their American colleagues and were willing to agree to a quid pro quo with them. "We tried to get him [Churchill] to agree to going along with the Andaman operation," Brooke wrote in his diary, "so as to get American agreement in the Mediterranean," but Churchill refused.[26]

Brooke attributed Churchill's contrariness to his ill health. "He is not fit," he noted, "and consequently not in the best of moods."[27] This was not the first time that Brooke had to deal with the mercurial mood swings of the prime minister. As mentioned earlier, Churchill's behavior was often erratic and posed problems for associates like Brooke.[28]

While the BCOS were trying to deal with the matter of operations in Southeast Asia and their linkage to plans for forthcoming offensives in the European theater, Roosevelt and the JCS were meeting at the American Legation to discuss the same issues.[29] During the course of the meeting, General Marshall pointed out that, due to a shortage of landing craft in Europe and Southeast Asia, it would be impossible to launch simultaneous operations in France, the Mediterranean, and the Andamans. According to Marshall, this meant that the Allies would be forced to choose between Operation Buccaneer and the British proposal to capture Rhodes. He warned Roosevelt that Churchill would press him to reconsider his promises to the Chinese.[30]

Roosevelt responded to Marshall's comments by pointing out that the Allies were "obligated to the Chinese" to carry out Operation Buccaneer.[31] That might well be the case, Harry Hopkins told the president, but Churchill considered the capture of Rhodes of much greater importance than the campaign in Burma. If a choice had to be made, the prime minister would opt to cancel Operation Buccaneer in spite of the promises that the president had made to Generalissimo Chiang.[32]

Roosevelt once again reiterated that promises had been made to the generalissimo and stated that these promises were not solely his. He reminded the JCS that Churchill himself had promised Chiang that the British would build up their fleet in the Bay of Bengal in anticipation of the offensive in Burma. "Of what value would the fleet be there," Roosevelt asked rhetorically, "unless some operations were carried out?"[33]

Marshall pointed out that while he was aware of Churchill's promises to Chiang Kai-shek, it was his belief that the prime minister would not feel bound to honor them if he believed that doing so would jeopardize operations in Europe.[34] In Marshall's view, Churchill was hoping that Russian demands for the speedy implementation of a cross–Channel invasion and supporting operations would force the cancellation of Operation Buccaneer.[35] He told Roosevelt that the prime minister would not consent to the Operation Buccaneer so long as he considered it a political rather than a military necessity.[36]

Roosevelt replied to Marshall by pointing out that the British might never be satisfied with Operation Buccaneer. Even if the campaign in Burma and the attack on Rhodes could be carried out simultaneously, the president felt Churchill would probably say, "Now we will have to take Greece."[37] It would be impossible to convert the prime minister and his aides to the virtues of any operation in Southeast Asia, according to Roosevelt, because they were obsessed with the Mediterranean.[38]

Roosevelt's meeting with the Joint Chiefs lasted until 1:00 P.M., after which he took his lunch and prepared for the move to the Russian legation.[39] At 3:00 P.M., the president, Leahy, Hopkins, and the president's son-in-law, John Boettiger, motored over to the Soviet compound.[40] Upon arrival at the Russian Legation, Roosevelt and his staff were given full run of the main building, which Stalin and his aides had vacated in favor of one of the smaller houses in the compound as a courtesy to the president.[41] "Pa" Watson and other members of the president's staff remained at the American Legation to give the appearance that the president was still in residence in the American diplomatic compound.[42]

Immediately after the president arrived at the Soviet compound, he had his first encounter with Marshal Stalin who came over to the main house to welcome Roosevelt.[43] After an initial exchange of pleasantries, Roosevelt and Stalin discussed the situation on the eastern front. According to minutes of the conversation kept by Charles Bohlen, the president told Stalin that he wished that the Allies could provide the Soviets with relief from the German onslaught and expressed the hope that by the time the Teheran conference ended, plans for Operation Overlord would be firmed up and agreed upon.[44] Stalin acknowledged that the launching of Overlord would provide such relief and thanked the president for his concern.[45]

Roosevelt then told Stalin about the Cairo conference and his conversations with Generalissimo Chiang Kai-shek, outlining plans for Mountbatten's proposed campaign in Burma and telling Stalin about the training of Chinese forces in India.[46] At this point, Stalin interrupted the president to suggest that he had a very poor opinion of the ability of the Chinese army and its leaders, singling out Chiang for particular criticism.[47] Roosevelt did not respond to Stalin and the conversation turned from a discussion of the Cairo conference to a more general discussion of the fate of colonialism in the post-war era.[48]

Stalin commented that considering the behavior of many French leaders during the war, he did not propose that the Allies should shed any blood to restore the French to their pre-war colonial empire.[49] Roosevelt agreed with Stalin, although he warned him that Churchill was of a different mind. According to Roosevelt, the prime minister believed that France would quickly emerge as a strong nation after the war and try to reclaim those of her colonies that had fallen under German, Italian, or Japanese control during the war.[50] The British would be likely to support French claims because they also wished to re-establish control in their Southeast Asian colonies.[51]

Roosevelt voiced his opposition to French colonialism and suggested that French colonies in Indochina be placed under an internationally supervised trusteeship when the war ended rather than being returned to the French.[52] The president also told Stalin that he had discussed this matter with Generalissimo Chiang in Cairo and that Chiang seemed to be in agreement with the concept of international trusteeship.[53] Stalin expressed his approval of this general proposition as well.[54]

Roosevelt engaged Stalin in this lengthy discussion to find out his views on the colonial question. When it became clear to the president that Stalin shared his abhorrence of imperialism, he tried to enlist Stalin's support in what was sure to be a difficult bout with Churchill over the post-war fate of the British Empire and treated the Russian leader to a discourse on the prime minister's sensitivity about this matter.

Roosevelt suggested that it might be best to avoid discussing the fate of India and other British colonies with Churchill until more immediate problems were resolved because it was a sore point with the prime minister, but he also made it clear to Stalin that it was his view that the British would have to prepare for the independence of their colonies in the post-war era or face the consequences.[55] Stalin replied that this question was complicated but moot since the British had not even gotten as far as considering the fate of imperialism in a new post-war world. To make too much of this issue might compromise the goodwill of the Allies and wreck the conference.[56]

After the war, Harriman observed that Stalin "showed rather more sophistication than Roosevelt" in the discussion of colonial matters and marveled at his knowledge of the outside world:

> I was struck time and time again by the extent of his knowledge of other countries, which I found remarkable in view of the fact that he had done so little traveling.[57]

The president, on the other hand, had traveled widely, but he was often naive about global issues.[58] Whereas Roosevelt favored abstract formulas and idealistic long-term goals, Stalin preferred to apply the principles of realpolitik, dealing with political issues far more pragmatically and realistically than the president.[59]

Soon after finishing his conversation with Stalin, Roosevelt opened the plenary session of the Teheran conference, delivering a rambling discourse on the war against Japan.[60] During the course of his remarks, the president emphasized that the war in the Pacific was a war of attrition, which the Allies would eventually win because they had more staying power than the Japanese.[61] China provided this extra staying power and had to be kept in the Allied camp at all costs.[62] Although it now seems clear that in the long term Japan might have lost the war with or without China's continuing participation, the president did not then have a sense that the disparity of resources available to the United States and Japan made the issue of staying power somewhat irrelevant.

Stalin responded to the president's discourse on the war against Japan by expressing his regrets that the Soviet Union had not been able to join the Anglo-American Allies in this struggle.[63] He then indicated that when the

Germans were defeated, the Russians would join their Anglo-American Allies in the final assault against Japan.[64] This marked the first time that Stalin had personally gone on record to assure Churchill and Roosevelt that the U.S.S.R. would ultimately declare war on Japan.

Stalin's assurance that the Soviet Union would eventually join the United Kingdom and the United States in the war against Japan made a considerable impression on Churchill and Roosevelt and, unknown to Marshal Stalin, proved to be a catalyst which contributed to the unraveling of agreements reached at Cairo only days before. For the moment, however, the implications of Stalin's remarks remained unclear because the timetable of Russian intervention in the Pacific war still seemed far off and uncertain.

President Roosevelt hosted a dinner for Churchill and Stalin at 8:30 P.M. in his quarters at the Russian Legation.[65] The meal was prepared by the president's Filipino stewards who had to hurriedly move ranges and kitchen equipment from the American Legation to the Russian compound while the plenary meeting was still in session.[66] As the president himself noted, "with their usual resourcefulness, they saw it done and came through in their usual fine style."[67]

Roosevelt's dinner party was an intimate gathering. Except for the president, the prime minister, and Marshall Stalin, the only others present were Bohlen, Eden, Hopkins, Molotov, Pavlov, Archibald Clark Kerr, the British minister in Teheran, and one of his aides.[68] After dinner, Roosevelt and his guests discussed a wide variety of matters, including the question of the post-war status of Japanese-occupied territories in east and Southeast Asia.

Stalin began this discussion with a blunt condemnation of France. According to Bohlen's minutes of the conversation, Marshall Stalin stated that France had "no right to retain her former empire" because the "French ruling class was rotten to the core and had delivered over France to the Germans."[69] Roosevelt agreed with Stalin, stating that in his opinion no one over the age of forty should be permitted to participate in the post-war French government.[70]

Stalin's tirade against the French and Roosevelt's support of his position was troubling to Churchill. According to Bohlen's recollection of the evening, the prime minister could barely contain his anger over the efforts of his peers to gang up on the French. At one point, Churchill interrupted Stalin's remarks, lecturing him that it was impossible to conceive of a world "without a flourishing and lively France."[71] Stalin did not budge one inch, replying to Churchill's remark with the comment that France might be a charming and pleasant country yet that did not mean that the French "should be allowed to play any important role in the immediate post-war world."[72]

Stalin's savage comments on the French reflected his contempt for their collaboration with the Germans rather than support of communist insurgencies in Indochina or elsewhere in the French empire. Although the capitulation of the French had come before the Germans violated the Molotov-Von Ribbentrop Pact and invaded Russia, Stalin believed that the collapse of the French military and the subsequent collaboration of the Vichy regime with German authorities had made it possible for the Germans to launch their invasion of the Soviet Union. The fact that his 1939 agreement with Hitler had opened the door to invasions of Poland and France seemed lost on him, at least for the moment.

Churchill, Roosevelt, and Stalin had been up rather late on November 28 and had no scheduled meetings the next morning. While they attended to their private business, the CCOS held a meeting with their Soviet counterparts at 10:30 A.M. on November 29 in the large meeting room in the Russian Legation.[73] As had by now become customary at CCOS meetings, Alan Brooke chaired the session.

Brooke welcomed Marshal Voroshilov and his translator, V.N. Pavlov, and then proceeded to give the Russians a brief account of the war, ending in an examination of Operation Overlord and its relationship to other operations of the war effort. Conscious that he was analyzing the war through a British prism, Brooke invited General Marshall to present the American perspective.[74] Marshall eagerly accepted this invitation.

Since Brooke's remarks contained no mention of the war against the Japanese, Marshall focused on this issue, pointing out that the United States was fighting a war on two fronts and had to balance these two wars.[75] While, as a general rule, there were enough men and supplies to fight both wars, some items, such as naval landing craft, were in short supply. This made it impossible to undertake more than two major new amphibious operations at one time in 1944.[76] While no mention was made of Operation Buccaneer, Marshall tried to make it clear that operations in Europe could not be discussed in a vacuum. A broader vision was necessary.[77]

Marshall expressed no disagreement with Brooke over the importance of Operation Overlord. Where he differed with his British colleague was over the importance of operations in the Mediterranean. Marshall indicated to Voroshilov that before plans for future Mediterranean operations could be approved, important logistical problems would have to be worked out, chief among these the availability of landing craft.[78] While saying nothing specific about Mountbatten's proposal for the 1944 offensive in Burma, Marshall's message made it clear that the United States considered operations in Southeast Asia to be at least as important as operations in the Mediterranean.

When Voroshilov expressed concern that the Allies launch Operation Overlord at the earliest possible date, Marshall took the opportunity to inform his Soviet colleague that the United States was involved in five amphibious operations in the Pacific and that four more, including Operation Buccaneer, were planned for 1944.[79] These operations could not be suspended or postponed so as to divert landing craft to the European theater and even if they could, there would be insurmountable logistical problems involved in moving landing craft from the Pacific and Southeast Asia to Europe.[80]

Marshall told Voroshilov that if Overlord was to be launched at an early date, there would have to be reduced operations in the Mediterranean. Conversely, if the Allies decided to go ahead with operations in the Mediterranean, Operation Overlord would have to be delayed.[81] Voroshilov may not have been aware that Marshall was chiding the British, but Alan Brooke and his associates clearly understood Marshall's message. Two could play the same game. If the British hoped to use the Russians to bring pressure on the United States to drop its support for Operation Buccaneer, the Americans could use the same ploy in the hope of forcing the British to abandon their plans for the capture of Rhodes.

Following the long but inconclusive CCOS meeting, Brooke and his colleagues met to plot strategy. During the course of their conversation, it was agreed that the British would continue to press their American friends to reconsider plans for forthcoming operations in Southeast Asia by taking a new approach, i.e., suggest that going ahead with Operation Buccaneer would threaten the cross–Channel invasion.[82]

Since Stalin had made it absolutely clear that Overlord must be launched at the earliest possible date, Brooke and his aides expected to toss the ball back into the American court by bluntly suggesting that it was America's obsession with aiding Generalissimo Chiang Kai-shek that threatened to delay the cross–Channel invasion. Their goal was to force President Roosevelt to reconsider his seemingly unstinting commitment to Operation Buccaneer.[83]

While Brooke and was discussing logistics at the British Legation, Marshal Stalin and Foreign Minister Molotov called on President Roosevelt.[84] The president treated his guests to a long and rambling discourse on need to set up a mechanism to guarantee peace in the post-war world, suggesting that China, the United States, the United Kingdom, and the U.S.S.R. could preserve the peace by acting as "policemen," with each of the Big Four monitoring developments in different parts of the world and intervening to maintain peace when necessary.[85]

Stalin was less than enthusiastic about the concept of the Four Policemen. According to Harriman, who was present during this conversation, Stalin was dubious about the elevation of China to great power status and expressed doubt that the nations of Europe would wish to have the Chinese given a position which would involve them in European affairs.[86] He suggested that it might be better to think in terms of regional policemen or committees, creating two separate groups, one to monitor affairs in Europe and a second to monitor events in Asia.[87]

According to Harriman, nothing that Roosevelt said at Teheran caused Stalin to change his view of China, although he did get a better fix on the president's thinking.⁸⁸ Churchill would later agree with Harriman's analysis, adding his own editorial comment that "the Soviet leader showed himself more prescient and possessed of a truer sense of values than the president" when it came to the China question.⁸⁹

Elliott Roosevelt, who was also present during the president's meeting with Stalin and Molotov, recalls that his father also raised the question of the post-war borders of China, specifically conveying Chiang Kai-shek's concern about Soviet recognition of the pre-war Manchurian borderline.⁹⁰ Stalin replied that this would be no problem.⁹¹ According to the president's son, Stalin told his father that since recognition of Soviet sovereignty was a cardinal point with him, he "would most certainly respect the sovereignty of countries large or small," implying that he would respect China's claims in Manchuria.⁹²

Elliott Roosevelt also mentions that his father and Stalin spoke about the generalissimo's concern over the post-war status of Hong Kong and the treaty ports.⁹³ According to the president's son, Roosevelt told Stalin that Chiang was particularly anxious to have the powers renounce their extraterritorial rights in China and hoped that they would all do so before the war was over.⁹⁴ Stalin voiced no objection over this from the Soviet point of view.⁹⁵ The question of Hong Kong was another matter. Stalin understood the problem, but he was in no position to help to resolve it.⁹⁶

Roosevelt and Stalin broke off their conversation at 3:30 P.M. to join Churchill and the members of the American, British, and Russian delegations on the front portico of the Russian Legation for a picture-taking opportunity, which lasted less than fifteen minutes.⁹⁷ The accredited members of the press who accompanied the Big Three to Teheran had no opportunity to pose questions. If the press had been quarantined in Cairo, security provisions were even more stringent in Teheran and there was no opportunity for reporters to get within ten feet of the principal players.⁹⁸

After the picture taking was over, the Big Three moved back into the conference room for the second plenary session of the Teheran conference.⁹⁹ This session was exclusively devoted to a discussion of Operation Overlord. There was no discussion of the Chinese question or the war in the Pacific. During the course of the plenary session, Alan Brooke and Churchill emphasized the need to maintain pressure on the Germans in the Mediterranean as a means of facilitating the ultimate success of Operation Overlord.¹⁰⁰ Stalin grew impatient and announced that he did not wish to delay Operation Overlord because of British preoccupation with the Mediterranean. Speaking quite bluntly to the prime minister, Stalin suggested that operations in the Mediterranean were minor diversions compared to the cross–Channel offensive.¹⁰¹ Churchill replied defensively, launching into a lengthy discourse on the strategic value of his plan for the capture of Rhodes.¹⁰²

Roosevelt sensed that Churchill and Stalin were on a collision course and suggested that a CCOS committee prepare a report analyzing the respective merits of operations in Europe and the Mediterranean and report back to the Big Three.[103] Stalin would buy none of this. Such questions, he suggested, should be decided by the Big Three not their lieutenants and these questions should be decided before the Teheran conference ended.[104]

At this point, Stalin lost his temper and asked Churchill whether the British really believed in Overlord or were merely paying lip service to the operation to lift the spirits of his government.[105] Churchill reassured Stalin that he was fully committed to the cross–Channel invasion and suggested the CCOS should work out a specific set of directives on Operation Overlord for discussion at the next plenary session of the Teheran conference, which was scheduled for 4:00 P.M. the next afternoon.[106] Since this was acceptable to Stalin and the time was getting late, Roosevelt adjourned the meeting at 7:20 P.M.[107]

The discussion that had taken place at the plenary session was haunted by the ghost of Operation Buccaneer. Although not one word was said about this amphibious operation in the Andamans, it was clearly on the mind of the Americans and the British. In urging support of operations in the Mediterranean, Alan Brooke and Churchill were implicitly advocating cancellation of Operation Buccaneer since it was clear that there was a critical shortage of landing craft available to the Allies. In trying to educate Stalin about the global perspective taken by the Americans, Marshall was making a case in favor of operations in Southeast Asia even if they had to be supported at the expense of possibilities in the Mediterranean because of the very same shortage of landing craft.

The last event on the calendar of the second day of the conference was a dinner party at the Russian Legation hosted by Stalin for Churchill, Roosevelt, Eden, Hopkins, Harriman, Molotov, and their aides.[108] After dinner, the Big Three engaged in a lengthy conversation, which lasted until midnight, discussing a wide variety of matters in an increasingly acrimonious manner.[109]

Charles Bohlen, Roosevelt's translator, recalled that the most notable feature of the evening was Stalin's antagonism toward Churchill:

> Marshall Stalin lost no opportunity to get in a dig at Mr. Churchill. Almost every remark that he addressed to the Prime Minister contained some sharp edge, although the Marshall's manner was entirely friendly.... At one occasion he told the Prime Minister that just because Russians are a simple people, it was a mistake to believe that they were blind and could not see what was before their eyes.[110]

Bohlen may have described Stalin's manner as "friendly," but his teasing of the prime minister was hardly friendly. Stalin's comments that the British were soft on the Germans and that the prime minister secretly liked the Germans could hardly have pleased Churchill. Although he would later suggest that he did not resent Stalin's remarks, Churchill's response to Stalin's chiding would suggest otherwise.[111]

Much has been made of Stalin's remarks that evening about the summary liquidation of 50,000–100,000 German war criminals when the war ended and Churchill's strong reaction to such cold blooded murder, but the real explosion between Churchill and Stalin came when the Soviet leader seemed to imply that the British were more interested in territorial gain and the re-establishment of their empire than in defeat of the Germans.[112] At that point Churchill could no longer contain his anger.

The British, Churchill told Roosevelt and Stalin, did not desire to acquire any additional territory as a result of the war, but they "intended to hold on to what they had," including Singapore and Hong Kong, and would not give up their colonies in Asia without a war.[113] In the future, Great Britain might "release" a portion of her empire, but that would be done voluntarily "in accordance with her own moral precepts" and not because of external pressures.[114]

Clearly, the question of colonialism touched a raw nerve with Churchill. Roosevelt had strong anti-colonial views, but he chose not to discuss them at length with the prime minister at this point because he did not want to disrupt the conference. He preferred to wait until the end of the war to address this question through the mechanism of the United Nations.[115] Marshall Stalin, on the other hand, was not as sensitive in dealing with Mr. Churchill on this matter and refused to treat him with kid gloves when it came to discussing the fate of colonialism in the post-war world.

Churchill had difficulty in accepting advice on colonial matters from men like Chiang and Stalin nor was he alone in rejecting their opinions on colonial affairs. His lieutenants also resented the interference of outsiders in the affairs of the Empire. Circumstances and fate had brought the British and Russians together as allies and Churchill was grudgingly forced to accept Stalin as his peer and listen to his advice. He did not feel it necessary to accord Chiang the same recognition.

The debate over the fate of Operation Buccaneer seemed, on the surface, to be an honest debate over strategy and priorities, but beneath the surface there lurked another issue, the question of whether to indulge the Chinese in their quest for aid and recognition or to protect imperial interests in places like Singapore and Hong Kong. Churchill and his associates clearly opted for the latter alternative.

To admit China into the council of the great powers had ominous overtones for supporters of the Empire like Churchill and Alan Brooke. Opening the door to China and recognizing her as a member of the country club might lead to opening the door to Indian independence, a frightening prospect to Churchill and his associates. Nor was this was their only concern. There was also the question of China's quest for sovereignty in Hong Kong and Tibet, not to say anything of Chiang's demand for the end of extra-territoriality in the treaty ports.

So strong were British concerns about the fate of their empire and their European interests that Churchill was willing to alienate his American and Soviet allies to ensure the sanctity of Great Britain's place in the world in the post-war era. In large measure, the failure of the Cairo conferees to come to a general understanding on future policy could be attributed to Churchill's stubborn defense of British interests. Now the Teheran conference seemed stalled as well.

11

November 30–December 1, 1943: The Teheran Interlude Part II

Despite the somewhat belligerent nature of his conversation with Roosevelt and Stalin on the evening of November 29, Churchill instructed his aides to work toward an understanding with the other Allies on the matter of fixing a date for Operation Overlord before the Teheran conference ended. To that end, Alan Brooke convened an early morning meeting of the BCOS on November 30.

Brooke and his colleagues discussed the reasons behind the continuing impasse between them and their American associates and what could be done to break the impasse.[1] They had no problem identifying the stumbling blocks to an agreement: Roosevelt's unwavering commitment to Chiang Kai-shek and Operation Buccaneer and Churchill's equally unwavering opposition to this venture. But as Brooke suggested, defining the problem was much easier than finding a solution to break the impasse.[2]

The British had tried to argue that Operation Buccaneer should be scrapped in favor of an operation in the Mediterranean, but that argument failed to move the Americans. Stalin also dismissed the idea that a Mediterranean operation was vital to the success of Operation Overlord, accusing Churchill of proposing such a plan as a means of delaying the cross–Channel attack. The BCOS were agreed that continuing to advance this line of thinking would be unproductive.[3] A new approach was called for.

During the course of their conversation, Brooke and Ismay suggested that it might useful to engage their American counterparts in a discussion of the implications of Stalin's promise to enter the war against Japan once Germany was defeated, with an eye toward persuading them to defer new operations in Southeast Asia in favor of an all-out effort in Europe.[4] There would be little or no mention of operations in the Mediterranean. Rather, the British would stress Overlord and Anvil, the planned landings in southern France, which were to complement the Normandy landings.[5]

Whereas Stalin was opposed to diverting resources to the Mediterranean, he was known to favor Operation Anvil, a second landing in France. Roosevelt could be made to believe that going ahead with Operation Buccaneer would cause delay in Operation Anvil, he might be willing to abandon or postpone new operations in Southeast Asia. As Brooke pointed out, although Roosevelt was interested in supporting Generalissimo Chiang, he was even more interested in establishing a good relationship with Marshal Stalin and would not likely risk alienating Stalin even if this meant alienating Chiang.[6] Brooke's associates agreed with this view and it was decided to test it at the meeting of the CCOS, which was scheduled for later that morning.[7]

Alan Brooke opened the CCOS meeting shortly after 9:30 A.M. and immediately raised the question of the timing of Operation Anvil and its relationship to Operation Overlord.[8] To his pleasure, he found the Americans in agreement that Anvil was a worthy venture and eager to support it.[9] He was somewhat surprised at Marshall's endorsement of Anvil, given the fact that in previous conversations the Americans did not seem enthusiastic about the plan, but welcomed the endorsement nevertheless.[10] The only area of disagreement between the British and American positions on Anvil and Overlord was the question of the availability of sufficient landing craft to launch both operations in France.

On this question, the British took a more pessimistic position than their American friends, arguing that coordinating Anvil and Overlord would necessitate the cancellation or postponement of Buccaneer. "If all other operations were put off," Brooke told the JCS, "we could do Overlord and Anvil in May."[11] This was what Stalin wanted, he suggested, and it could be guaranteed by diverting some of the landing craft from the Bay of Bengal to Europe.[12] Never once in his remarks did Brooke even mention the Mediterranean.

Surprisingly, the JCS did not react with alarm to Brooke's argument. Leahy was the first to respond and he merely asked whether the release of landing craft destined for use in Operation Buccaneer would really help facilitate Operations Anvil and Overlord.[13] Brooke replied in the affirmative, but in so doing he almost gave away the secret agenda of the British when he suggested these landing craft could be used in the Aegean or the south of France. Fortunately for Brooke, Admiral Cunningham picked up on this faux pas and reiterated that all landing craft diverted from Burma would be applied to strengthening Operation Anvil.[14]

Having reached what appeared to be a consensus, the CCOS agreed to recommend that Churchill and Roosevelt inform Stalin that Anvil and Overlord would be launched sometime in May 1944 "on the largest scale that is permitted by the landing craft available at that time."[15] The cancellation or postponement of Operation Buccaneer was implied in this resolution, at least in so far as the BCOS were concerned, but there was no clear statement of this in the CCOS recommendation.

The consensus mentioned above was built on quicksand. Although there appeared to be no overt opposition to Alan Brooke's agenda among the JCS, they did not agree formally or informally to urge the president to abandon Operation Buccaneer nor was he yet ready to do so. For their part, the BCOS were in much the same position. Although they had not mentioned the Mediterranean, except for Brooke's faux pas, they did not agree formally or informally to give up on an attack against Rhodes in 1944 nor was the prime minister yet ready to consider abandoning one of his favorite projects.

As he mused about the new ploy he and Ismay introduced at the CCOS meeting, Brooke noted in his diary that while the Americans had not dismissed the idea of relocating some of their landing craft from the Indian Ocean to the English Channel, they were hardly ready to abandon Operation Buccaneer and certainly would not release these landing craft if there was any hint of the fact that they were to be used in the Mediterranean.[16] Still, some progress had been made in weaning the Americans away from the Andaman operation.[17]

Ironically, at the same time that Brooke, Ismay, and the other British Chiefs were working on this new strategy to force the cancellation of Operation Buccaneer, Mountbatten had just caught up with Generalissimo Chiang Kai-shek in India where he hoped to secure the generalissimo's written consent to that very same operation.

At the Cairo conference, Chiang had agreed in principle to support Mountbatten's proposed offensive in Burma at least three times, but each time he had qualified his support of the proposal so as to alienate the CCOS and make it difficult to arrive at a firm understanding with the Anglo-American Allies.[18] Part of the problem, as Mountbatten later noted, was that Chiang was elusive:

> It had been difficult, at Cairo, to obtain a precise statement from the Chinese on any major point; for unlike the President and the Prime Minister, the Generalissimo did not delegate authority to members of his staff, with the result that points which were understood to have been agreed to by all the staffs concerned were subsequently changed by the Generalissimo in person.[19]

While in Cairo, Mountbatten was not able to obtain Chiang's undivided attention nor could he obtain the generalissimo's unqualified support of his proposal for the campaign in Burma. Chiang and his wife were too busy socializing with Churchill and Roosevelt and lobbying with the president for more assistance to pay much attention or give much time to the SEAC commander. In Ramgarh on November 30, the situation was quite different. The only item on Chiang's agenda was to review the Chinese troops stationed there.

Mountbatten found Generalissimo and Madame Chiang much more sympathetic to his ideas in Ramgarh. Chiang Kai-shek conceded everything that he [Mountbatten] had asked for in Cairo.[20] On one hand, Mountbatten was delighted at the generalissimo's change of heart; on the other hand, he found it most frustrating:

> I must say that this job is enough to turn my few remaining hairs grey.... I could not have believed so difficult a job would have been invented for anybody and those who envy me my job (if there are any) must be mad.[21]

Little did Mountbatten realize that at the very moment that he had finally persuaded Generalissimo Chiang to give his blessings to operational plans in Southeast Asia for 1944, his colleagues among Churchill's military advisors had laid the foundation to eliminate these same operations. Had he known this, he might not have bothered to make the trip to Ramgarh.

If Mountbatten was operating in the dark, Generalissimo Chiang was likewise laboring under false pretenses. He left India on his return flight to Chungking with the distinct impression that all was set for 1944 and expected to make a triumphal announcement to this effect when he arrived home. The generalissimo would soon be in for a rude shock, the consequences of which were to be profound.

While Mountbatten and the Chiangs were engaged in dialogue in far-off Ramgarh and the CCOS were finishing their meeting at the British Legation in Teheran, Churchill was trying to arrange a meeting with Stalin to familiarize him with British views and correct whatever erroneous impressions Stalin may have formed about British intentions based on his private conversations with Roosevelt.[22]

Churchill was very much concerned that Stalin had fallen under the influence of Roosevelt and that the president was using the Soviet leader to advance American policies at the expense of the previously close relationship between him and Mr. Roosevelt.[23] He was even more concerned about the icy reception he had received from Stalin since the opening of the Teheran conference, which he attributed, in part, to Roosevelt's influence on Stalin.[24]

Churchill was not mistaken in his belief that Stalin was giving him the cold shoulder. As Harriman would later observe in his memoirs:

> When the President spoke, Stalin listened closely with deference whereas he did not hesitate to interrupt or stick a knife into Churchill whenever he had the chance.[25]

Harriman felt that Stalin's treatment of the president was based on his recognition that the United States had replaced the United Kingdom as the leader of the democratic nations and his feeling that Roosevelt's politics were closer to his own.[26] Harriman was not suggesting that Stalin thought that Roosevelt was a comrade in arms, but that his political vision was more acceptable than Churchill's, particularly with regard to the elimination of colonialism in the post-war world.[27]

Churchill was able to see Marshal Stalin alone before lunch on November 30. It was his purpose to persuade the Soviet leader that the British did not mean to put obstacles in the path of Operation Overlord and that they were not obsessed with the idea of a Mediterranean offensive and a subsequent invasion of the Balkans, as Roosevelt may have led Stalin to believe.[28]

Churchill lost no time in telling Stalin that if there were to be any delay in launching Operations Anvil and Overlord, it would be due to Roosevelt's insistence on the implementation of Buccaneer and not British intransigence.[29] According to the prime minister, Roosevelt's commitments to Chiang Kai-shek were draining resources, which could be best used in Europe.[30] The prime minister assured Stalin that if the president could be persuaded to abandon "the enterprise in the Bay of Bengal," Operations Anvil and Overlord would most definitely be initiated by the end of May 1944.[31]

Churchill told Stalin that the choice the Allies had to make was between Operation Buccaneer and the date of Operation Overlord and not between Mediterranean operations and Overlord as Roosevelt may have suggested to him.[32] Churchill admitted that he preferred to spend his resources in the Mediterranean as opposed to the Bay of Bengal if such resources were available after implementing Operations Anvil and Buccaneer.[33] Given the near collapse of the Italian government, Churchill suggested that there was much more to be gained in the Mediterranean arena than in the jungles of Southeast Asia.[34]

Lest Stalin might think him to be anti–American, Churchill reminded the Soviet leader that he was half American and "had a great affection for the American people."[35] The issue between him and the Americans, Churchill suggested, was "a very narrow one" which could have been reconciled at Cairo had Chiang Kai-shek not arrived so early and had Chinese questions not taken up nearly all of the time available for deliberations.[36]

Despite the differences which still separated the American and British positions, Churchill said that he believed that they could be compromised in light of Stalin's announcement that Russia would enter the war against Japan at the earliest possible moment after the defeat of Germany. The promise of Soviet intervention into the war against Japan provided a sound reason to urge Roosevelt to reconsider his support of Operation Buccaneer. Surely, the U.S.S.R. would be a more valuable ally in the war against Japan than the Chinese. Once Roosevelt understood this fact, he would do everything necessary to bring about the earliest possible defeat of Germany, including canceling Buccaneer.[37]

Churchill's conversation with Stalin was more a monologue than a dialogue, with the prime minister doing most of the talking and Stalin doing most of the listening. According to Churchill's recollection of this discussion, Stalin said little in response to his remarks except to emphasize that the Red Army was depending upon the success of Operations Anvil and Overlord and that the Russians would be most disappointed if these operations were delayed.[38]

Churchill and Stalin broke off their conversation shortly before 1:30 P.M., at which time they joined Roosevelt for lunch at the president's quarters.[39]

Before sitting down to their meal, Stalin was informed that the CCOS had agreed to a May 1944 timetable for Operation Overlord. According to Bohlen's minutes of the gathering, Stalin expressed great satisfaction with this decision and promised that the Red Army would launch a new attack against German forces at the same time.[40]

As lunch was served, the conversation turned to a discussion of the Cairo communiqué. In response to a question posed by Churchill, Stalin indicated that he had read the communiqué and that he "thoroughly approved" of its contents.[41] He told the president and the prime minister that it was "right" that Manchuria, Formosa, and the Pescadores should be returned to China, but he also indicated that the Chinese should be made to fight against Japan, "which they had not done thus far."[42] Stalin also indicated he approved of the creation of an independent Korean state when the war was over.[43]

In commenting on the Cairo Declaration, Stalin indicated that the Soviet Union had no territorial designs in the Far East, but later in the conversation, he expressed Soviet interest in obtaining access to a warm water port on the Pacific, suggesting that Vladivostok was only partly ice free and too vulnerable to attack.[44] Roosevelt suggested that Dairen might be a good possibility if the Chinese consented to turning that city into a free port under international guarantee. That was quite likely, Roosevelt assured Stalin, based on what the generalissimo had told him in Cairo.[45]

Stalin thought that Roosevelt's suggestion was a good one, assuming that the president was right about Chiang's willingness to see Dairen under international control.[46] Churchill echoed this sentiment and indicated that there was nothing wrong in satisfying the legitimate needs of those nations that had united to defeat the Axis powers. Bohlen summarized Churchill's remarks on this subject as follows:

> The Prime Minister then said it was important that the nations who would govern the world after the war ... should be satisfied and have no territorial or other ambitions.... He said that hungry nations and ambitious nations are dangerous, and he would like to see the leading nations of the world in the position of rich, happy men.[47]

The next event of the day was the third plenary session of the conference, which Roosevelt convened at 4:00 P.M.[48] All of the discussion at the plenary session focused on plans for Operations Anvil and Overlord and the arrangements that would have to be completed if these operations were to launched by the end of May 1944. There was no consideration of plans for the Mediterranean or Southeast Asia.

November 30 was Churchill's birthday and he hosted a gala dinner party that evening at the British Legation to celebrate having reached his 69th birthday. It was to be the largest gathering of the Teheran conference with all of the high-ranking members of the three delegations in attendance. The prime minister had intended the evening to be an informal social affair, but it turned out to be a celebration of Allied cooperation, sparked by the agreement which had been reached earlier in the day about the timetable for launching the cross–Channel invasions.

Churchill occupied the place of honor at the main table, flanked by the leaders of the Allied powers. Churchill would later remember this evening as one of the most memorable occasions of his life:

> On my right sat the President of the United States, on my left the master of Russia. Together we controlled practically all the naval and three-quarters of all the air forces in the world, and could direct armies of nearly twenty millions of men, engaged in the most terrible of wars that had yet occurred in human history.[49]

The dinner party got off to a good start with Churchill, Roosevelt, and Stalin exchanging toasts and congratulating each other on the achievements of the Allied nations and drinking to their eventual victory over the Axis powers, but as the evening wore on and the heavy drinking continued, the pleasantries gave way to some moments of rancor and tension.[50] At one point during the course of the evening, Roosevelt toasted Alan Brooke, congratulating him on the heroism of the British army.[51] The president had barely finished his toast when Stalin offered some remarks of his own, acknowledging Brooke's genius, but criticizing him for his unfriendly attitude toward the U.S.S.R.[52] As he drank to Brooke's health, Stalin observed that when the general got to know the Russians better, he would find that they "were not so bad after all."[53]

There was a moment of still silence when Stalin sat down and after what must have seemed to be an eternity, Brooke rose to reply to Roosevelt and Stalin. First, he thanked the president for his kind remarks and then he chastised the Soviet leader for his remarks, looking Stalin straight in the eye and telling him, "I am surprised that you should have found it necessary to raise accusations against me that are entirely unfounded."[54] Brooke then went on to suggest that he was far more amiably disposed toward the Soviet Union than the Soviet leader was disposed toward him.[55]

As Stalin rose to respond to Brooke, some comic relief was provided when a waiter tripped as he passed the Soviet leader's translator, V.N. Pavlov, and spilled ice cream all over his suit. Admiral Andrew Cunningham, Chief of Staff of the Royal Navy, was sitting next to Mr. Pavlov and described what happened in the aftermath of this accident:

> He [Pavlov] dared not stop interpreting and stood there decoding Stalin's ... speech while those sitting on each side of him, of whom Brooke was one, did their best to clean him up with their napkins.[56]

This comic-opera episode broke the tension. Stalin, who apparently appreciated the boldness of Brooke's remarks, laughed and told Churchill that he "liked" Brooke because he spoke candidly; he even proposed to have a talk with him when the dinner party was over.⁵⁷ After dinner when Churchill's guests moved to the living room, Stalin did seek Brooke out, telling him, "The best friendships are those founded on misunderstandings."⁵⁸

Churchill's birthday party lasted until nearly 2:00 A.M. Since Roosevelt left the party at 11:45 P.M., Churchill and Stalin had some time to talk alone.⁵⁹ Both men had consumed a considerable amount of alcoholic refreshment and were in a reasonably good mood, but as Alan Brooke would later note, the tension between them still was palpable.⁶⁰ Churchill's efforts to befriend Stalin had not been entirely successful. Because of the late hour at which Churchill's party ended, the Big Three had no scheduled activity until noon on December 1, at which time they met for a long session in Roosevelt's quarters.⁶¹ They were joined by Eden, Harriman, Hopkins, Kerr, and Molotov and their three translators, Major Arthur Birse, Charles Bohlen, and V. N. Pavlov.⁶²

Much of this session was devoted to the question of bringing Turkey into the war against the Axis powers and the incentives that could be offered to Turkish officials to end their neutrality when they met with Churchill and Roosevelt in Cairo after the Teheran conference. During the course of this discussion, the prime minister once again raised the issue of launching new operations in the Mediterranean, arguing that an attack on Rhodes would provide an incentive for the Turks to join in the war against Germany.⁶³

Churchill's comment prompted Roosevelt and Hopkins to suggest that there were no landing craft available for an attack on Rhodes and that even if additional landing craft could be found, they could probably be used with more profit elsewhere.⁶⁴ Undaunted, Churchill suggested that it might be possible to divert some landing craft from the Pacific.⁶⁵ Roosevelt replied that this would be "absolutely impossible."⁶⁶ At this point, the prime minister dropped the matter and the conversation turned to other questions, but Churchill had not given up on his campaign to sabotage Operation Buccaneer and substitute a campaign in the Mediterranean.

The discussion over how to bring Turkey into the war was followed by a long and somewhat acrimonious debate on the Finnish and Polish questions, which lasted until dinnertime with two intermissions.⁶⁷ During and after dinner, efforts were made to draft a communiqué on the course of action to be pursued by the three Allies in 1944 based on the understandings reached by Churchill, Roosevelt, and Stalin during the preceding three days. By this time, everyone was quite exhausted and in such ill humor that they were arguing over the pettiest of issues, including whether to use the name Persia as opposed to Iran to designate the venue of the conference.⁶⁸

The Teheran Declaration which Churchill, Roosevelt, and Stalin and their aides finally hammered out and agreed to sign was purposefully vague, even more so than the Cairo Declaration. As to the future course of the war, all the conferees were willing to say in public was that they had "reached complete agreement" on the operations they would undertake in 1944. As to the post-war peace, all the conferees were willing to suggest was that they were sure that their cooperation and concord would make for "an enduring peace."[69]

The Teheran Declaration was designed for public consumption. A second secret agreement noting details of future military plans was also drafted and signed by Churchill, Roosevelt, and Stalin before the evening was over. This agreement included an understanding that Operation Overlord would be launched in May 1944 in conjunction with an operation against southern France [Anvil] which was to be undertaken "in as great a strength as the availability of landing craft permitted."[70]

On the surface, this statement about the opening of the long-anticipated second front seemed innocuous enough, but it was to prove to be a bone of contention when Churchill and Roosevelt returned to Cairo to complete their talks and wrap up plans for the cross–Channel attacks. After the war, Churchill suggested that plans for Operation Anvil had not been examined in detail at Teheran and that Roosevelt never quite understood the implications of endorsing Anvil, which virtually dictated the cancellation of Operation Buccaneer.[71] If the president failed to realize this, Churchill would try to make it clear to him upon their return to Cairo.

Roosevelt did not share Churchill's belief that the agreements reached at Teheran would force the eventual cancellation or postponement of Operation Buccaneer. In his mind, nothing that the Allies had agreed to in Teheran suggested that he would have to renege on the promises he had made to Chiang Kai-shek in Cairo. In Roosevelt's opinion, it was Churchill who had been forced to concede defeat in terms of his efforts to get Stalin to support his Mediterranean strategy. The president saw nothing incompatible between operations in Europe and Southeast Asia.

From Roosevelt's perspective, the Teheran conference had been a success. Not only had he and Stalin hit it off on a personal level, but he also found that Stalin shared many of his views on military strategy and plans for the post-war peace. Elliott Roosevelt recalls his father telling him that Stalin understood that the best way to kill the most Germans was "to mount one big invasion and slam 'em with everything we've got."[72] Stalin also understood that Churchill was more preoccupied with devising means to preserve Great Britain's position in the post-war era than he was in providing relief to the Soviet Union and this was why he kept pushing for offensives in the Mediterranean and the Balkans.[73] Fortunately, according to Roosevelt, Stalin would not buy into this strategy.

If Roosevelt had reason to be happy with the outcome of the Teheran conference insofar as plans for the European theater were concerned, he was well aware that Stalin did not share his opinions about China's role in the war and her place among the powers in the post-war era. Still, Stalin's antipathy toward Generalissimo Chiang and his regime were manageable compared to his hostility toward General Charles de Gaulle and the French government in exile.

Churchill had often suggested that Roosevelt was playing Papa Gepetto to Chiang Kai-shek's Pinocchio, but he could have been accused of playing the same role in relationship to General de Gaulle. The prime minister's advocacy of the importance of France and her heroic wartime leader often mirrored the president's advocacy of Chiang and his brave government. Both Churchill and Roosevelt succumbed to hyperbole when advancing the causes of their clients.

One might suggest that this strange *ménage-à-quatre* haunted both the Cairo and Teheran conferences, partially blinding both Churchill and Roosevelt. The president lost no opportunity to urge support of the Chinese cause and the prime minister lost no opportunity to advance the French cause. Roosevelt talked about the concept of the Four Policemen and the United Nations, suggesting that it was impossible to conceive of a nation of over 400 million people that should not one day play a major role in world affairs. Churchill talked of post-war balances of power, suggesting that Europe could not be made whole again unless the French were helped to regain their former place at the European table. Stalin did not accept either of these arguments.

In some respects, Churchill and Roosevelt were forced to accommodate each other's patronage of Chiang and de Gaulle, but there were some questions on which they could not compromise. Churchill refused to afford the Chinese a full place of honor among the great powers and Roosevelt refused to acquiesce in the re-establishment of the French colonial empire when the war was over. This tension influenced the deliberations at the first Cairo conference and in Teheran. It would emerge again when the president and the prime minister returned to Cairo on December 2.

After more than ten hours of discussion on December 1, Churchill, Roosevelt, and Stalin had finally drafted and signed a communiqué and a secret military agreement. This accomplished, Roosevelt bade his companions farewell at 10:30 P.M. and left Teheran, staying overnight at an American military base near the Soviet airfield, from which he would leave for Cairo the next morning.[74] Marshall, the Joint Chiefs of Staff, and the British Chiefs of Staff had already left for Cairo.[75] Churchill spent the night at the British Legation and left for Cairo on his own aircraft the next day.[76]

12

December 2–7, 1943: Cairo: The Final Act

Churchill and Roosevelt returned to Cairo on December 2 and spent much of the day recuperating from their trip.[1] The deliberations in Teheran had been grueling, leaving both the president and the prime minister emotionally and physically exhausted. Except for this first day of their return stay in Cairo, there would be little time for rest or relaxation. Too many unresolved issues awaited solutions.

Like their bosses, the CCOS also took much of the day off on December 2, but on December 3, it was back to business as usual, the main item on their agenda being the conclusion of final plans for Operations Anvil and Overlord. Agreeing on plans for the cross–Channel attacks could not be accomplished unless the CCOS also came to some understanding on plans for Southeast Asia and the Mediterranean. This was the hidden agenda at the second Cairo conference.

Once again comfortably ensconced in their quarters at the Mena House Hotel, the BCOS met at 10:00 A.M. to plot strategy for the final round of the Cairo summit.[2] Alan Brooke directed their discussion, focusing attention on the inter-relationship between Operations Anvil and Buccaneer. In the course of their discussion, Brooke and his colleagues agreed that to properly carry out Operation Anvil, it would be necessary to divert equipment and supplies from Southeast Asia.[3] Such a diversion of resources would also have a salutary effect on Aegean operations, permitting an attack on Rhodes early in March 1944.[4]

Alan Brooke was well aware that his American friends were still unbending in their opposition to new campaigns in the Mediterranean so he suggested that when the CCOS met later that afternoon, the British chiefs should make little or no mention of Aegean operations. Rather, they would focus on Operation Anvil, telling the American chiefs that Operation Anvil could not be carried out with adequate strength and vigor unless Operation Buccaneer was deferred or cancelled or unless the United States "could make good any deficiencies in terms of landing craft and supplies."[5]

With Ismet Inonu, the Turkish president, due to arrive in Cairo the next day, it was unnecessary for the BCOS to push in favor of operations in the Mediterranean at the CCOS meeting. Hopefully, the Turkish president would do the job for them when he met with Churchill and Roosevelt on December 4, bringing more pressure on Roosevelt to abandon plans for Operation Buccaneer.[6] Even Stilwell realized this, telling General Marshall to be prepared for a concerted effort on Churchill's part to press for an offensive against Rhodes once the Turkish president arrived in Cairo.[7]

The Combined Chiefs of Staff met at 2:30 P.M. at the Mena House Hotel to consider the implications of the military conclusions reached in Teheran.[8] There was a lengthy discussion of the minimum number of troops and equipment needed for a successful execution of the attack in southern France. The British argued that no fewer than two divisions must be committed to the operation while their American counterparts argued that Anvil could be successfully carried out with smaller numbers.[9] Although there was no overt mention of Operation Buccaneer, it was very much on the minds of the CCOS. No decision was reached on the matter of the minimum troop strength necessary for Operation Anvil, much to the displeasure of Alan Brooke who was already agitated about Leahy's announcement that Roosevelt might be leaving Cairo as early as December 5. With no agreement on the details of Operation Anvil yet in hand and other equally important problems unresolved, Brooke believed it would be a "calamity" if the president should leave Cairo precipitously.[10]

Although he avoided an explosion at the CCOS meeting, Brooke was furious that Roosevelt would think of leaving Cairo before finalizing plans for Anvil and Overlord and he blamed the president and his advisors' preoccupation with Chiang Kai-shek for the roadblock the Anglo-American Allies now faced:

> They have completely upset the whole meeting by wasting all our time with Chiang K'ai-shek and Stalin before we [BCOS] had settled any points with them. And now—with nothing settled—they propose to disappear into the blue and leave all of the main points associated with this Conference unsettled.[11]

Reflecting on the same issue years after the war, Brooke admitted he may have been unnecessarily bitter and at the end of his tether on December 3, 1943, but he reiterated his conviction that the American desire to meet the generalissimo at the start of the Cairo conference had "set matters adrift."[12]

Alan Brooke and his peers spent the entire day of December 3 pursuing two objectives: pressuring the United States into postponing or cancelling Operation Buccaneer and trying to secure American agreement to redeploy landing craft and other equipment from Southeast Asia to Europe and the Mediterranean. They did not succeed in either of these efforts, but as Leahy warned Roosevelt, it was not likely that the British would give up on these goals.[13] He was right.

According to Leahy, when Churchill joined the president for dinner that evening, he used "every artifice in his large repertoire to induce Roosevelt to drop the amphibious operation in the Bay of Bengal and to use those naval, air, and ground forces to seize his pet island of Rhodes."[14] The president would have none of this and repeatedly told the prime minister that he would not abandon the Chinese or renege on the promises he had made to Generalissimo Chiang at the first Cairo conference.[15]

Roosevelt stressed the importance of the moral obligation the Anglo-American Allies had to the Chinese, but that was not the only reason he refused to budge. There was the broader question of ensuring the continuity of American policy in East Asia, which had been constant for nearly a half century. Ever since the articulation of the Open Door doctrine at the end of the nineteenth century, American policy in East Asia had been premised on the existence of a strong and independent China. Helping the Chinese to realize this situation would allow American merchants to exploit the potential of the China market and provide for a more stable balance of power in Asia.[16] Franklin Roosevelt accepted these axioms even more eagerly than his predecessors.

There were also other reasons why Roosevelt championed the Chinese cause, chief among them his conviction that China would be a valuable ally of the United States in the United Nations, helping to create and maintain a Pax Americana and insuring American interests and hegemony in Asia.[17] A strong China, playing her appropriate role in the family of nations, would also serve as an ally of the president in his anti-imperialist crusade.

For these reasons, Roosevelt refused to alter any of the commitments he had made to the generalissimo unless there was "some very good reason to do so."[18] Churchill tried to argue that two such reasons existed, these being the importance of Operation Overlord and Stalin's promise to assist in the war against Japan. Roosevelt's mind was set, however, and he was not yet ready to give in on these matters.[19] The prime minister would have another opportunity to argue with the president the next day.

The BCOS met again at 9:45 on the morning of December 4 for the purpose of further discussion of the Southeast Asian debacle. Since their previous efforts to persuade the Americans that Operation Buccaneer must be abandoned in favor of Operations Anvil and Overlord had failed to convert the JCS to the cause, Alan Brooke's aides now set about to prove to their American counterparts that Operations Buccaneer and Tarzan, the effort to open a new land route to China through northern Burma, were unnecessary and irrelevant in light of logistical problems and decisions reached in Teheran.[20]

Discussion of how to initiate this new strategy of winning over the Americans was cut short when Brooke was summoned to Churchill's villa at 10:15 A.M.[21] When he arrived at the prime minister's residence, Brooke found

Churchill to be in a snit over a memorandum he had just received from Mountbatten informing him that Chiang had finally agreed to endorse plans for Operation Tarzan and outlining the manpower that would be necessary to implement that operation.[22]

At first, Brooke thought that Churchill was upset because the generalissimo had agreed to support Mountbatten at the very moment the British were trying to scuttle plans for all operations in and adjacent to Burma.[23] He soon learned that this was not the principal reason for Churchill's ire. That was due to Mountbatten's suggestion that implementation of operations in Southeast Asia would require a commitment of at least fifty thousand British troops in addition to the hundreds of thousands of Chinese troops that Chiang was now prepared to commit to the fray.[24]

Mountbatten's memorandum could not have come at a worse time for Churchill. Despite all of the prime minister's efforts to persuade the president to abandon plans for a large scale Southeast Asian offensive, Roosevelt remained obdurate in insisting that his pledges to Chiang Kai-shek must be honored. If Roosevelt remained firm and Mountbatten's predictions were correct, the offensive in Burma would have to be mounted on a scale that astounded Churchill.[25]

There was not much that Brooke could say or do to comfort Churchill except to suggest that the British must turn this adversity to their advantage when they joined the president and the JCS for the plenary session scheduled to begin at 11:00 A.M. at Roosevelt's villa. He could have told the prime minister that Mountbatten was trying to "out–MacArthur MacArthur," as some of Mountbatten's subordinates in the SEAC command believed, but that would have only upset Churchill even more.[26] Prudence dictated calming the prime minister down before he met the president.[27]

Mountbatten's memorandum was not the only cause of Churchill's political indigestion. Equally irritating were reports of Generalissimo Chiang's triumphant return to Chungking and the exaggerated stories of his success in Cairo that were being circulated in Chinese newspapers, excerpts of which arrived in Cairo via cable on morning of December 4. "Chinese reaction to the Cairo conference," as John Paton Davies would later describe it, "was expressed with typical celestial sophistication."[28] Chinese editorial writers hailed the conference in hyperbolic fashion. *Su Tung Pao* suggested that the Cairo conference was "a great event without precedent in history."[29] The *Central Daily News*, an organ of the Kuomintang in Chungking, hailed the conference as "the greatest step in the realization of President Roosevelt's world policy."[30]

Normally, Churchill would have had little interest in the ranting of Chinese journalists, but he was well aware that if he were familiar with the adulatory comments of the Chinese press, Roosevelt would be as well. If the president had taken a hard line about honoring the promises that had been made to Chiang before learning of the reaction of the Chinese public, his position would now be set in concrete.

Little did Churchill imagine that the comments of the Chinese press masked a growing uncertainty among Chinese leaders that their allies would really honor the promises made at Cairo. At the very moment that Churchill was expressing his frustration to Alan Brooke about the difficulty of getting Roosevelt to change his mind now that the news was in from China, Chiang Kai-shek made this entry in his diary:

> The press here and abroad hailed the Cairo Communiqué as an unprecedented victory of Chinese diplomacy. But my mind is filled with anxiety and apprehension.[31]

Churchill and Brooke had little time to mull over Mountbatten's memorandum and the news from China as Roosevelt was due to open the next plenary session of the conference at 11:00 A.M. They hurried over to the president's villa, arriving just in time to hear him confirm his intention to leave Cairo on the morning of December 6.[32] Whereas the British expressed apprehension about Roosevelt's early departure, he did not feel that it posed any real problems:

> Apart from Turkish participation in the war, the only outstanding problem seems to be the provision of about twenty landing craft or their equipment. It is unthinkable to be beaten by a small item like that.[33]

Roosevelt's comment was a direct reference to the debate over Operation Anvil versus Operation Buccaneer and suggested that agreement on Anvil did not dictate the cancellation of Buccaneer. Churchill did not share this view and responded quite forcefully to the president's remarks, suggesting that in light of new information he and Brooke had just received from Mountbatten, it was clear that operations in Southeast Asia must be reconsidered "in their relation to the predominant importance of Overlord."[34]

It was at this point that Churchill outlined Mountbatten's report, stressing the admiral's suggestion that seizure of the Andamans would require a British troop commitment in excess of fifty thousand men plus the landing craft and equipment necessary to support such a large-scale operation.[35] Surely, such an operation could not be undertaken with only a few dozen additional landing craft as Roosevelt had suggested.[36]

Churchill went on to suggest that in light of Stalin's pledge that the U.S.S.R. would enter the war against Japan, SEAC operations had lost a great deal of their value while, at the same time, the cost of mounting new operations in Southeast Asia had become prohibitive as Mountbatten's memorandum made only too clear.[37] Chiang Kai-shek may have left Cairo under the impression that Operation Buccaneer was a fait accompli, but in light of events that had occurred since his departure, it was necessary for the Anglo-American Allies to reconsider their options.[38]

Roosevelt was quite shocked to hear Mountbatten's analysis of the manpower necessary to secure the Andamans and suggested to Churchill that it should be possible to execute Operation Buccaneer with approximately one-third of the troops Mountbatten thought were needed.[39] The president may have been stunned by Churchill's bombshell, but he was not ready to throw in the towel on Operation Buccaneer. He suggested that Mountbatten be instructed "to do his best with the resources which had already been allocated to him" and to seek the assistance of American officers who had successfully mounted such operations against the Japanese in the Pacific.[40]

Realizing Roosevelt's sensitivity to bolstering Chinese morale and his hesitancy to renege on promises he had made to Generalissimo Chiang, Churchill suggested that Operation Buccaneer might be postponed until after the monsoon season. This would put off the launching of Buccaneer until October 1944, giving the Allies plenty of time to complete the initial phase of the cross–Channel attacks and return needed landing craft to the Bay of Bengal.[41]

Admiral King dismissed Churchill's suggestion, pointing out that the Allies had made a definite commitment to Chiang that there would be an amphibious operation in the spring of 1944.[42] At this point, Churchill could not contain himself. He reminded his American friends that although the generalissimo had said it was essential that Operations Buccaneer and Tarzan be launched simultaneously and they had supported him on this point, the British had never agreed to such linkage and that he had made this absolutely clear to Chiang at the first Cairo conference.[43]

Churchill's effort to postpone the implementation of Operation Buccaneer was also rejected by Roosevelt, who once again raised the question of the moral obligation the Allies had "to do something" for China.[44] Marshall seconded the president's judgment, going even further than Roosevelt to suggest that there would be very serious consequences if the Allies reneged on their promise of aid to the Chinese.[45]

Whereas Churchill and his colleagues saw the question of Operation Buccaneer as a political one, a position that was also shared by some of his peers on the JCS, Marshall saw the matter in a very different light. He warned the prime minister and the CCOS that if Operation Buccaneer were postponed, Chiang Kai-shek would cancel Operation Tarzan.[46] If no campaign took place in Burma, there would be repercussions in the Pacific as the Japanese would be able to withdraw some troops from Burma and reposition them elsewhere.[47]

Churchill was not swayed by Marshall's comments and stated yet another time that he had never committed himself to any amphibious operation in Southeast Asia, particularly one as questionable as Operation Buccaneer.[48] He did not rule out some kind of operation on a much-reduced scale, but that would have to worked out by his military aides in conjunction with the

JCS.⁴⁹ In light of Churchill's position, there was little that Roosevelt could do except to adjourn the plenary session and hope that the CCOS could reach some agreement on Southeast Asian policy before the conference ended.⁵⁰

When the Combined Chiefs of Staff met at 2:30 P.M., the dispute over Southeast Asian policy once again dominated the agenda. Alan Brooke suggested that the Americans needed to rethink their policy in light of promises made by Stalin in Teheran.⁵¹ He also suggested that even if the Russians had not promised to enter the war against Japan, Operations Buccaneer and Tarzan would have been of very dubious merit because they were at odds with the main thrust of Anglo-American planning, namely that the main effort against the Japanese would take place in the Pacific.⁵² At best, the proposed offensive in Burma was a diversion; at worst, Brooke likened it to a vacuum cleaner, which would suck up resources but not clean the rug.⁵³

Alan Brooke's efforts to wear down his American friends were beginning to bear fruit. Responding to his appeal to reason, Leahy admitted that Buccaneer and Tarzan were indeed diversionary efforts. He also admitted that the Joint Chiefs of Staff had not realized just how costly these operations could be in terms of manpower and other resources until they were informed of Mountbatten's memorandum at the just-concluded plenary session with Churchill and Roosevelt.⁵⁴

Arnold, King, and Marshall were not willing to go as far as Leahy in recognizing the potential problems posed by Roosevelt's promises to Chiang, but they too were growing weary of the continued debate over whether the president's pledges to the generalissimo were sacrosanct. They were aware that Churchill and Roosevelt were the only two people in Cairo with the power to break the impasse which now faced the Allies and that continued debate by the CCOS of the relative merits of Anvil versus Buccaneer and Overlord versus Tarzan was becoming increasingly counter-productive. That being the case, they joined their British friends in proposing that each side prepare one last position paper on the matter of military priorities in 1944 for submission to Churchill and Roosevelt the next day.⁵⁵ On that note, the CCOS meeting was adjourned.

Fatigue was fast becoming the common ground of the members of the CCOS. The same fatigue was overtaking the president and the prime minister, who seemed to be increasingly at odds on almost every issue. In their case, fatigue was being exacerbated by their friendly but fierce personal rivalry. Elliott Roosevelt cites an amusing but telling example of this rivalry:

> I ran into John Boettiger, who told me that there had been a diplomatic contest between the P.M. and Father: both had dispatched planes to Adana [on December 4], in Turkey, to bring President Inonu back to Cairo; John had been Father's emissary and he had won. How important it was that the Turkish president should arrive in an American Army plane rather than a British [plane], nobody seemed to know.⁵⁶

How much of the deadlock over Southeast Asian policy and Chinese politics was due to such rivalry between the president and the prime minister is not entirely clear, but surely this contest of wills between Churchill and Roosevelt was contributing to the impasse at Cairo. It was not merely the *ménage-à-quatre* between Churchill, de Gaulle, Chiang, and Roosevelt that complicated the proceedings in Cairo and Teheran. Egos were also interfering with coming to terms with the hard decisions the Allies had to make.

The members of the Combined Chiefs of Staff were caught in the middle of this web of egocentrism. They were increasingly trying to protect the men they served, often at the expense of their own views and reason. Alan Brooke had to deal with the mood swings and mindset of Churchill on an almost-daily basis and even though he usually agreed with the prime minister on matters of policy, he found him to be difficult. Marshall and Leahy had an easier job dealing with Roosevelt, who was more even-tempered than Churchill, but they recognized that on certain issues, the China tangle among them, the president had to be humored.

When the CCOS met for their fifteenth session of the Cairo/Teheran conferences on the morning of December 5, the mood was somber and restrained. The issues were well defined and the position of the parties also well understood. What made this session unique was that it would be the last time each side would have to argue the merits of the positions of the president and the prime minister. The members of the CCOS knew this and seemed to welcome the imminent resolution of their mutual dilemma.

Prior to their meeting, final drafts of position papers prepared by the BCOS and the JCS had been mimeographed and circulated to the CCOS. The contents of these papers could hardly have come as a surprise to their readers. The American position paper stressed the importance of operations in Southeast Asia; the British position paper stressed their irrelevance. The debate was meant to frame the issues one last time.

The paper prepared by the Joint Chiefs of Staff was taken up first. Admiral Leahy, in many ways the most sympathetic to the British position, outlined the American view. He argued that Operations Buccaneer and Tarzan were "essential" and warned that postponing or cancelling these operations would have serious military consequences, not the least of which would be to threaten the supply line from India to China.[57] General Marshall carried the argument even further, suggesting that American intelligence had revealed that the Japanese were poised to take the offensive in Burma and would do so if Operation Tarzan were not implemented.[58] Without a substantial commitment from the Allies, which Chiang Kai-shek defined as a pledge to go ahead with Operation Buccaneer, Marshall believed that the Chinese would not choose to engage the Japanese in Burma and some, he warned, even predicted that the generalissimo would make a separate peace with Japan, which would have disastrous consequences for the Allies.[59]

When pressed by his British colleagues to express his opinion on the respective merits of Operations Buccaneer and Tarzan, Marshall admitted that if it were possible to abandon Buccaneer and go ahead with Tarzan, "he would not be personally disturbed," but he quickly added that these operations were absolutely linked in the mind of Chiang and his generals.[60] Thus, to abandon or even scale down Operation Buccaneer might well lead to the cancellation of Operation Tarzan.[61]

Alan Brooke responded for the BCOS. He made it clear that they believed that the JCS had overstated the importance of operations in Southeast Asia and the consequences that might follow should Buccaneer be cancelled.[62] Even if Leahy and Marshall were correct in assuming that Chiang would refuse to commit his forces to Tarzan in the aftermath of the postponement or cancellation of Buccaneer, the chances of success in Burma were slim, Brooke argued, if past Chinese performance on the battlefield was any indication of what the future might have in store.[63]

In Brooke's opinion, Operations Buccaneer and Tarzan were unnecessary diversions from the main goals of the Anglo-American Allies. If they were abandoned, the BCOS estimated that some 35,000 troops could be transferred from the SEAC theater to Europe where they would make a great contribution to the success of Operations Anvil and Overlord.[64] Surely the Americans should see the merits of such a transfer of forces.[65]

Since it was clear that there was no point in continuing the debate any further, Brooke and Marshall agreed that they would forward concise summaries of the conflicting views held by the BCOS and the JCS to Churchill and Roosevelt and urge them to make some decisions with regard to policies in the CBI and SEAC theaters as soon as possible, preferably before the day was out.[66] These summaries were to be extracted from the papers that had been prepared and circulated before the CCOS meeting that morning.

The summary prepared by the Joint Chiefs of Staff presented the American case cogently and concisely:

> Political and military considerations make it essential that Operation Tarzan and an amphibious operation in conjunction therewith [Buccaneer] should take place. Apart from political considerations, there will be serious military repercussions if this is not done, not only in Burma and China, but also in the Southwest Pacific.[67]

The summary prepared by the British Chiefs of Staff was equally concise and to the point:

> We fully realize that there are political and military repercussions in the postponement of Buccaneer. As regards the political implications, we must leave these to be taken into consideration by the President and the Prime Minister. As regards the military disadvantages, these are overridden by the far greater advantages to be derived from a successful invasion of the continent and the collapse of Germany.[68]

Churchill and Roosevelt joined the CCOS at 11:30 A.M.[69] The president acknowledged the summaries that had been prepared for him and the prime minister and suggested that some way must be found to reconcile conflicting British and American positions.[70] Sensing that even some of his own advisors may have been leaning toward the British view, Roosevelt made a valiant effort to salvage Operation Buccaneer. Turning to Churchill, he suggested that Soviet promises of aid in the war against Japan were helpful, but he warned against counting one's chickens before they were hatched. Elaborating on this metaphor, Roosevelt argued that the Allies should not risk forfeiting Chinese support by putting all of their eggs in the Russian basket.[71] After all, what were the Allies to do if Stalin could not make good on his promises and Chiang decided to hold his forces in reserve?[72]

Churchill would buy none of this argument. The Chinese, he told Roosevelt, would not drop out of the war should Operation Buccaneer be postponed or cancelled. The only reason they would be forced to make a separate peace with Japan would be if the supply route from India into China via the Hump was closed and that was not likely, given the declining fortunes of Japan's Imperial Air Force.[73] Churchill also raised the question of Mountbatten's estimate of the troop strength necessary to successfully execute Operation Buccaneer, asking Roosevelt and the JCS whether they really thought that a commitment of fifty thousand men was worth what the Allies might get out of the operation.[74] He also posed two additional questions: Did it make sense to pour this large a number of men against a Japanese garrison in the Andamans estimated to be in the neighborhood of five thousand men? Couldn't these troops be put to better use in Europe?[75]

Churchill's questions were designed to point out that the problems in implementing Operation Buccaneer were not limited to the scarcity of landing craft; there was also the very real problem of allocating scarce manpower resources. The British were not about to give Mountbatten the troops he requested for Buccaneer and Churchill made it very clear why they refused to do so:

> We cannot get away from the fact that we would be doing wrong strategically if we used vital resources on insignificant operations instead of using these resources to strengthen Overlord and Anvil where it looks like we are working to a dangerously narrow margin.[76]

In framing his comments, Churchill made it clear to Roosevelt that he realized the difficulty the president would face in dealing with Chiang should Operation Buccaneer be cancelled. He suggested that Roosevelt might ease the blow to Chiang that would result from a scaling down or cancellation of Buccaneer by informing the generalissimo that things had changed substantially since Chiang had left Cairo. Specifically, Chiang would have to be told that Mountbatten's new estimates of the resources needed to launch Buccaneer would prohibit the Allies from honoring the commitments made to Stalin in Teheran and this they could not do.[77]

A reading of the minutes of this meeting reveals that Roosevelt was nearly silenced by Churchill's remarks. He did not interrupt the prime minister to challenge or question him except to ask what operations Mountbatten could carry out with the forces he already had in hand and even this was done in a half-hearted fashion.[78] Clearly, a turning point was near in the discussion of future operations in Southeast Asia and the British view seemed to be prevailing. Still, no final decisions were made when the conferees adjourned for lunch just after 1:00 P.M.[79]

Roosevelt returned to his villa in time to greet Ismet Inonu, the Turkish president, and his entourage.[80] They were soon joined by Churchill and much of the afternoon was spent discussing Turkey's entry into the war.[81] When the president's guests left at 4:30 P.M., he worked on his mail which included a long and friendly cable from Madame Chiang Kai-shek informing him of her safe return to Chungking and the state of Chinese public reaction to the first news of the Cairo conference.

Madame Chiang was effusive in her praise of the president and his support of the Chinese cause: "The consensus of opinion [here] is that President Roosevelt is a great man and he does things in a truly great spirit."[82] She was equally ebullient in her assessment of Chinese press reaction to the publication of the Cairo Declaration, informing Roosevelt, "Its effect of uplifting the morale of our army and the people has been electric."[83]

This good news from Chungking could not have been welcome news to Roosevelt, who was at that very moment giving very serious consideration to accepting the inevitable and agreeing to the postponement or cancellation of Operation Buccaneer. Would the Chinese continue to think of him as a man of "truly great spirit" if he abandoned the promises he had made to them earlier in Cairo?

Roosevelt did not have much time to mull over Madame Chiang's cable because he had asked the Joint Chiefs to meet with him at 5:00 P.M.[84] Although no minutes of this meeting exist, it is quite clear from other sources that the president called his advisors together to inform them that he had decided to give up the ghost on Operation Buccaneer.

Leahy recalls that Roosevelt told them that he had "reluctantly" come to the conclusion that he must abandon the Andaman amphibious assault and would propose "some substitute to Chiang."[85] Marshall recalled much the same thing and later told Forest Pogue, his biographer, that the president told the Joint Chiefs he had been "stubborn as a mule" for days, but, alas, had not been able to budge Churchill.[86] Now, he was ready to give in to the prime minister.[87]

The Joint Chiefs of Staff must have been surprised at Roosevelt's decision to capitulate for they had just come from a second meeting of the CCOS where, once again, they stated what they believed to be Roosevelt's bedrock position: a scaled down version of Operation Buccaneer must be launched to fulfill promises to Generalissimo Chiang. Now they found themselves in the position of being at odds with their own commander-in-chief. Even Leahy, who had questioned the wisdom of Roosevelt's promises to Chiang, found himself wondering what the implications might be if the president failed to fulfill his promises to the generalissimo, but, as he later noted in his memoirs, Roosevelt was the commander-in-chief and "that ended the argument."[88]

Having made his decision, Roosevelt sent a terse note to Churchill telling him that "Buccaneer is Off."[89] He then drafted the following cable to Generalissimo Chiang Kai-shek with the aid of Marshall and Hopkins:

> Conference with Stalin involves us in combined grand operations on European continent in late spring giving fair prospect of terminating war with Germany by end of summer 1944. These operations impose so large a requirement of heavy landing craft as to make it impracticable to devote a sufficient number to the amphibious operation in the Bay of Bengal simultaneously with launching of Tarzan to insure success of operation.
>
> This being the case: Would you be prepared to go ahead with Tarzan as now planned...? If not, would you prefer to have Tarzan delayed until November to include heavy amphibious operation. Meanwhile concentrating all air transport on carrying supplies over the hump to air and ground forces in China.
>
> I am influenced in this matter by the tremendous advantage to be received by China and the Pacific through the early termination of the war with Germany.[90]

After drafting the cable to Chiang, a copy of which was sent to Churchill's villa for his information, Roosevelt retired to his bedroom to relax. The president's son, Elliott, visited him shortly before 6:00 P.M. and found his father in bed reading a detective story.[91] Although he felt that his father looked quite fatigued, Elliott Roosevelt found him to be in much better spirits than the last time he had seen him in Teheran.[92] The two men joked and chatted for almost an hour.[93] It was as if a weight had been lifted from the president's shoulders.

Roosevelt said little to his son about the decision he had just announced to the Joint Chiefs of Staff nor did he share his reasons for finally agreeing to cancel Operation Buccaneer with his aides. Since Roosevelt kept his own counsel, they were forced to guess as to why he had finally changed his mind on this issue after maintaining what had seemed to be an unwavering commitment to the Chinese that coordinated land and naval offensives would be launched in Southeast Asia early in 1944.

After the war, Marshall suggested that Roosevelt finally gave in on the question of SEAC operations because he could not budge Churchill and continued debate with the prime minister threatened to weaken the strong personal bond between them and the Anglo-American alliance.[94] He also suggested that the president wished to relieve the Joint Chiefs of Staff from the pressures of continued bickering with their British counterparts so the

CCOS could devote their undivided attention to planning Operations Anvil and Overlord.[95]

Robert Sherwood provided another insight into Roosevelt's turnabout in his classic postwar study of the relationship between the president and Harry Hopkins. Whereas Marshall argued that it was Roosevelt's desire to preserve Anglo-American harmony that ultimately forced him to capitulate to Churchill on Southeast Asian policy, Sherwood suggested that it was Stalin's "sudden and voluntary" statement of Russia's intention to join the war against Japan that led the president to change his mind on Operation Buccaneer.[96]

Sherwood suggests that Roosevelt believed that a Soviet declaration of war against Japan would make air bases in eastern Siberia available to the United States Army Air Force from which long range bombers might launch a direct attack against the Japanese home islands. This, according to Sherwood, led the president to conclude that recapture of similar bases in eastern China would be less critical, thus eliminating the necessity of mobilizing Chinese forces for an expanded role in the war against Japan and minimizing the need for major new campaigns in the CBI theater.[97]

Sherwood's hypothesis is interesting, but it does not seem to stand up to close scrutiny. When Elliott Roosevelt and his father talked on the afternoon of December 5, the president certainly mentioned Stalin's commitment to enter the war against Japan, but he told his son that Soviet intervention was far from imminent and that Stalin's promise was more symbolic than real:

> I think he offered to declare war against Japan and start fighting in the Far East in order to win finally the argument for a second front in the west. He was willing to get in as soon as he could move troops to Siberia, if we could just promise the May first invasion in the west. But after all, it makes more sense, militarily, to have the Russians bringing all their weight against Hitler on an eastern front. Time enough for him to fight against Japan after Hitler's licked.[98]

Roosevelt was certainly not unaware that Stalin's willingness to join in the war against Japan might ultimately mark an important turning point in that conflict, but the time was still far off when the Russians would be able to honor this commitment. In his conversation with his son, the president seemed more interested in the post-war implications of the Soviet-American alliance against Japan than in its wartime significance, telling Elliott that he hoped to enlist Stalin's help in bringing the Kuomintang and the Chinese Communists to the bargaining table and assisting him in persuading Churchill to give up British control of Hong Kong and extraterritorial privileges in China after the war ended.[99]

Neither Marshall nor Sherwood comment on how Roosevelt's experiences with Generalissimo and Madame Chiang at the first Cairo conference may have contributed to his decision to abandon Operation Buccaneer, but the president did comment on this very matter when he met with General Stilwell and John Paton Davies on December 6, the day after he decided to inform the generalissimo that there would be a major change in allied plans for 1944.

As Elliott Roosevelt recalls this meeting, the president told Stilwell and Davies that Operation Buccaneer was off after listening to Stilwell fulminate against Chiang and the Kuomintang regime in Chungking for nearly twenty minutes.[100] Davies recalls that although Roosevelt told them that he had decided to yield to Churchill on Southeast Asian operations because the prime minister had yielded to Stalin on the matter of the cross–Channel invasions, he also indicated his concern with the reliability of Chiang and the stability of his government.[101]

The president's comments seem to have caught Stilwell somewhat by surprise, leading him to ask Roosevelt whether he had changed his view of the Kuomintang regime.[102] Roosevelt responded to Stilwell's question with one of his own, asking the general how long he thought Chiang would be able to maintain control of the Chinese government.[103] Stilwell indicated that the generalissimo's situation was "serious" and intimated that Chiang would not be helped by the president's reneging on his promise to support Operation Buccaneer, especially in light of the praise lavished on the generalissimo by the Chinese press in the wake of his return from Cairo.[104]

Stilwell's analysis of the tenuousness of Chiang's position did not surprise Roosevelt. Indeed, he suggested to Davies and Stilwell that the United States should look for some other man or group of men to carry on in China should Chiang's leadership collapse.[105] Stilwell and Davies respectfully told Roosevelt that although some Kuomintang leaders might be happy to see the generalissimo fall, there was no other man or group of men waiting in the wings capable of filling Chiang's shoes should his control of the Kuomintang slip. That, the general suggested, was why the United States must be careful to help Chiang maintain face.[106]

This conversation must have been almost surreal from Stilwell's point of view. For more than a year, he had tried to persuade Roosevelt take a more realistic view of the generalissimo and his government, urging him not to present Chiang to the American public as a saint whose government was as solid as the Rock of Gibraltar. Now he found the president all too ready to write off Chiang without giving any thought as to the political void this would cause. Stilwell was confused and angry. In a diary entry later that day, Stilwell described Roosevelt as "a flighty fool" and suggested that he felt like "puking" after listening to the president.[107]

As bizarre as their meeting with the president must have seemed to Stilwell and Davies, it revealed that the White House was now no longer completely under the spell of Chiang and his entourage, a change of heart that could be attributed to Roosevelt's experiences with Chiang and his wife at the first Cairo conference.[108] Still, the president mentioned no specific candidates to replace Chiang in the course of his conversation with Davies and Stilwell nor could they come up with any likely names.

While Roosevelt's associates were trying to figure out why the president had reversed himself, Churchill and his aides were absolutely jubilant about the news that Roosevelt had agreed to cancel Operation Buccaneer. When Churchill received the president's terse message that "Buccaneer is Off" on the afternoon of December 5, he immediately called Ismay to share the good news, praising Roosevelt as a man who had restrained his passions in favor of reason.[109]

Alan Brooke was similarly pleased and attributed Roosevelt's decision to cancel Operation Buccaneer to his having been converted by the force and logic of the case made by the BCOS and Churchill.[110] Writing in his diary on December 6, Brooke expressed his delight at Roosevelt's change of heart and speculated on the impact his decision might have in the immediate future:

> To our joy this morning, we discovered that the President had at last agreed to cancel the Andaman Islands attack. He had sent a wire to that effect to the Generalissimo. This may lead to the latter's refusal to carry out his part of the Burma campaign. If he does, it will be no very great loss. At any rate, we can now concentrate all our resources on the European theatre.... I shall rest very well tonight and feel very satisfied at the final results of the meeting.[111]

After two weeks of often-heated exchanges over promises made to Chiang Kai-shek and the Chinese government, the Anglo-American Allies were now at ease. A new mood swept over the conferees during the last day of the conference, a mood described by Churchill as one of conciliation and cooperation as opposed to confrontation and stalemate. There was even time for the prime minister and the president to pay a return visit to the Sphinx where they gazed at her inscrutable smile in silence before returning for the final session of the Cairo and Teheran conferences.[112]

13

A Postscript on the Cairo Conference

Having settled the dispute over policy in Southeast Asia, at least for the moment, Churchill and Roosevelt were able to spend their remaining hours together in Cairo attending to other and more pressing issues, such as the appointment of a commander for Operation Overlord and related matters. Compared to the often-acrimonious discussions of priorities in Burma and China, these matters were disposed of relatively easily and without rancor, allowing the president and the prime minister to savor their accomplishments in Cairo and Teheran.

On the whole, Churchill and Roosevelt were pleased with results of their meetings, but as Roosevelt remarked to his son Elliott before leaving Cairo on December 7, 1943, it remained to be seen how Sino-American relations would be affected when the Chinese received word that Operation Buccaneer had been cancelled.[1] Roosevelt had a visceral feeling that Chiang Kai-shek would not react kindly to the news contained in the cable he sent him from Cairo on December 5. He was right.

Chiang received Roosevelt's cable on December 6. According to Mountbatten, Chiang was "jolted" by the news from Cairo, which he believed to be "a breach of faith."[2] When the SEAC commander saw Chiang on December 7, the generalissimo told him that since the Anglo-American leaders apparently felt no responsibility to honor the promises made to him at Cairo, he was no longer obligated to them to commit Chinese forces to any operation in Burma.[3] Chiang also suggested that the Chinese would have to re-examine all of their options in light of the latest news from Cairo.[4]

Except for venting his spleen at Mountbatten, Chiang reserved his energies for an assault on Roosevelt. With the help of Madame Chiang and T.V. Soong, who was called back to Chiang's inner circle from his Babylonian exile at the Foreign Ministry in Chungking, the generalissimo drafted a long cable to the president suggesting the grave consequences that would likely occur when the Chinese people learned that their allies were now reneging on promises:

> If it should now be known to the Chinese army and people that a radical change of policy is being contemplated, the repercussions would be so disheartening that I fear the consequences of China's ability to hold out much longer.[5]

Chiang had often intimated that China might be forced to drop out of the war and seek a separate peace with Japan if certain conditions were not met. Now he was making this point directly and suggesting that the Allies would face "serious problems" should Chinese resistance collapse.[6]

Since it did not appear likely that Roosevelt would reverse himself again, Chiang offered him another way to demonstrate his good faith:

> The only seeming solution is to assure the Chinese people and army of your sincere concern in the China theater of war by assisting China to hold on with a billion dollar gold loan to strengthen her economic front and relieve her dire economic needs.[7]

The generalissimo also suggested that doubling supply drops into China to twenty thousand tons per month might be another appropriate demonstration of American goodwill.[8]

Chiang hoped to play Roosevelt's guilt over the decision to cancel Operation Buccaneer to the hilt, extracting as much from the United States as possible in payment for the president's capitulation to Churchill. The generalissimo was quite upset over the president's betrayal and saw nothing untoward in suggesting that the Americans should compensate him for the losses China would suffer as a consequence of the change of plans made in Cairo on December 5. The loss that Chiang was most concerned about was his loss of face and it was this loss for which he sought the greatest compensation. The cancellation of Operation Buccaneer wounded the generalissimo's ego, not the Chinese nation. If anything, the cancellation of the campaign in Burma spared the Chinese army countless casualties in the jungles of Southeast Asia.

When Stilwell returned to Chungking on December 12, he was informed that Chiang was crazy with anger over Roosevelt's seeming change of heart over policy in Southeast Asia.[9] When he met with Chiang on December 15, he realized that this was true.[10] The generalissimo seemed totally irrational and even Madame Chiang was at a loss as to how to calm her husband, telling Stilwell that Chiang had not slept well for days after receiving Roosevelt's cable and that she had done "everything but murder him" to get the generalissimo to quiet down and rest.[11]

John Paton Davies heard much the same story from Wang Chung-hui, the highest-ranking Chinese diplomat to accompany Chiang to Cairo. Wang told him that members of the Chinese delegation to the conference were amazed to hear that Operation Buccaneer was now off and feared that news of Roosevelt's capitulation to Churchill would undermine the generalissimo's position in Chungking.[12] Davies could say little to reassure Wang because he agreed with him that the Kuomintang regime would be less secure in China as a consequence of the decisions reached in Cairo after Chiang's departure.[13]

Although no details of the agreements reached at Cairo had been given to the press when Chiang and his entourage returned to Chungking, specifics were provided to the generalissimo's intimates in the Kuomintang leadership. Given the fact that it was virtually impossible to maintain secrecy in Chungking, discussion of the promises made to the generalissimo by Roosevelt in Cairo circulated widely enough to fuel the rumor mills in this city of rumormongers. Should it now become known that the president had reneged on these promises without making appropriate compensation in other ways, Chiang was sure to lose face with his peers, an intolerable situation in the context of Chinese politics.

Roosevelt had brought Chiang to Cairo to plump up his ego and to provide graphic evidence to the Chinese people that their leader was accorded an honored place among world leaders. The images brought back from the summit by Chinese journalists and Chiang's initial enthusiastic comments about his reception at Cairo seemed to indicate that Roosevelt had accomplished these goals, but with the latest news from Cairo, the bubble might soon burst unless the president agreed to the terms contained in Chiang's cable of December 9.

Saving face for the generalissimo was so critical that T.V. Soong volunteered to press Chiang's case with his friend, Harry Hopkins. If anyone was able to reach Roosevelt, it would be Hopkins and Soong was very well aware of this. Soong was preparing to return to Washington to resume his lobbying on behalf of the Kuomintang regime, but he did not wait until returning to the United States to alert Hopkins to the crisis brewing in Chungking. He sent a lengthy message to Hopkins in mid–December pleading with him to urge the president to provide Chiang with some face-saving way out of the crisis that was sure to occur when it became known that all promises made to the Chinese at Cairo were now off.[14]

Roosevelt returned to the White House on December 18 and found Chiang's message on his desk.[15] Later that day, Roosevelt briefed Secretary of War Stimson on the deliberations in Cairo and discussed Chiang's demands with him.[16] According to Stimson, the president told him that the conferences at Cairo and Teheran had been successful save for the "Burma situation" which he blamed on Churchill's unwillingness to support any significant operation in Southeast Asia.[17] Roosevelt also told Stimson about Chiang's request for a large new loan and increased supplies and indicated that he was leaning toward providing some additional assistance.[18] Musing on their conversation in his diary, Stimson wondered how high a price the president might be willing to pay to compensate Chiang for his disappointment.[19]

Stimson had good reason to be concerned about Roosevelt's willingness to stroke Chiang Kai-shek's ego. In the past, Stimson had found the president to be too supportive of the generalissimo, but in this instance, Roosevelt reacted quite differently. Replying to Chiang's cable of December 9, Roosevelt politely but firmly informed Chiang that doubling the supplies flown into China over the Hump was a virtual impossibility. He also made no promises on the matter of a new loan except to suggest that he would take the matter up with the Treasury Department.[20]

Roosevelt's cable also urged Chiang not to withdraw his forces from Operation Tarzan, intimating that to do so would weaken the generalissimo's support in the United States and make it difficult for him to lobby the Congress for the increased aid Chiang was requesting.[21] Although this suggestion was couched in polite language, the implication of the president's comment was clear. He now expected a quid pro quo for going to bat for the generalissimo.

Roosevelt's message upset Chiang. Replying to the president's cable of December 20, the generalissimo stated that while he still had "confidence" in Roosevelt's judgment, the president's relegation of the CBI theater to the back burner was giving rise to "serious misgivings" in Chungking.[22] Chiang also balked at Roosevelt's advice on Operation Tarzan:

> I have nothing to say if the Combined Chiefs of Staff wants to divert all materials for an assault on Germany because I have not been consulted.... But the Burma operations are a life or death problem to China and without a large scale amphibious operation in South Burma, the Yunnan Force would be committing suicide if they moved into North Burma ... I could not agree to this plan.[23]

Before the Cairo conference, Chiang Kai-shek had usually been able to manipulate Roosevelt by hinting at the problems American policy was causing in Chungking, but the president did not respond to Chiang's message of December 23 in this manner. To the contrary, he warned the generalissimo about the repercussions that might follow if he chose to boycott Operation Tarzan:

> Considerable critical materials ... for the Yunnan divisions are currently scheduled to be moved by air to China. The rate of this buildup to my mind depends to a large degree upon the use to be made of these divisions in the near future.[24]

Chiang was laboring under the impression that Roosevelt would capitulate to his demands as a payoff for the decision of the Allies to renew on commitments made to him in Cairo. With the receipt of Roosevelt's message of December 27, it was clear that this would not be the case and the generalissimo began to panic. The president had not only refused to be rushed into approving the billion dollar loan Chiang had requested, he was now insisting that the Chinese participate in some kind of offensive in Burma as a prerequisite for receiving additional military aid.

In light of this frightening turn of events, T.V. Soong was ordered to return to Washington immediately to plead China's case with Hopkins and

Roosevelt. While Soong was en route to the United States, Chiang attempted to maintain a calm facade, stressing his accomplishments in Cairo and praising Roosevelt's support of China. In his first public address on the Cairo conference, delivered before a large crowd in Chungking on January 1, 1944, the generalissimo lavished compliments on the president:

> I may tell you that the deepest impressions I have of President Roosevelt are of his unflinching faith, his firm determination to emancipate all the worlds oppressed peoples and his sincere desire to help China become a truly free and independent nation.[25]

If Chiang's public statements were filled with praise of Roosevelt and the results of the Cairo conference, his private comments were hardly as laudatory. In a memorandum submitted to Stanley Hornbeck on December 27, 1943, Ambassador Gauss informed Hornbeck that Chungking gossipmongers were clicking their tongues over the generalissimo's snide comments about Roosevelt and Churchill, although no one wanted to speak "on the record" to confirm these remarks.[26]

Hornbeck shared Gauss' memo with Secretary of State Hull, who suggested that Roosevelt was now reaping the harvest of his propensity to circumvent the State Department by allowing Chiang to communicate through private channels. Had the Department of State been permitted to deal with China "exclusively," as Hull thought advisable, the Chinese would have been forced to pursue a stable and resolute course instead of bullying the United States for aid.[27] Now it might be too late to teach Chiang new tricks.

Neither Hornbeck nor Hull could appreciate just how unnerved Chiang was becoming over Roosevelt's seeming change of heart about aid to China because they were out of the loop of Chinese lobbying in Washington. Soong and his subordinates in the Chinese diplomatic corps wasted few of their efforts on outsiders in Roosevelt's administration. They preferred to concentrate on the president's intimates such as Harry Hopkins. Thus, when T.V. Soong arrived back in the United States in January 1944, it was to his door that he went, not to the State Department.

Normally, Soong had easy access to Hopkin's office, but this time things were somewhat different. Hopkins had taken ill in Cairo and had to be hospitalized upon his return to Washington. Hopkins was too sick to receive visitors and was on doctor's orders to refrain from conducting business from his hospital bed. This did not stop Soong from trying to see Hopkins in the hospital to talk about the Cairo conference. Denied access to him by hospital authorities, Soong sent the following note to Hopkins:

> Several years ago when you were in the hospital, I recall that against the injunction of your doctor you hurried from the hospital back to the White House when a vital international principle was at stake. Today a fateful decision is again being made and you must be a part of the process.[28]

No one had ever accused Soong of being shy in conducting China's foreign policy, but, in this instance, he went too far, prompting an angry response from Hopkins. "I can't do this sort of thing from out here," Hopkins told one of his aides, "tell them I'm sick."[29] Soong was not to see Hopkins until several weeks after his release from the hospital and after this incident their relationship would never be quite the same. Hopkins had seen enough of the Chinese at Cairo to cause him to reconsider his support of the China lobby. It was too late for Soong to salvage the situation.

As Soong made the rounds in Washington, it soon became clear to him that the Cairo conference had been a public relations disaster in terms of the negative impressions that Generalissimo and Madame Chiang had made on the members of the American delegation, including Hopkins and Roosevelt. The ineffectiveness of the Chinese delegates and Chiang's seemingly constant change of mind and mood had a sobering affect on the president and his aides. As Soong noted in a memorandum to Victor Hu, his assistant at the Foreign Ministry, "my absence from the deliberations at Cairo proved more costly than I could have imagined."[30]

While Soong was hardly a humble man, his comment to Hu was not an exaggeration. Had he accompanied the generalissimo to Cairo, he could have orchestrated things so as to present Chiang and his entourage in a more positive light. No one in the Kuomintang leadership was more familiar with American manners and mores than Soong. No one had a better working relationship with Roosevelt's intimates than Soong. Surely he would have been more effective at the summit than Dr. Wang Chung-hui who had no clout with Churchill, Roosevelt, or any of the Combined Chiefs of Staff.

T.V. Soong was savvy about public relations and what he did not know about the art of manipulating public or private opinion, he relied on Hollington Tong to find out. As Soong indicated to Hu, it was bad enough that he had been forced to remain in Chungking while Chiang went off to Cairo, but it was mind boggling that Tong had been taken to Cairo but relegated to the role of an occasional interpreter because of his association with Soong.[31] After Tong's success in arranging the itineraries for Wilkie's visit to China and Madame Chiang's triumphant tour of the United States, it was folly not to allow him to manage the generalissimo's itinerary in Cairo.[32]

What Chiang needed at Cairo was a good stage manager and a competent script supervisor. He had had neither of these services at his disposal during his stay in Cairo. Madame Chiang was forced to play these roles at the summit, but she was neither up to the job nor able to orchestrate the Chinese players. Madame Chiang had arrived in Cairo suffering from influenza and dysentery. Given the fact that she was quite ill, Madame Chiang was barely able to keep up with the round of appointments and social obligations that filled her husband's days in Egypt; she was certainly not able to provide the kind of support services that could have turned the conference into a public relations triumph for the generalissimo.

Without Soong or Tong to shield the generalissimo from his peers and orchestrate the activities of his subordinates, the performance of the Chinese delegation at Cairo was a poor one and even Chiang seems to have realized that things had not gone well at the conference, although he could not pinpoint the problem. Writing in his diary immediately after his return to China, Chiang expressed continued misgivings about Churchill and, perhaps for the first time, fear that Roosevelt might be falling under the influence of the prime minister.[33] It was for this reason that he ended T.V. Soong's exile in Chungking and sent him off to Washington.

Better stage management of Chiang's activities in Cairo might not have altered the ultimate outcome of the conference, given the overwhelming importance of launching Operation Overlord, but it would have gone a long way to ensure that Roosevelt continued to think of the generalissimo as an asset. Continued American support was critical for the Kuomintang regime. If, as Chiang now feared, the president viewed him as a liability, this would have serious implications for his future political fortunes in China.

By the time T.V. Soong arrived in the United States to survey the damage caused by Chiang's performance in Cairo, it was too late to salvage much for the generalissimo. In less than one week, he and Madame Chiang had undone much of Soong's previous efforts to cultivate a favorable image of the Kuomintang regime and its leaders. For two years, Soong had fine-tuned a propaganda apparatus in the United States second to none in attracting good press for his government's cause. Now, in the aftermath of Chiang's dismal performance in Cairo, even friends of China were beginning to wonder about the discrepancies between Chinese propaganda and Chinese realities.

Hopkins' refusal to see Soong and intervene with the president on behalf of Chiang Kai-shek was a clear sign to him that the situation in Washington had changed dramatically since he was last in that city. He counted Hopkins as one of his most trustworthy allies among Roosevelt's intimates and a much better friend to China than others in the White House. With Hopkins sidelined in the hospital and unwilling to leave his sick bed to intercede on behalf of the Chiangs, Soong feared that Roosevelt would fall under the influence of Marshall, Morgenthau, Stimson, and others less friendly to the Chinese.

Soong's fears were not unfounded. There seems little doubt that Roosevelt was taking a new and harder line with Chiang and nowhere is this more clearly illustrated than in his response to the generalissimo's request for a new billion-dollar loan. Prior to the Cairo conference, Roosevelt had ignored the advice of the Treasury Department and lavished money on China as a gesture of good faith. After Cairo, he was less inclined to buy the generalissimo's goodwill with additional cash grants or loans.

When Roosevelt received Chiang's request for a huge new loan, he immediately shared the generalissimo's cable with Morgenthau and solicited his advice. As Soong knew only too well, Morgenthau was no friend of the China lobby. When the Chinese had requested a $500 million loan in 1942, Morgenthau had warned the president against extending such a credit to the Kuomintang regime without extracting a quid pro quo. Roosevelt ignored this advice and the loan was advanced. Now, Morgenthau was even more adamant in urging Roosevelt to deny Chiang's request for an even larger loan.[34] This time, the president heeded Morgenthau's advice.

Morgenthau told Roosevelt that the Chinese had spent less than half of the loan provided by the United States in 1942 and that this money "made no significant contribution to the control of inflation and had little effect except to give additional profit to insiders."[35] While there was no suggestion that Chiang had personally profited from this money, it was clear, according to Morgenthau, that some of his associates had diverted funds to their own bank accounts and that little of the money was being used to further the war effort.[36]

After his experiences at Cairo, Roosevelt was not shocked by Morgenthau's analysis of the situation in Chungking and was ready to get tough with Chiang. Sensing this, Morgenthau and Stimson joined forces in urging him to refuse the generalissimo's latest demands. This would not be easy because the Chinese had been pushing Roosevelt very hard. Still, if the president could be persuaded to discount Chiang's threats to drop out of the war and negotiate a separate peace with Japan, he might initiate a new course of action vis-à-vis the Kuomintang regime.

Roosevelt had no illusions about the capacity or the willingness of the Kuomintang regime to wage an aggressive war against Japan nor was he much interested in this. As long as the Chinese were even nominally at war with Japan, the Japanese would be forced to maintain forces well in excess of one million men in China and Manchuria and could not divert these units to the Pacific battlefields. This was more important to the president than whipping the Chinese armies into fighting shape to engage the Japanese on a massive scale in China proper.

At first, Roosevelt took Chiang's threats to drop out of the war quite seriously. American intelligence was well aware of the efforts of Wang Ching-wei's puppet regime in Nanking to negotiate an alliance with Chiang. While such a possibility was discounted, it was not dismissed entirely. With Anglo-American forces retreating all over Asia, Roosevelt could not afford to alienate the generalissimo and risk the loss of his Chinese ally. As Allied fortunes brightened in 1943, the president could afford to take a more realistic view of the situation in China and his meetings with the generalissimo in Cairo convinced him that Chiang was less likely to drop out of the war than he had previously believed. Still, Roosevelt did not feel confident enough to dismiss Chiang's threats entirely.

Churchill had already softened the president up on the question of Chinese threats to drop out of the war during the second Cairo conference.

Although Roosevelt continued to cling to the notion that China was a nation which would count in the world of tomorrow and was less given to overt racism than Churchill, he was not blind. His first-hand experiences with Chiang and his entourage at the first Cairo conference had given him pause for thought that the generalissimo was really ready to lead China into the modern age without American tutelage and pressure or that any other Chinese leader could do so.[37]

The efforts of Morgenthau and Stimson bore fruit. Roosevelt refused to support the extension of an additional billion-dollar credit to China. On January 5, 1943, as Soong was still en route to the United States, the president informed Chiang that he could not support his request for additional funds because the Chinese had not been able to curb inflation and stop currency speculation with the proceeds of the 1942 loan.[38] Adding insult to injury, Roosevelt also suggested that his refusal to support a new loan to China was influenced by Chiang's unwillingness to make a clear commitment to action in Burma.[39]

As might have been expected, Chiang reacted angrily to Roosevelt's message, castigating him for treating Sino-American relations as if they were a "commercial transaction" and warning of the very real possibility that China might have to drop out of the war if he did not reconsider his decision.[40] Before the Cairo conference, such threats would have been taken very seriously by Roosevelt. After Cairo, he tended to discount them because he had come to understand that the very existence of the Chiang's regime depended upon continued participation in the war. The growing rift between Roosevelt and Chiang was kept from the general public in China and the United States thanks to the effectiveness of the propaganda machines in Chungking and Washington that seemed to be governed by the lyrics of a popular wartime tune which urged people "to accentuate the positive, eliminate the negative, and don't mess with Mister Inbetween." For wartime propagandists concerned with maintaining the facade of Sino-American unity, ignorance was bliss but beneath the veneer of business as usual, major changes were in the offing.

One of the first changes in American policy in China to follow in the wake of Roosevelt's return from Cairo was the effort to establish direct diplomatic and military liaison with the communist regime in Yenan. Prior to the president's journey to Cairo, efforts had been made to send American emissaries to Yenan, but Chiang and Soong had been successful in persuading Roosevelt that such contacts would be detrimental to the Kuomintang regime and its conduct of the war effort. After Cairo, such arguments carried less weight in Washington.

While in Cairo, Roosevelt had observed to his son, Elliott, that the Chinese communists were more actively engaged in the war against Japan than the Kuomintang regime and that it was time for the United States to consider funneling aid to Yenan as well as Chungking.[41] He had also observed that much of the aid that the United States had sent to China was being hoarded for a future civil war with the communists.[42] He had pressed Chiang to allow the communists to play a role in the national government and the generalissimo had agreed to this idea in principle, but Roosevelt was not sure he would really include the communists in future deliberations.[43]

Although the president was not given to poring over lengthy memoranda or intelligence reports, it is clear that he read summaries of critical intelligence from the field including synopses of reports from the American embassy in Chungking and General Stilwell's command headquarters. Such reports were filled with information about the energy of the communist leaders and the activities of the Yenan regime. While Roosevelt distrusted State Department "types" and tended to feel that Stilwell was somewhat of a crank, he could not completely discount their warnings about the political inroads being made my Mao and his colleagues and was influenced by such reports. Still, for the public record, he remained a steadfast supporter of the Kuomintang regime.[44]

By the time Roosevelt returned to Washington from the Cairo conference, he seems to have concluded that, left to himself, Chiang would do little to create a genuine united front with the communists. Furthermore, in light of the fact that the generalissimo was unwilling to engage the Japanese in Burma in any substantial campaign without the simultaneous launching of Operation Buccaneer, Roosevelt was ready to act more forcefully on establishing contacts with Mao's Yenan government despite Chiang's wishes.

Roosevelt might well have pressed Chiang to allow an American mission to visit Yenan immediately after his return from Cairo, but the moment was not auspicious. Stilwell had just launched a new campaign in Burma, using the Ledo forces under his command to dislodge the Japanese from northern Burma, and things were going very poorly. Unless Chiang could be persuaded to commit his Yunnan armies, Stilwell might well have to beat another humiliating retreat from Burma. Under these circumstances, it was not prudent to push the generalissimo on the Yenan connection.

Ironically, Stilwell's problems in Burma proved to be a blessing in disguise for Roosevelt. With American and Chinese forces suffering very heavy losses in Burma, Chiang's unwillingness to commit his Yunnan armies to the fray was becoming an increasingly untenable position for the Chinese government to maintain and Roosevelt's patience with the generalissimo was wearing thin. Roosevelt warned Chiang that unless he came to Stilwell's assistance with the Y-Force, continued American aid to the Kuomintang would be jeopardized. After waiting for several weeks without receiving an appropriate reply from Chiang, a presidential ultimatum was delivered to the generalissimo by General Frank Dorn sometime between April 10 and 14, 1944. Either Chiang was to commit his forces immediately or all aid to China would be suspended.[45] The generalissimo capitulated.

Still smarting from the president's ultimatum, Chiang was faced with an even more serious problem when the Japanese launched a major military offensive in China in the spring of 1944. Code-named Operation Ichigo, this campaign threatened the very existence of the Kuomintang regime. At first, the Japanese offensive seemed to be aimed at the destruction of Chennault's forward air bases in central China, but as Japanese forces quickly steamrolled through these bases, the campaign was expanded to include a direct attack on Kuomintang strongholds in Szechwan and Yunnan provinces.

Chiang's armies proved unable to prevent the Japanese advance and he was forced to recall some of his best units from the area surrounding the communist base in Yenan to the defense of Chungking and Kunming. Once again, Chiang's misfortune proved to be a hidden blessing for Roosevelt.

Now more than ever, it was imperative that some accommodation be reached between the communists and the Kuomintang regime that would permit the communists to play a vital role in beating back Operation Ichigo. If this were to be done, American aid would have to be funneled to the communists so they could launch counter-attacks against the Japanese. To facilitate this, an American mission would have to be sent to Yenan. Even Chiang could not dispute this logic and he reluctantly gave his assent to such a mission, which finally reached Yenan by July.

Given the location of communist bases in China and the logistical problems of moving supplies to them, American aid to Mao's guerillas never amounted to much, but symbolically the dispatch of American observers to Yenan, however lowly their status, marked a major change in Roosevelt's perception of the war in China and the future of the Kuomintang regime. Although he never wavered from his public praise of Chiang's government in Chungking, Roosevelt was a political realist who was prepared to deal with more than one man in China.

Chiang was reeling from the one-two blow delivered by Roosevelt between January and April 1944. He and Soong had resorted to their usual tricks in dealing with the president, but nothing seemed to work. Roosevelt was relying more heavily on Morgenthau and Stimson and less on members of the China lobby, resulting in a growing sense of panic in Chungking. With Hopkins sidelined by illness and increasingly cool to their cause, Chiang and Soong had to get through to one of the president's other intimates or lose their access to him.

In March, Soong indicated to Hull, Stimson, and whoever else would listen to him that Chiang would welcome the visit of yet another personal emissary of the president.[46] He stressed that such a visit was urgent in light of events that had occurred since the Cairo conference.[47] When asked who Roosevelt might send as his representative, Soong suggested Vice President Henry Wallace.[48] Much to Soong's surprise, Roosevelt jumped at the chance to send Wallace to China.

Chiang's invitation came at a time when Roosevelt was preparing to announce that he would seek another term as president and encountering considerable opposition to this idea from party leaders who would not endorse his bid for a fourth term unless he dumped Henry Wallace from the ticket. Although he was quite fond of Wallace, Roosevelt understood that Wallace was a political liability because of his increasingly liberal views and was looking for some way to ease him off the ticket and the political center stage in Washington. Soong's suggestion that Wallace make a fact-finding trip to Chungking provided the perfect vehicle for accomplishing both of these ends.

Chiang was pleased to hear that Wallace was coming to China. Little did he realize Roosevelt's motives in sending the vice president to Chungking. The Chinese spared no effort in arranging Wallace's visit and orchestrating things so that he would be able to see things from the generalissimo's perspective. Soong was in charge of the planning and served as Wallace's personal escort during his visit in China from June 18 to 30, 1944.

Despite all of their efforts, Chiang and Soong failed to convert Wallace to their cause. The situation in 1944 was quite different from that in 1942 when Lauchlin Currie and Wendell Willkie had visited China at Roosevelt's request. At that time, the Sino-Japanese war was quiet and it was possible to stage events so as to maximize the heroic struggle of the Kuomintang regime. By the time Wallace arrived in Chungking, the Japanese offensive was well under way and it was impossible to stage manage the war in China for Wallace's benefit. What he saw was a government under siege and on the brink of disaster.

The entreaties of Chiang and Soong were largely lost on Wallace, who paid more attention to the advice he received from his principal political aides, Owen Lattimore and John Carter Vincent, than to the nostrums doled out by the generalissimo's associates. Upon his return to the United States, Wallace advised Roosevelt that continued American aid to Chiang must be seen as "a short term investment" and that in the longer term, new leaders would be thrust forward "by evolution or revolution."[49]

Wallace's assessment of the situation in China could hardly have come as a surprise to Roosevelt. He had made some of these same observations to Stilwell and John Paton Davies on December 6, 1943, his last full day in Cairo. On that occasion, the president told them that the United States must be prepared for the possible collapse of Chiang's regime, although he indicated that nothing should be done in Washington that would precipitate such a collapse.[50]

Contrary to the views of some of his critics, Roosevelt was not totally naive in his assessment of the situation in China. He realized the vulnerability of Chiang's regime, but he also realized that there was no understudy in the wings waiting to play the generalissimo's role should he falter. The collapse of Chiang's government might well lead to political chaos and paralysis, which would hardly contribute to the war effort. Even the Chinese communists recognized this. As Chou En-lai had often told visiting Americans, including Henry Wallace, no Chinese leader, not even Mao Tse-tung, had Chiang's broad appeal and capacity to balance the various political cliques in China. Chiang's demise was not necessarily an event to be welcomed.

Chou En-lai's endorsement of Chiang must have struck Wallace as somewhat peculiar coming, as it did, from one of the generalissimo's most impressive political opponents. There was clearly no love lost between the Chinese Communist Party and the Knomintang and yet Chou and his colleagues in Yenan were still willing to put in a good word for the generalissimo. Why should this have been the case?

The Chinese communists were increasingly aware that the burden of trying to maintain a stable government in Chungking while attempting to wage war against Japan was crippling the Kuomintang. They had no interest, for the moment, in putting themselves in this impossible situation. It was in their interest to keep Chiang in the driver's seat since it seemed inevitable that his car was going to crash at a later point in time when the CCP would better be able to take the wheel. Mao made this point, albeit in a more Chinese fashion, in one of his wartime essays.[51] There were also other reasons why the communists found it in their immediate interest to appear supportive of the generalissimo's leadership.

As 1944 dawned, CCP leaders believed that they were on the brink of receiving direct aid from the United States. It was well known in Yenan that Roosevelt was becoming increasingly impatient with Chiang's unwillingness to commit his forces and more inclined to listen to the advice he was receiving from American diplomats and military experts in China, many of whom were encouraging him to establish closer relations with the CCP. Mindful that the president could not publically abandon the generalissimo, CCP leaders did not wish to cause Roosevelt any embarrassment, especially if such embarrassment threatened the aid they hoped to obtain from the United States. Thus, their strategy was to muffle their anger with Chiang and appear to be conciliatory.[52]

Given the realities of the Chinese political scene in 1944, Roosevelt had to walk a tightrope in his dealings with Chiang, talking bluntly with the generalissimo when necessary, but making sure that he did nothing to cause Chiang to lose face publically. To avoid falling off this tightrope, the president often had to act in what appeared to be a somewhat inconsistent manner. His handling of Stilwell's recall is a good example of this dilemma.

For nearly two years, Chiang had urged Roosevelt to recall Stilwell and replace him with an officer more sympathetic to the Kuomintang regime. For nearly two years, Roosevelt had resisted capitulating to the generalissimo and removing Stilwell. Things changed after the Cairo conference. Having reneged on promises made to Chiang at the conference and refused his request for a billion-dollar compensation package after the conference, Roosevelt was ready to make some major concession to the generalissimo, providing such a concession did not compromise the interests of the United States. Recalling Stilwell met both of these standards.

After Roosevelt had informed Chiang that the United States would not grant the loan and credits he demanded, the generalissimo concentrated his energies on trying to secure the recall of General Stilwell. By the time Wallace returned from China, the president was ready to replace the general. The question was not whether Stilwell would be recalled, but, rather, when he would be recalled. On the one hand, Roosevelt wanted to make a gesture to Chiang; on the other hand, he did not wish to appear to be caving to the generalissimo's demands.

Roosevelt postponed removing Stilwell until October 1944, by which time Chiang had toned down his calls for Stilwell's recall and the American presidential campaign was nearly over. The president's decision buoyed Chiang's morale and standing for the short term, but provided no additional aid or commitments for the long term. It was a consummate public relations gesture, accomplished at minimal political cost in Washington and providing maximum good press in Chungking.

General Albert Wedemeyer replaced Stilwell as the president's chief military representative in China, but his arrival in Chungking changed little. Except for establishing a cordial relationship with Chiang and his associates, something that Stilwell had never quite managed to accomplish, Wedemeyer was in no position to assist the Chinese in obtaining any additional aid, a fact which Chiang and Soong learned very quickly.

In the aftermath of the Cairo conference, the Kuomintang regime had to acclimate itself to a new relationship with the Roosevelt administration, one in which they were now dealing with Washington from a distinct disadvantage. Whereas Soong and Chiang had once been effective in lobbying the president to provide massive amounts of aid to their government, they now had to settle for mere crumbs.

The post–Cairo relationship between Roosevelt and Chiang was also characterized by a toning down of the president's rhetoric in support of the generalissimo and his regime. Roosevelt spoke less and less about China's role as a great power and was increasingly sparing in his praise of Chiang's leadership abilities. To be sure, Roosevelt never publically criticized Chiang, but his endorsements of the generassimo were less enthusiastic and less frequent than before the Cairo conference.

By the end of 1944, Soong realized that little additional American aid would be forthcoming. The climate in Washington had changed substantially since Madame Chiang had completed her triumphant tour of the United States and Roosevelt and Chiang had met in Cairo. The most that Soong could hope to achieve was to persuade Roosevelt to honor some of the commitments he had made to Chiang prior to the Cairo conference, such as providing arms and funds to complete the retraining of ninety Chinese divisions. Even this would prove to be a difficult task because none of these agreements were written down and the president was in no rush to make good on his word.⁵³

Soong may have accepted the fact that the Kuomintang's glory days in Washington were now over, but Chiang Kai-shek never quite got the message. After years of being puffed up by Roosevelt's praise and support, the generalissimo found it difficult to adjust to the new realities of Sino-American relations nor was he alone in failing to make this adjustment. The American and Chinese publics were also trapped in this propaganda time warp.

By accentuating the positive and eliminating the negative, Chinese and American propagandists had created an image that was no more real than a Potemkin village, leaving neither side ready or able to deal with the post-war situation in China. Americans, when they thought about it at all, had come to think of the Kuomintang regime as a force for democracy and stability while the Chinese had come to think of the United States as a stalwart supporter of the generalissimo and a cash cow for his regime. Neither of these views reflected the realities of Sino-American relations.

By the time of his death in April 1945, Roosevelt had reluctantly come to agree with the view of many of the China hands at the State Department that Chiang Kai-shek might not survive the post-war struggle for power that was sure to take place in China. Unfortunately, he did not share his view with the American public, who continued to labor under the impression that Chiang was some kind of savior who would lead China to her rightful place in the family of nations when the war ended. He also failed to share these views with Vice President Truman, who was left to pick up the pieces of the China puzzle after Roosevelt's death and deal with the China tangle.

If Roosevelt refused to publicize his misgivings about the Kuomintang for fear of harming the war effort, Chiang also preferred to keep his concerns about the president's new China policy quiet for fear that his control of the Kuomintang might be jeopardized if his rivals became aware of the erosion of Roosevelt's support of his regime. Thus, even after Roosevelt had reneged on many of the promises he had made to Chiang in Cairo, the generalissimo missed no opportunity to praise Roosevelt and emphasize the president's unqualified support of his leadership. Chinese newspapers bombarded their readers with this line on a daily basis, leaving many of them somewhat bewildered in the post-war era when American support of the Kuomingtang government seemed to falter.

Since there were no specific accords signed by Chiang and Roosevelt at the Cairo conference, save for the purposefully vague Cairo Declaration, illusion was everything. Roosevelt was happy to give Chiang his moment in the center stage and the generalissimo was only too happy to bask in the glow of the stage lights. When the curtain came down on the summit, both actors returned to their real worlds, which were markedly different from the ambiance of the set at the Mena House Hotel in Cairo. The actors in this drama may have realized the illusory nature of the images that were presented to their audiences after Cairo, but their audiences did not. That was the problem.

At best, summit conferences give world leaders an opportunity to break impasses and resolve differences between friend or foe at the highest level. At worst, summit conferences are a genre of theater, carefully orchestrated to present the actors in the best possible light, but often lacking in substance. The Cairo conference of 1943 occupies a place somewhere between these two extremes.

The original purpose of the Cairo conference, as conceived by Roosevelt, was to give Chiang Kai-shek the public recognition he so desperately desired and needed. The president's mission was to stroke the generalissimo's ego so as to ensure China's continued participation in the war against Japan and also to take the measure of the man who headed the Kuomintang regime. Roosevelt had no agenda for the talks at Cairo beyond these two goals, both of which he felt he had accomplished at the summit.

The purpose of the Cairo conference, as perceived by Chiang, was to lobby the president for increased aid and full recognition of China's place among the powers. He had no agenda beyond this. When the generalissimo left for Cairo, he had every reason to be optimistic that he would achieve his goals. When he left Cairo, he believed he had accomplished his mission. He would soon learn that this was not the case, although he never quite understood why Roosevelt had abandoned him. Chiang could not publically admit that the conference was a bitter disappointment, but he often shared this view with his intimates, chastising Roosevelt for abandoning the China lobby.[54]

Although neither Chiang nor Roosevelt had any premonition that the Cairo conference would mark an important turning point in Sino-American relations, it did. Roosevelt had come to Cairo to take the measure of Chiang and found him wanting. Never again would he offer the generalissimo his unquestioning support. Chiang had come to Cairo to extract more aid and moral support from Roosevelt and found him untrustworthy and wanting as well. Never again would he be able to count on the president's unlimited largesse.

The Cairo conference marked the zenith of Chiang Kai-shek's prestige as a world leader; after the conference, it was all downhill for the generalissimo and his regime. Chiang had managed to ride the proverbial Chinese tiger for almost two decades, but he was soon to fall off. Thanks to the effectiveness of Sino-American wartime propaganda, neither the American nor the Chinese people were prepared for Chiang's fall and this was to cause them both considerable pain and suffering after 1943.

Chapter Notes

Introduction

1. Whatever Chiang Kai-shek's limitations as a leader and strategist, he was quite prescient in predicting that Japan's effort to create a Greater East Asia Co-Prosperity Sphere would lead to conflict with the United States whose interests in China and Southeast Asia would not coincide with Japan's assertion of a Monroe Doctrine of their own. For additional detail on Chiang's views on this matter see Jay Taylor's recent biography, *The Generalissimo: Chiang Kai-shek and the Struggle for Modern China* (Cambridge: Harvard University Press, 2009).
2. R. J. C. Butow, "A Notable Passage to China, Myth and Memory in FDR's Family History: A Note on the Sources," *Prologue*, 31, no. 3 (Fall 1999): 173.
3. *Ibid.*, 170.
4. *Ibid.*, 173.
5. Stilwell Diaries, hereafter cited as JSD, February 9, 1942.
6. *Ibid.*
7. Henry Luce's advocacy on behalf of the Kuomintang regime and his use of *Time* and *Life* to support the work of Generalissimo and Madame Chiang Kai-shek is well documented in Alan Brinkley's definitive biography of Luce, *The Publisher: Henry Luce and His American Century* (New York: Knopf, 2010).
8. For an account of Rabe's efforts see Iris Chang, *The Rape of Nanking* (New York: Penguin, 1997), 109–121.
9. Brinkley, *Luce, The Publisher*, 255.
10. *Ibid.*, 264.

Chapter 1

1. For a detailed description of Roosevelt's management of foreign affairs see James MacGregor Burns, *Roosevelt the Soldier of Freedom* (New York: Knopf, 1970) and Alexander Dallek, *Roosevelt's Foreign Policy: 1937–1945* (New York: Oxford University Press, 1979).
2. Nearly all of Gauss' associates in China shared the view that he was remiss in not being more aggressive in cultivating better relations with Chinese leaders. Some of them believed this was a reflection of his shyness and introversion. Others believed that Gauss simply did not like China or the Chinese and his feelings were well known to the people he had to work with in Chiang's retinue and the Foreign Office. Although Ambassador Gauss represented the United States for many years in China, there have been few studies of his tenure there. These include a Ph.D. dissertation, "Ambassador Clarence E. Gauss and United States relations with China, 1941–1944," written by James Larry Durrence and submitted to the University of Georgia in 1971 and a recent essay by Hannah Gurman, "'Learn to Write Well': The China Hands and the Communistification of Diplomatic Reporting," published in the *Journal of Contemporary History*, 45(2), 430–453.
3. For a detailed explanation of Hu Shih's relationship with Chiang Kai-shek and the Kuomintang leadership see Chou Min-chih, *Hu Shih and Intellectual Choice in Modern China* (Ann Arbor: University of Michigan Press, 1984), chapter 7.
4. The most detailed and objective study of Stilwell's career in China is Barbara Tuchman's *Stilwell and the American Experience in China* (New York: Macmillan, 1970).
5. *Ibid.*, chapter 13.
6. *Ibid.*
7. *Ibid.*
8. Dallek, *Roosevelt's Foreign Policy*, 388.
9. Chiang Kai-shek (CKS) to Franklin D. Roosevelt (FDR), May 27, 1942, cited in *Foreign Relations of the United States: China: 1942*, hereafter referred to as *FRUS: China: 42*, 57.

10. Mme. CKS to Currie, May 31, 1942, *FRUS: China: 42*, 60.
11. Cable, T. V. Soong to CKS, June 21, 1942, T. V. Soong Papers, hereafter referred to as TVS.
12. Memo: Currie to FDR, June 1, 1942, *FRUS: China: 42*, 61.
13. Memo: Currie to FDR, June 3, 1942, *FRUS: China: 42*, 62.
14. The text of this cable is contained in a memo sent by Currie to FDR on June 26, 1942 which is cited in *FRUS: China: 42*, 89.
15. Mme. CKS to Currie, June 27, 1942, *FRUS: China: 42*, 89.
16. Currie informed FDR of his conversation with Soong in a memo dated June 26, 1942 and cited in *FRUS: China: 42*, 89.
17. Hull to Gauss, July 3, 1942, *FRUS: China: 42*, 94–95.
18. Gauss to Hull, July 11, 1942, *FRUS: China: 42*, 110.
19. Report on Visit to China, August 24, 1942, Currie Papers, Hoover Institute, Stanford University, 2.
20. *Ibid.*, 2.
21. *Ibid.*, 6.
22. *Ibid.*, 8.
23. *Ibid.*
24. *Ibid.*, 2.
25. *Ibid.*, 4.
26. *Ibid.*, 5–6.
27. *Ibid.*, 6.
28. Although Chiang Kai-shek offered no explanation for the recall of Ambassador Hu Shih, U.S. experts on China in the State Department at the time believed this to be the result of personal animosity between Chiang and Hu and Chiang's desire to have a more reliable K.M.T. man in Washington.
29. *Ibid.*, 1–2.
30. FDR to CKS, July 4, 1942, *FRUS: China: 42*, 95.
31. Guass to Maxwell Hamilton (assistant head, Far Eastern Affairs Department of the Department of State), August 3, 1942, *FRUS: China: 42*, 120.
32. Currie, *FRUS: China: 42*, 34.
33. *Ibid.*
34. *Ibid.*, 37.
35. *Ibid.*, 43.
36. In an entry in his diary dated August 26, 1942, Secretary of War Henry L. Stimson recalls talking to General Marshall about some aspects of Currie's report, particularly his call for the replacement of General Stilwell by a more appropriate representative. Although Stimson and Marshall did not necessarily agree with Currie's recommendation in this matter, they considered it seriously along with other recommendations in the conclusion of the report.
37. Willkie had already announced his plans to make a world tour to visit Allied nations and leaders when Roosevelt asked him to extend his tour to include a visit to China.
38. FDR to CKS, August 21, 1942, *FRUS: China: 42*, 140.
39. Hull to Gauss, August 24,1942, *FRUS: China: 42*, 142.
40. Soong to CKS, August 21, 1942, Soong Papers (hereafter referred to as TVS), Hoover Institute, Stanford University.
41. Wendell Willkie, *One World* (New York: Simon & Schuster, 1943), 48.
42. *Ibid.*, 53.
43. *Ibid.*
44. Prior to Willkie's visit to China, T. V. Soong convened a special meeting at the Foreign Ministry in Chungking for the express purpose of improving publicity services in the Chinese capital and focusing on the development of a public relations strategy to improve China's image in the United States. A five page summary of the findings of this group was prepared by Vice Minister Victor Hu on June 29, 1942, and can be found in the Victor Hu Papers, Hoover Institute, Stanford University. A reading of this memorandum makes it clear that Soong and his associates were keenly aware that "to increase the effectiveness of our propaganda, we must constantly be aware of, and bear in mind, the feelings and reactions in the U.S.A." The Willkie visit gave them an opportunity to test new ideas and techniques.
45. Gauss to Hull, October 8, 1942, *FRUS: China: 42*, 163.
46. *Ibid.*
47. A number of Madame Chiang's biographers have alleged that she had a one night stand with Wendell Willkie when he visited China in 1942, including Sterling Seagrave, in his best seller, *The Soong Dynasty* (New York: Harper and Row, 1985), and Hannah Pakula, in her well reviewed biography of the generalissimo, *The Last Empress: Madame Chiang Kai-shek and the Birth of Modern China* (New York: Simon & Schuster, 2009). This story is based on comments made by Gardner Cowles, publisher of *Look* magazine, who accompanied Willkie on his China trip and later stated in his memoirs that Willkie shared the savory details of his seduction of Madame Chiang. When Cowles was later called to testify under oath in a lawsuit brought by Madame Chiang against columnist Drew Pearson, who had repeated this allegation in one of his books, *Pearson Diaries*, Cowles re-

neged on his previous accusation and apologized to Madame Chiang.
48. Willkie, *One World*, 53–55.
49. Currie, *FRUS: China: 42*, 34.
50. Willkie, *One World*, 55.
51. *Ibid.*
52. *Ibid.*, 57.
53. *Ibid.*, 59.
54. *Ibid.*, 58.
55. *Ibid.*
56. Gauss to Hull, October 8, 1942, *FRUS: China: 42*, 163.
57. *Ibid.*
58. Willkie, *One World*, 60.
59. *Ibid.*
60. CKS to FDR, October 6, 1942, *FRUS: China: 42*, 160.
61. Kung to FDR, October 7, 1942, *FRUS: China: 42*, 161.
62. FDR to CKS, October 26, 1942, *FRUS: China: 42*, 172.
63. FDR to Kung, October 26, 1942, *FRUS: China: 42*, 172.

Chapter 2

1. Urticaria is a transient condition of the skin usually caused by allergic reaction and characterized by pale elevated irregular patches, severe itching, nettle rash, and hives. It may be brought on by nervous tension and psychological stress as was surely the case with Madame Chiang. Before commencing her barnstorming trip across the United States, Madame Chiang checked into Columbia-Presbyterian Hospital in New York City where she had a full diagnostic workup, surgery of an unspecified nature, and some dental work. Her attending physician was Dr. Robert E. Loeb. In Dr. Loeb's discharge report given to Madame Chiang's brother, T. V. Soong, for transmittal to Generalissimo Chiang, Dr. Loeb indicated that Madame Chiang would need to convalesce for several months to secure some relief from her urticaria and urged Soong to use what influence he had on his sister to insure that she spend the next several months resting. She did not heed this advice. Dr. Robert E. Loeb to Soong, TVS, Box 64-10, February 25, 1943.

2. *The First Lady of China* (New York: International Business Machines Corporation, 1943), 16. This privately published commemorative volume of Madame Chiang's 1943 tour of the United States, hereafter referred to as FLC, contains the complete texts of all of her public speeches and press conferences. Copies of this commemorative volume were circulated, free of charge, to "friends of China" by Thomas Watson, founder of IBM and co-sponsor of Madame Chiang's visit.
3. *Ibid.*
4. *Ibid.*
5. Stimson Diary, hereafter referred to as SD, May 4, 1943.
6. *New York Herald Tribune*, February 19, 1943.
7. FLC, 20.
8. *Ibid.*
9. *Washington Post*, February 20, 1943.
10. FLC, 20.
11. *Ibid.*, 23.
12. SD, February 26, 1943.
13. *Ibid.*
14. FLC, 32.
15. Part of the Chinese propaganda effort in the United States involved promoting a pro-China lobby among leaders of the business community. This effort was a successful one, judging by the roster of American business leaders, e.g., Thomas Watson and John D. Rockerfeller Jr., who sponsored and participated in Madame Chiang's tour. Along with men like Henry Luce, the founder of the Time-Life Media conglomerate, they formed the powerful "China Lobby" which would play a major role in influencing American foreign policy even after the end of the Second World War.
16. *New York Times*, March 3, 1943.
17. *Ibid.*
18. *Ibid.*
19. FLC, 52.
20. *Ibid.*, 53.
21. *Ibid.*
22. *Ibid.*
23. *Ibid.*, 56.
24. For an interesting insight into Tong's grasp of the use of propaganda to influence American public opinion, see his post-war memoir, *Dateline China* (Shanghai: Commercial Press, 1947).
25. *Boston Globe*, March 10, 1943.
26. FLC, 52.
27. *Ibid.*, 102.
28. *San Francisco Chronicle*, March 26, 1943.
29. FLC, 102–104.
30. *San Francisco Chronicle*, March 28, 1943.
31. FLC, 109.
32. *San Francisco Chronicle*, March 28, 1943.
33. For an amusing account of this gathering from the point of view of Hollywood insiders see the front page story in the *Hollywood Reporter*, April 1, 1943.
34. The other "escorts" of Madame Chiang were Joan Bennett, Ida Lupino, Ginger

Rogers, Irene Dunne, Deanna Durbin, Kay Francis, Judy Garland, Janet Gaynor, Rita Hayworth, Dorothy Lamour, Rosalind Russell, Norma Shearer, Barbara Stanwyck, Shirley Temple, Lana Turner, and Loretta Young.

35. *Los Angeles Times*, April 5, 1943.
36. FLC, 149.
37. *Ibid.*
38. *Ibid.*, 154.
39. *Ibid.*
40. Roosevelt to Chiang Kai-shek, June 30, 1943, *FRUS: China: 1943*, 69.
41. *Ibid.*
42. Chiang Kai-shek to Roosevelt, July 9, 1943, *FRUS: China: 1943*, 73.
43. *Ibid.*
44. *FRUS: China: 43* contains dozens of memoranda sent by Ambassador Gauss and John Carter Vincent describing the deteriorating political situation in China and the unwillingness of Chiang's government to conduct and active war against Japan on the battlefields of China.
45. Examples of the growing disillusionment of American journalists covering events from Chungking can be found in Theodore White's articles in Time and his post-war China memoir, *Thunder Out of China* (New York: Sloane, 1946), Graham Peck's *Two Kinds of Time* (Boston: Houghton-Mifflin, 1950), and Jack Belden's *Still Time to Die* (New York: Harper, 1944).
46. George Acheson to Hull, August 2, 1943, *FRUS: China: 43*, 80.
47. *Ibid.*

Chapter 3

1. SD, November 6, 1941.
2. *Ibid.*
3. SD, December 13, 1941.
4. SD, January 19, 1942.
5. Morgenthau Diary, January 29, 1942, cited in John Morton Blum, *From the Morgenthau Diaries: Years of War 1941–1945* (Boston: Houghton Mifflin, 1967), hereafter cited as MD.
6. A close reading of Stimson's diary entries reveals that Soong did make an effort to point out the shortcomings of appointing General Stilwell, although he did not specifically state that he or the generalissimo objected to the appointment.
7. Victor Hoo (Hu Chi-tsai) was the son of a Chinese diplomat who was educated at the *Ecole Libre des Sciences Politique* and the School of Law of the University of Paris from which he obtained a doctorate in 1918. He was a member of the Chinese delegation to the Paris Peace Conference and later served at the League of Nations and in other diplomatic posts. When T. V. Soong was appointed as China's foreign minister and Chiang Kai-shek's personal representative to President Roosevelt, Hu went along with Soong to the United States where he served as Soong's deputy and chief of staff.
8. "Memorandum on the Improvement of the Publicity Service in Chungking," Victor Hu to T. V. Soong , June 29, 1942, Victor Hoo Papers (hereafter referred to as VH), Hoover Institute, Stanford University, 1.
9. *Ibid.*
10. Soong to Han Lin-wu, TVS, September 17, 1942.
11. *Ibid.*
12. VH, 2–3.
13. *Ibid.*, 3–4.
14. *Ibid.*, 4–5.
15. *Ibid.*, 5.
16. H. H. Kun, Chiang Kai-shek's other brother-in-law and his minister of finance, was among those who opposed giving Soong control of China's propaganda machinery. Ch'en Li-fu, co-leader of the powerful C-C clique of the Kuomintang, also opposed the idea of a consolidated propaganda ministry.
17. John Davies to Clarence Gauss, "Memorandum on Conversation with Chou En-lai," March 16, 1943, *FRUS: China: 43*, 216.
18. The Casablanca Conference took place in January 1943. Discussions of the military situation in Europe dominated the deliberations, although there was some discussion of events in the CBI theater. It was at Casablanca that Roosevelt suggested the idea of unconditional surrender from the Axis powers as the only possible acceptable condition for ending the war with the enemies of the Allies.
19. J. Edgar Hoover to Adolf Berle, "Memorandum on Chinese Reaction to the Casablanca Conference," February 11, 1943, found in Stanley Hornbeck Papers (hereafter referred to as SH), Hoover Institute, Stanford University.
20. *Ibid.*
21. *Ibid.*
22. Soong to Victor Hu, TVS, January 27, 1943.
23. SD, February 23,1943.
24. SD, February 27, 1943.
25. Pearl Buck to Roosevelt, March 22, 1943, Official File 200, Franklin Delano Roosevelt Library (hereafter referred to as FDR), Hyde Park, New York.
26. *Ibid.*

27. Soong to Chiang Kai-shek, TVS, n.d. (probably March 22,1943).
28. *Ibid.*
29. TVS, "Memorandum of Conversation with Roosevelt," May 10,1943.
30. *Ibid.*
31. TVS, "Notes on Meeting with Churchill and Hopkins," May 13,1943.
32. *Ibid.*
33. *Ibid.*
34. *Ibid.*
35. Soong to Hopkins, TVS, May 13, 1943.
36. Soong to Chiang Kai-shek, TVS, May 14, 1943.
37. Chiang Kai-shek to Hull, May 15, 1943, *FRUS: China: 43*, 53.
38. TVS, "Notes on Meeting of Pacific War Council," May 21, 1943.
39. *Ibid.*
40. As a consequence of his meetings with Chennault and Stilwell and his desire to prove his good faith to Chiang Kai-shek, Roosevelt agreed at the Washington Conference to increase the amount of supplies flown into China and ordered Stilwell to divert more of these supplies to Chennault so that he could mount his aerial offensive. Churchill reluctantly promised to have his subordinates look into what they could do to assist Chiang and prepare for a campaign in Burma.
41. Chennault held two commissions, one in the United States Army Air Force and a second as an officer in the Chinese Air Force. In that latter capacity, he had an open line into Generalissimo Chiang Kai-shek's headquarters and often discussed matters with Chiang without getting prior approval from General Stilwell, his superior in the American command in China. Chennault was, undoubtedly, the most popular American in Chungking.
42. TVS, "Memorandum of Conversation with Roosevelt and Hopkins," July 16, 1943.
43. *Ibid.*
44. *Ibid.*
45. *Ibid.*
46. TVS, "Notes on Conversation with Anthony Eden and V. Wellington Koo," August 3, 1943.
47. TVS, "Memorandum on Meeting of Pacific War Council," August 4, 1943.
48. *Ibid.*
49. *Ibid.*
50. *Ibid.*
51. Soong to Hull, TVS, August 18, 1943; also found in *FRUS: China: 43*, 94–95.
52. *Ibid.*
53. *Ibid.*
54. *Ibid.*
55. SH, "Memorandum of Conversation with T. V. Soong ," August 19, 1943.
56. *Ibid.*
57. *Ibid.*
58. *Ibid.*
59. TVS, "Memorandum of Conversation with Roosevelt," August 30,1943.
60. *Ibid.*
61. TVS, "Notes on Conversation with Hopkins," September 5, 1943.
62. *Ibid.*
63. TVS, "Notes on Conversation with Hopkins," September 15, 1943.
64. *Ibid.*
65. *Ibid.*
66. *Ibid.*
67. *Ibid.*
68. TVS, "Memorandum of Conversation with Roosevelt," September 16, 1943.
69. *Ibid.*
70. TVS, "Notes on Conversation with Hull and Hornbeck," September 22, 1943.
71. TVS, "Notes on Conversation with Stimson," September 30, 1943.
72. SD, September 30, 1943.
73. *Ibid.*
74. This view of the feud between Chiang and Soong was based on Chungking gossip and newspaper accounts, which were summarized in a cable sent from Gauss to Hull on December 10, 1943. The cable may be found in *FRUS: China: 43*, 387–388.
75. This view of the feud between Chiang and Soong was put forward by Drew Pearson. A summary of Pearson's views and some of his sources may be found in a cable sent by Alfred Sze to Soong, TVS, on February 14, 1944.

Chapter 4

1. George Atcheson to Cordell Hull, May 21, 1943, *FRUS: China: 43*, 55.
2. An examination of T. V. Soong 's papers and documents published in *FRUS: China: 43* illustrate the importance the Chinese attached to the Chiang-Roosevelt summit.
3. There are more than one dozen memoranda and cables concerning Baldwin's essay in the Reader's Digest and other critical treatments of the situation in China in *FRUS: China: 43*. Typical of these is a lengthy memo sent by Atcheson to Hull on August 26, 1943 which may be found on p. 107 of the aforementioned collection.
4. Hanson Baldwin, "Too Much Wishful Thinking About China," *Reader's Digest*, August 1943, 129–133.

Notes—Chapter 4

5. *Ibid.*, 131.
6. This translation of *Ta Kung Pao*'s editorial response to the Baldwin article and samples of other Chinese editorial responses to such criticism are found in a memorandum from Hull to Stimson, August 26, 1943, *FRUS: China: 43*, 102–103.
7. *Ibid.*, 103.
8. Atcheson to Hull, August 26, 1943, *FRUS: China: 43*, 107.
9. *Ibid.*
10. Soong to Chiang, "Memorandum on the Improvement of the Publicity Service in Chungking," June 29, 1942. This is a copy of the memo that Victor Hu had prepared for Soong, the complete text of which can be found in VH Papers.
11. Excerpts of Senator Lodge's speech may be found in a cable from Assistant Secretary of State Stettinius to Ambassador Gauss, October 19, 1943, *FRUS: China: 43*, 151.
12. Gauss to Hull, October 18, 1943, *FRUS: China: 43*, 149.
13. *Ibid.*, 150.
14. A full account of Hurley's mission may be found in Don Lohbeck's biography of Hurley, *Patrick J. Hurley* (Chicago: Henry Regnery, 1956), 202–220. A copy of Hurley's report to Roosevelt can be found in FDR, Official File 200, November 20, 1943.
15. Roosevelt to Chiang, October 27, 1943, *FRUS: China: 43*, 154.
16. Roosevelt to Chiang, October 30, 1943, *FRUS: China: 43*, 156.
17. Chiang to Roosevelt, November 2, 1943, *FRUS: China: 43*, 156–157.
18. Chiang to Roosevelt (carried by General Brehon Somervell), October 30, 1943, *FRUS: China: 43*, 156. It is clear from this message that Generalissimo Chiang was still very wary of the sincerity of Churchill and the British government and concerned that Churchill's presence at Cairo could serve to complicate Sino-American discussions.
19. SD, November 1, 1943.
20. SD, November 4, 1943.
21. *Ibid.*
22. *Ibid.*
23. *Ibid.*
24. JSD, November 5, 1943.
25. *Ibid.*, November 6, 1943.
26. *Ibid.*
27. *Ibid.*
28. Roosevelt to Chiang, November 8, 1943, FDR, Map Room 10. Text of cable also found in *FRUS: China: 43*, 160.
29. *Ibid.*
30. *Ibid.*
31. Chiang to Roosevelt, November 9, 1943, FDR, Map Room 10. Text of cable also found in *FRUS: China: 43*, 161.
32. *Ibid.*
33. *Ibid.*
34. Roosevelt to Chiang, November 10, 1943, FDR, Map Room 10. Text of cable also found in *FRUS: China: 43*, 162.
35. *Ibid.*
36. Hurley to Roosevelt, "Report to Roosevelt on visit to China," November 20, 1943, FDR, Official File 200-3-N.
37. *Ibid.*
38. *Ibid.*
39. *Ibid.*
40. *Ibid.*
41. JSD, November 13, 1943.
42. Hurley to Roosevelt, FDR, Official File 200-3-N.
43. Tong, *Dateline China*, 194.
44. *Ibid.*
45. Stilwell to Chiang, "Proposals for the Cairo Conference," November 11, 1943, Stilwell Papers (hereafter referred to as JSP), Hoover Institute, Stanford University.
46. *Ibid.*
47. *Ibid.*
48. *Ibid.*
49. Throughout his diaries and in much of his correspondence, General Stilwell took a very cynical and dim view of the commitment of the British government to the war in the CBI theater. He, like the generalissimo, found Churchill more interested in preserving the empire than in waging war against Japan.
50. Tong, *Dateline China*, 195.
51. *Ibid.*
52. For a fuller biographical sketch of Wang Ch'ung-hui see Howard Boorman, et. al., *Biographical Dictionary of Modern China: Volume III* (New York: Columbia University Press, 1970), 376–379.
53. During Lauchlin Currie's visit to China in 1942, Chiang Kai-shek suggested to him that T. V. Soong was had more valuable contacts in the United States than Wang Ch'ung-hui and that this was the principal reason why Wang was replaced as foreign minister by Soong. Report on Visit to China, August 24, 1942. Currie Papers, Hoover Institute, Stanford University.
54. One of the main reasons for Soong's fall from the generalissimo's good graces in the autumn of 1943 was his propensity to act on his own initiative and upstage Chiang. Most associates of Chiang Kai-shek were well aware that it was not wise to challenge the generalissimo's leadership or stray too far from his guise. Soong had the kind of panache that most members of the Kuomintang inner circle lacked. This was sometimes to his advantage;

other times, it made for strained relations with Chiang and other members of the family.
55. JSD, November 12, 1943.
56. Boorman, *Biographical Dictionary of Modern China*, 90.
57. *Ibid.*
58. *Ibid.*
59. JSD, November 12, 1943.
60. Boorman, *Biographical Dictionary of Modern China Volume I*, 390.
61. *Ibid.*
62. *Ibid.*
63. *Ibid.*, 391.
64. JSD, November 12, 1943.
65. Sir Adrian Carton De Wiart, *Happy Odyssey* (London: Jonathan Cape, 1950), 237.
66. After the Quebec conference in August 1943 and T. V. Soong's protest over the insensitivity of the Allies to the generalissimo's government, Churchill decided it would be prudent to have a reliable personal emissary posted to Chungking and chose Carton De Wiart for this post. Winston Churchill, *The Second World War: Closing the Ring* (Boston: Houghton-Mifflin, 1951), 94–95.
67. De Wiart, *Happy Odyssey*, 238.
68. *Ibid.*
69. *Ibid.*, 254.
70. *Ibid.*
71. John Paton Davies, *Dragon by the Tail* (New York: Norton, 1972), 277.
72. *Ibid.*
73. "Log of the President's Trip to North Africa and the Middle East: November–December 1943," (hereafter referred to as FDR-LOG), FDR, Official File 200-3-N (Box 65), November 12, 1943.
74. *Ibid.*
75. *Ibid.*
76. Forrest Pogue, *George C. Marshall: Organizer of Victory, 1943–1945* (New York: Viking, 1973), 302.
77. *Ibid.*
78. This anecdote is contained in the postwar memoir of General Henry A. Arnold, *Global Mission* (New York: Harper, 1949), 455.
79. William D. Leahy, *I Was There* (New York: Whittlesey House, 1950), 196.
80. FDR-LOG, November 15, 1943.
81. *Ibid.*, November 16, 1943.
82. Churchill, *Closing the Ring*, 326.
83. *Ibid.*
84. *Ibid.*, 327.
85. *Ibid.*
86. FDR-LOG, November 19, 1943.
87. The president's log and the post-war memoirs of JCS make it quite clear that Roosevelt had many long discussions of issues to be taken up at Cairo and Teheran. There is no similar record that Chiang Kai-shek discussed any aspect of the upcoming talks while en route to Cairo or before departure except with his wife and General Stilwell.
88. Arnold, *Global Mission*, 457.
89. FDR-LOG, November 20, 1943.
90. *Ibid.*
91. *Ibid.*, November 21, 1943.
92. *Ibid.*
93. *Ibid.*
94. Churchill, *Closing the Ring*, 325.
95. *Ibid.*, 326.
96. *Ibid.*
97. *Ibid.*, 329–333.
98. After the war, Churchill stated that "the talks of the British and American staffs [at Cairo] were sadly distracted by the Chinese story, which was lengthy, complicated, and minor." *Ibid.*, 328.
99. In a diary entry made on November 18, 1943, as Churchill's party was making its way to Cairo, Alan Brooke states that the prime minister was "piqued" and upset by Chiang's efforts to meddle in Indian affairs and concerned that the generalissimo and the president might gang up on him during the course of the Cairo conference. As Alan Brooke also noted, the Chinese were determined to prevent the British from reclaiming their primacy along the south China coast and Hong Kong and played the India card as a "trump." ABP, November 18, 1943.

Chapter 5

1. Furuya Keiji, *Chiang K'ai-shek: His Life and Times* (New York: St. John's University Press, 1981), entry for November 21, 1941. This is an abridged translation of the author's *Sho Kai-seki Hiroku* [*From the Private Files of Chiang K'ai-shek*] (Tokyo: Sankei Shimbun, 1976), hereafter referred to as CKS.
2. Claire Lee Chennault Papers (hereafter referred to as CLC), Hoover Institute, Stanford University, Box 1, Biographical File, November 21, 1943.
3. JSD, November 21, 1943.
4. Barbara Tuchman, *Stilwell and the American Experience in China* (New York: Bantam, 1972), 514.
5. Tong, *Dateline China*, 194.
6. *Ibid.*
7. *Ibid.*, 195.
8. *Ibid.*
9. Alan Brooke Papers (hereafter referred to as ABP), Liddell-Hart Military Archives, King's College, University of London, November 21, 1943.
10. Churchill, *Closing the Ring*, 328.

11. ABP, November 21, 1943.
12. CKS, November 21, 1943.
13. Philip Ziegler, *Mountbatten* (New York: Knopf, 1985), 262.
14. *Ibid.*
15. *Ibid.*
16. *Ibid.*
17. *Ibid.*
18. *Ibid.*
19. *Ibid.*
20. Mountbatten's early experiences in Chungking are chronicled in his *Report to the Combined Chiefs of Staff by the Supreme Allied Commander Southeast Asia: 1943-1945* (London: His Majesty's Stationary Office, 1951).
21. Pogue, *George C. Marshall*, 304.
22. Arnold, *Global Mission*, 459.
23. JSD, November 21, 1943.
24. *Ibid.*
25. *Ibid.*
26. *Ibid.*
27. *Ibid.*
28. *Ibid.*
29. ABP, November 21, 1943.
30. *Ibid.*
31. Lord Hastings Ismay, *The Memoirs of General Lord Ismay* (New York: Viking, 1960), 334.
32. FDR-LOG, November 22, 1943.
33. *Ibid.*
34. Elliott Roosevelt, *As He Saw It* (New York: Duell, Sloan, and Pearce, 1946), hereafter referred to as ER, 146.
35. *Ibid.*
36. *Sextant: Record of British Chiefs of Staff Proceedings at Malta, Cairo, and Teheran between 18th November and 7th December, 1943* (London: War Cabinet Chiefs of Staff Committee, 1943), hereafter referred to as BCOS, 4.
37. *Ibid.*, 3.
38. *Ibid.*
39. JSD, November 22, 1943.
40. Churchill, *Closing the Ring*, 329.
41. *Ibid.*
42. *Ibid.*
43. *Ibid.*
44. *Ibid.*
45. V. K. Wellington Koo Diary, December 3, 1943, V. K. Wellington Koo papers, Columbia University, hereafter referred to as WK.
46. *Sextant Conference: Minutes of the Combined Chiefs of Staff* (London: War Cabinet, Chiefs of Staff Committee, 1944), hereafter referred to as CCOS, 410.
47. *Ibid.*
48. *Ibid.*
49. *Ibid.*, 411.
50. *Ibid.*
51. *Ibid.*
52. *Ibid.*
53. *Ibid.*, 412.
54. *Ibid.*
55. *Ibid.*
56. FDR-LOG, November 22, 1943.
57. Pogue, *George C. Marshall*, 304.
58. *Ibid.*
59. *Ibid.*
60. *Ibid.*
61. *Ibid.*
62. Carton De Wiart, *Happy Odyssey*, 240.
63. Ismay to Somerville, December 20, 1943, Ismay Papers, hereafter referred to as IP, Liddell-Hart Military Archives, King's College, University of London.
64. ABP, November 22, 1943.
65. *Ibid.*
66. Arthur Bryant, *Triumph in the West: A History of the War Years Based on the Diaries of Field-Marshal Lord Alanbrooke* (New York: Doubleday, 1959), 53.
67. FDR-LOG, November 22, 1943.
68. JSD, November 22, 1943.
69. *Ibid.*
70. CCOS, November 22, 1943.
71. JSD, November 22, 1943.
72. Arnold, *Global Mission*, 461.
73. ABP, November 23, 1943.
74. *Ibid.*
75. FDR-LOG, November 22, 1943.
76. JSD, November 22, 1943.
77. *Ibid.*
78. ABP, November 18, 1943.
79. *Ibid.*
80. *Ibid.*
81. *Ibid.*
82. JSD, November 22, 1943.
83. Tong, *Dateline China*, 195.

Chapter 6

1. BCOS, 6.
2. *Ibid.*, 7.
3. *Ibid.*
4. *Ibid.*
5. *Ibid.*, 7-8.
6. *Ibid.*, 8.
7. Pogue, *George C. Marshall*, 305.
8. *Ibid.*
9. *Ibid.*
10. JSD, November 23, 1943.
11. *Ibid.*
12. *Ibid.*
13. ABP, November 23, 1943.
14. FDR-LOG, November 23, 1943.
15. *Ibid.*
16. CKS, November 23, 1943.
17. Leahy, *I Was There*, 198.

18. CCOS, 376.
19. *Ibid.*
20. Ismay, *Memoirs*, 336.
21. CCOS, 377–378.
22. *Ibid.*, 379.
23. *Ibid.*
24. *Ibid.*
25. *Ibid.*
26. *Ibid.*
27. *Ibid.*
28. *Ibid.*
29. *Ibid.*
30. Ibid
31. *Ibid.*
32. *Ibid.*
33. *Ibid.*, 379–380.
34. *Ibid.*, 380.
35. *Ibid.*
36. *Ibid.*
37. *Ibid.*
38. *Ibid.*
39. *Ibid.*
40. *Ibid.*
41. *Ibid.*
42. CKS, 781.
43. *Ibid.*
44. *Ibid.*
45. *Ibid.*
46. CCOS, 381.
47. *Ibid.*
48. *Ibid.*
49. *Ibid.*
50. APB, November 23, 1943.
51. *Ibid.*
52. *Ibid.*
53. Ziegler, *Mountbatten*, 260.
54. *Ibid.*
55. *Ibid.*, 261.
56. *Ibid.*
57. In a memorandum on the Cairo conference ("Notes on Cairo/Teheran") from Ismay to Churchill, which was sent to Churchill to assist him in writing his history of the war, Ismay elaborates on the Mountbatten's deficiencies and the resentment of many of the BCOS toward the admiral. It is in this memo that Mountbatten is described as a "lightweight." IP/II/3, June 15, 1949.
58. ABP, November 23, 1943.
59. Ziegler, *Mountbatten*, 262.
60. *Ibid.*
61. *Ibid.*
62. *Ibid.*
63. *Ibid.*
64. Arnold, *Global Mission*, 461; Leahy, *I Was There*, 200.
65. Leahy, *I Was There*, 200.
66. Arnold, *Global Mission*, 461.
67. JSD, November 23, 1943.
68. *Ibid.*

69. *Ibid.*
70. *Ibid.*
71. *Ibid.*
72. CCOS, 47.
73. The complete text of Stilwell's memorandum, "The Role of China in the Defeat of Japan," was published as report number 405 and appended to the *Minutes of the Combined Chiefs of Staff, CCOS Reports*, 212–214, hereafter referred to as CCOS-405.
74. CCOS, 47.
75. *Ibid.*
76. *Ibid.*
77. *Ibid.*
78. *Ibid.*, 47–48
79. *Ibid.*, 50.
80. *Ibid.*
81. *Ibid.*
82. ABP, November 23, 1943.
83. CCOS, 50.
84. *Ibid.*
85. Bryant, *Triumph in the West*, 55.
86. *Ibid.*
87. *Ibid.*
88. JSD, November 23, 1943.
89. Pogue, *George C. Marshall*, 305.
90. JSD, November 23, 1943.
91. *Ibid.*
92. *Ibid.*
93. *Ibid.*
94. *Ibid.*
95. *Ibid.*
96. FDR-LOG, November 23, 1943.
97. *Ibid.*
98. CKS, 781–783.
99. ER, 142.
100. CKS, 783.
101. *Ibid.*
102. *Ibid.*
103. *Ibid.*
104. *Ibid.*
105. *Ibid.*
106. *Ibid.*
107. *Ibid.*
108. *Ibid.*
109. *Ibid.*
110. *Ibid.*
111. FDR-LOG, November 23, 1943.
112. CKS, 783; SJD, November 24, 1943.
113. ER, 142.
114. Ibid
115. *Ibid.*
116. *Ibid.*
117. JSD, November 24, 1943.

Chapter 7

1. ER, 142.
2. *Ibid.*, 142–143.

3. *Ibid.*, 143.
4. *Ibid.*
5. *Ibid.*
6. *Ibid.*
7. *Ibid.*, 142.
8. *Ibid.*, 143.
9. FDR-LOG, November 24, 1943.
10. Averell Harriman and Elie Abel, *Special Envoy to Churchill and Stalin* (New York: Random House, 1975), 261, hereafter referred to as AH.
11. "Comments on Reports that the Generalissimo is Deeply Concerned over the Soviet Government's Attitude toward his Regime and its Intention to Support the Chinese Communists," found in AH, 261–262.
12. *Ibid.*
13. *Ibid.*
14. *Ibid.*
15. *Ibid.*, 261.
16. *Ibid.*
17. *Ibid.*
18. *Ibid.*
19. *Ibid.*, 259.
20. *Ibid.*
21. *Ibid.*
22. *Ibid.*
23. *Ibid.*
24. BCOS, 12.
25. The matter of Chinese representation on Allied war councils had been raised repeatedly by T. V. Soong. As indicated in Chapter 3, Soong had taken exception to the absence of Chinese representatives at previous summit meetings between Churchill and Roosevelt and their military lieutenants, especially on those occasions when matters relating to China and Chinese interests were discussed. To solve this problem, he advanced the idea of a permanent Chinese presence on such councils as the CCOS. This idea had the blessing of Generalissimo Chiang and his government in Chungking and the generalissimo had on several occasions raised this matter with the president in his cables and letters.
26. BCOS, 12.
27. *Ibid.*
28. *Ibid.*
29. *Ibid.*
30. *Ibid.*
31. *Ibid.*
32. FDR-LOG, November 24, 1943.
33. CCOS, 28–33.
34. FDR-LOG, November 24, 1943.
35. JSD, November 24, 1943.
36. *Ibid.*
37. *Ibid.*
38. *Ibid.*
39. *Ibid.*
40. *Ibid.*
41. *Ibid.*
42. Pogue, *George C. Marshall*, 343.
43. JSD, November 24, 1943.
44. Pogue, *George C. Marshall*, 344.
45. *Ibid.*
46. *Ibid.*
47. JSD, November 24, 1943.
48. *Ibid.*
49. *Ibid.*
50. In his diary Alan Brooke recalls that Marshall was late in arriving at the CCOS meeting. ABP, November 24, 1943.
51. Although the CCOS rejected Chiang's call for an expansion of their group, they agreed that he should be told that Chinese representatives would be invited to participate in CCOS deliberations when matters of interest to the Chinese were taken up. It was hoped that such a promise would reassure the generalissimo and be satisfactory to him. CCOS, 52.
52. *Ibid.*, 53.
53. *Ibid.*
54. *Ibid.*
55. *Ibid.*
56. ABP, November 24, 1943.
57. *Ibid.*
58. CCOS, 53.
59. *Ibid.*
60. *Ibid.*
61. *Ibid.*
62. *Ibid.*
63. *Ibid.*
64. *Ibid.*, 54.
65. *Ibid.*
66. *Ibid.*
67. *Ibid.*, 55.
68. *Ibid.*
69. *Ibid.*
70. *Ibid.*
71. *Ibid.*
72. ABP, November 24, 1943.
73. *Ibid.*
74. *Ibid.*
75. According to Stilwell, he had drafted all of the questions raised by Shang Chen at the CCOS meeting on November 24 in order to avoid a repetition of the fiasco of the CCOS meeting of the day before when the Chinese generals seemed at a total loss for words. JSD, November 24, 1943.
76. *Ibid.*
77. *Ibid.*
78. CCOS, 55.
79. *Ibid.*
80. *Ibid.*
81. *Ibid.*
82. *Ibid.*, 56.
83. *Ibid.*

84. *Ibid.*
85. *Ibid.*
86. *Ibid.*
87. *Ibid.*, 57.
88. *Ibid.*
89. In a sense, Brooke and Chiang were on the same side on this issue; neither of them was really interested in fully tying up their resources in Burma. *Ibid.*, 57.
90. *Ibid.*
91. *Ibid.*
92. Arnold, *Global Mission*, 462.
93. *Ibid.*
94. *Ibid.*
95. FDR-LOG, November 24, 1990.
96. ER, 151.
97. Although Churchill did not comment on this dinner with the Chiangs in his postwar history, details of the evening are cited in CKS, November 24, 1943 and Liang Chintung, *General Stilwell in China, 1942–1944: The Full Story* (New York, St. John's University Press, 1972).
98. ER, 152.
99. *Ibid.*
100. *Ibid.*
101. *Ibid.*
102. *Ibid.*
103. *Ibid.*
104. *Ibid.*
105. *Ibid.*, 153–154.
106. *Ibid.*, 154.
107. *Ibid.*
108. Arnold, *Global Mission*, 463.
109. *Ibid.*
110. *Ibid.*
111. *Ibid.*
112. *Ibid.*
113. *Ibid.*
114. FDR-LOG, November 24, 1943.
115. *Ibid.*
116. ER, 155.
117. *Ibid.*
118. *Ibid.*
119. *Ibid.*
120. FDR-LOG, November 24, 1943.
121. ER, 155.
122. *Ibid.*
123. Liang, *Stilwell in China*, 151.
124. *Ibid.*
125. *Ibid.*
126. *Ibid.*

Chapter 8

1. Eden arrived in Cairo on November 24, 1943.
2. WK, January 5, 1944.
3. *Ibid.*
4. Anthony Eden, *The Reckoning: The Memoirs of Anthony Eden, Earl of Avon* (Boston: Houghton Mifflin, 1965), 491, hereafter referred to as AE.
5. *Ibid.*, 492.
6. *Ibid.*
7. *Ibid.*
8. WK, January 5, 1944.
9. *Ibid.*
10. FDR-LOG, November 25, 1943.
11. *Ibid.*
12. *Ibid.*
13. SH, "Newspaper File re: Cairo Conference," December 1943.
14. AE, 491.
15. SH, Newspaper File re Cairo Conference, December 1944.
16. Robert E. Sherwood, *Roosevelt and Hopkins: An Intimate History* (New York: Harper and Row, 1950), 771.
17. *Ibid.*
18. *Ibid.*
19. SH, "Clipping File re: Cairo Conference," December 1943.
20. FDR-LOG, November 25, 1943; AE, 491.
21. AE, 491.
22. *Ibid.*
23. *Ibid.*
24. *Ibid.*, 493.
25. *Ibid.*
26. *Ibid.*
27. ABP, Alan Brooke to Sunderland, May 23, 1949. .
28. ABP, Sunderland to Alan Brooke, June 21, 1949.
29. *Ibid.*
30. Roosevelt to Eleanor Roosevelt, OF 200–3N (Box 64).
31. ER, 163–165.
32. CCOS, 58.
33. *Ibid.*
34. According to Mountbatten, Chiang Kai-shek's proposal for a much-expanded offensive in Burma would have required the Americans and British to commit an additional 535 supply planes to the CBI. This was nothing short of impossible. *Ibid.*
35. *Ibid.*
36. *Ibid.*
37. *Ibid.*
38. *Ibid.*
39. *Ibid.*
40. *Ibid.*
41. *Ibid.*
42. *Ibid.*
43. *Ibid.*
44. ABP, November 25, 1943.
45. Somerville to Ismay, December 10, 1943, IP, IV/Som/3d.

46. *Ibid.*
47. *Ibid.*
48. JSD, November 25, 1943.
49. *Ibid.*
50. FDR-LOG, November 25, 1943.
51. JSD, November 25, 1943.
52. *Ibid.*
53. *Ibid.*
54. *Ibid.*
55. Stilwell also suggested that Chiang had another reason for refusing to accept a more modest Allied commitment to the Burma campaign, that being that he really preferred to husband his forces for a future confrontation with the communists and saw this as an opportunity to get out of a commitment in Burma entirely. *Ibid.*
56. *Ibid.*
57. ER, 158.
58. FDR-LOG, November 25, 1943.
59. CKS, November 25, 1943.
60. ER, 158.
61. *Ibid.*
62. CKS, November 25, 1943.
63. *Ibid.*
64. *Ibid.*
65. *Ibid.*
66. ER, 158.
67. *Ibid.*
68. *Ibid.*
69. *Ibid.*
70. CKS, November 25, 1943.
71. An examination of Roosevelt's correspondence with T. V. Soong and other Chinese diplomatic representatives makes it clear that the president was well briefed on the importance of face in Chinese politics. By the time the Cairo conference convened, Roosevelt was somewhat of an expert on the question of ego in Chinese political life and one of his main purposes of bringing the Chiang's to Cairo was to attend to their egos and give them the place and face they had felt denied to them in the past.
72. FDR-LOG, November 25, 1943.
73. *Ibid.*
74. *Ibid.*
75. Accompanying Roosevelt to Cairo was a cache of turkeys sufficient to feed all of the Americans at the conference and their British and Chinese friends. As mentioned earlier, in Chapter 4, the president's chef and stewards were brought to Cairo to attend to Roosevelt's dietary needs and the feeding and entertainment of his guests.
76. Churchill, *Closing the Ring*, 341.
77. *Ibid.*
78. JSD, November 25, 1943.
79. *Ibid.*
80. *Ibid.*

81. *Ibid.*
82. ER, 161.
83. Stilwell's diary entry for November 25, 1943 contains surprisingly little detail about the hour the general spent with the president. The only detailed account of the conversation is found in Elliott Roosevelt's post-war reminiscences, which I used to reconstruct the details of the president's chat with Stilwell.
84. ER, 161.
85. *Ibid.*
86. *Ibid.*
87. *Ibid.*
88. JSD, November 25, 1943.
89. ER, 162.
90. *Ibid.*
91. *Ibid.*
92. *Ibid.*, 161.
93. *Ibid.*, 162.
94. Frank Dorn, *Walkout with Stilwell in Burma* (New York: Crowell, 1971), 76.
95. In his book (75–79), Dorn goes into considerable detail outlining contingency plans he developed at General Stilwell's request to assassinate Generalissimo Chiang and his wife, but there is no evidence of any such directive in the Stilwell Papers or any other sources. In his fine study of Sino-American relations, *The U. S. Crusade in China, 1938–1945* (New York: Columbia University Press, 1979), 153–154, Michael Schaller relates this incident without offering a view on its authenticity.
96. Roosevelt had used much the same technique to placate Chiang Kai-shek earlier in the day when the generalissimo had complained about the difficulty of dealing with Churchill and the president agreed with him.
97. In his diary entry for November 25, Stilwell notes that the president expressed some anger and frustration over Chiang's obstructionism, but this seems to be a reference to his earlier conversation (4:30 p.m.) with Marshall and Roosevelt. JSD, November 25, 1943.
98. ER, 163.
99. *Ibid.*
100. *Ibid.*
101. *Ibid.*, 163–164.
102. *Ibid.*, 164.
103. *Ibid.*
104. *Ibid.*, 165.
105. *Ibid.*
106. *Ibid.*

Chapter 9

1. FDR-LOG, November 26, 1943.
2. CCOS, 57.

3. FDR-LOG, November 26, 1943.
4. ER, 166.
5. *Ibid.*
6. Ziegler, *Mountbatten*, 373.
7. Davies, *Dragon by the Tail,* 278.
8. *Ibid.*
9. FDR-LOG, November 26, 1943.
10. *Ibid.*
11. FDR to H.H. Kung, November 26, 1943, *FRUS: China: 1943,* 455.
12. In his post-war memoirs, Elliott Roosevelt suggests that his father made absolutely no mention of his conversation with Mountbatten to Madame Chiang. ER, 166.
13. JSD, November 26, 1943.
14. *Ibid.*
15. *Ibid.*
16. *Ibid.*
17. *Ibid.*
18. *Ibid.*
19. *Ibid.*
20. Arnold, *Global Mission,* 464.
21. *Ibid.*
22. JSD, November 26, 1943.
23. *Ibid.*
24. AE, 493.
25. *Ibid.*
26. *Ibid.*
27. *Ibid.*
28. CCOS, 243.
29. The full text of Mountbatten's draft is contained in Report 411/2, which may be found in CCOS, 243.
30. *Ibid.,* 64.
31. *Ibid.*
32. *Ibid.*
33. *Ibid.*
34. *Ibid.*
35. *Ibid.*
36. *Ibid.*
37. *Ibid.*
38. *Ibid.*
39. *Ibid.*
40. *Ibid.*
41. *Ibid.*
42. *Ibid.*
43. *Ibid.*
44. *Ibid.*
45. *Ibid.*
46. *Ibid.*
47. Pogue, *George C. Marshall,* 308.
48. ABP, November 26, 1943.
49. CCOS, 64.
50. *Ibid.*
51. Leahy, *I Was There,* 202.
52. *Ibid.*
53. *Ibid.*
54. *Ibid.*
55. Pogue, *George C. Marshall,* 308.
56. *Ibid.*
57. *Ibid.,* 304.
58. *Ibid.*
59. *Ibid.*
60. FDR-LOG, November 26, 1943.
61. *Ibid.*
62. Liang, *Stilwell in China,* 151.
63. *Ibid.*
64. *Ibid.*
65. *Ibid.*
66. *Ibid.*
67. *Ibid.*
68. FDR-LOG, November 26, 1943.
69. *Department of State Bulletin,* December 4, 1943.
70. Hopkins had told Roosevelt of his meeting with Cyrus Sulzberger and other reporters who had come to complain to him on November 26 about efforts being made to isolate the three leaders and their aides from the press and Sulzberger's inference that quarantining the press was a sure sign that things were not going well. Sherwood, *Roosevelt and Hopkins,* 771.
71. *Department of State Bulletin,* December 4, 1943.
72. According to Herbert Feis, in Hopkin's original draft of the Korean section of the Cairo Declaration, the text called for granting independence to Korea "at the earliest possible moment." Roosevelt then changed this to read "at the proper moment" and this wording was changed to "in due course" at the suggestion of the British. What Roosevelt had in mind was the creation of a trusteeship for Korea, which would postpone Korean independence for a brief period while the Koreans were tutored in the art of self-government. Herbert Feis, *Churchill, Roosevelt, and Stalin: The War They Waged and the Peace They Sought* (Princeton, Princeton University Press, 1957), 251-252.
73. ER, 142.
74. *Ibid.*
75. CKS, November 23, 1943.
76. Roosevelt was not totally naive about the fact that giving the Soviets a place in the Korean condominium could pose problems when the war ended, but, according to Bruce Cummings, Roosevelt was more concerned about having the Soviets play a major role in the United Nations, including its trusteeship operations than in the possibility that the Russians would be an impediment to Korean independence. Cummings, *Child of Conflict: The Korean American Relationship, 1943-1953* (Seattle: University of Washington Press, 1983), 13-15.
77. Bruce Cumings, *The Origins of the Korean War* (Princeton: Princeton University Press, 1981), 104-106.

78. Bruce Cumings, *Child of Conflict*, 11–13.
79. *Department of State Bulletin*, December 4, 1943.
80. FDR-LOG, November 26, 1943.
81. *Ibid.*
82. According to the president's log, the meeting between Roosevelt, Churchill, and the Chiangs began at 4:30 p.m. and was over just after 5:30 p.m.. FDR-LOG, November 26, 1943.
83. *Ibid.*
84. *Ibid.*
85. JSD, November 26 1943.
86. Liang, *Stilwell in China*, 161.
87. *Ibid.*
88. CKS, November 30, 1943.
89. *Ibid.*
90. *Ibid.*
91. JSD, November 27, 1943.
92. *Ibid.*
93. Ibid
94. *Ibid.*
95. *Ibid.*
96. *Ibid.*
97. *Ibid.*
98. *Ibid.*
99. *Ibid.*
100. *Ibid.*
101. Churchill, *Closing the Ring*, 328.
102. *Ibid.*
103. *Ibid.*
104. *Ibid.*
105. *Ibid.*
106. *Ibid.*

Chapter 10

1. FDR-LOG, November 27, 1943.
2. *Ibid.*
3. *Ibid.*
4. Churchill, *Closing the Ring*, 342.
5. *Ibid.*
6. *Ibid.*
7. *Ibid.*, p 342–343.
8. FDR-LOG, November 27, 1943.
9. *Ibid.*
10. *Ibid.*
11. *Ibid.*
12. *Ibid.*
13. *Ibid.*
14. *Ibid.*
15. *Ibid.*
16. *Ibid.*
17. *Ibid.*
18. BCOS, 22.
19. *Ibid.*
20. *Ibid.*
21. *Ibid.*
22. *Ibid.*
23. *Ibid.*
24. *Ibid.*
25. ABP, November 28, 1943.
26. ABP, November 29, 1943.
27. *Ibid.*
28. See Chapter V, p .
29. FDR-LOG, November 28, 1943.
30. *Foreign Relations of the United States: The Conferences at Cairo and Teheran* (Washington: United States Government Printing Office, 1961), hereafter referred to as *FRUS: C/T*, 479.
31. *Ibid.*
32. *Ibid.*
33. *Ibid.*
34. *Ibid.*
35. *Ibid.*
36. *Ibid.*
37. *Ibid.*, 480.
38. *Ibid.*
39. FDR-LOG, November 28, 1943.
40. *Ibid.*
41. *Ibid.*
42. *Ibid.*
43. *Ibid.*
44. *FRUS: C/T*, 483.
45. *Ibid.*
46. *Ibid.*
47. This comment is contained in Charles E. Bohlen's post-war memoir, *Witness to History* (New York: Norton, 1973), 139.
48. *FRUS: C/T*, 484.
49. *Ibid.*, 485.
50. *Ibid.*
51. *Ibid.*
52. *Ibid.*
53. According to Bohlen's minutes of the conversation, Roosevelt told Stalin that the Chinese "had no designs on Indochina" and supported the idea of a United Nations trusteeship. *Ibid.*, 485.
54. *Ibid.*
55. *Ibid.*
56. *Ibid.*, 486.
57. AH, 266.
58. *Ibid.*
59. Lloyd C. Gardner, *Architects of Illusion: Men and Ideas in American Foreign Policy, 1941–1949* (Chicago: Quadrangle Books, 1970), 36.
60. According to Hopkins' biographer, Robert Sherwood, Roosevelt was under the impression that Stalin knew very little about the war in the Pacific and wanted to educate him about the status of the war against Japan before the prime minister had a chance to do so. Sherwood, *Roosevelt and Hopkins*, 779.
61. *FRUS: C/T*, 488.
62. *Ibid.*

63. Ibid, 489.
64. *Ibid.*
65. *Ibid.*
66. *Ibid.*
67. *Ibid.*
68. *Ibid.*
69. *Ibid.*, 509.
70. *Ibid.*
71. *Ibid.* 514.
72. *Ibid.*
73. *Ibid.*, 515.
74. *Ibid.*
75. *Ibid.*, 518.
76. *Ibid.*
77. *Ibid.*, 518–519.
78. *Ibid.*
79. *Ibid.*, 520.
80. *Ibid.*
81. *Ibid.*
82. BCOS, 24.
83. ABP, November 30, 1943.
84. FDR-LOG, November 29, 1943.
85. *FRUS: C/T*, 529–531.
86. AH, 271.
87. *Ibid.*
88. *Ibid.*
89. Churchill, *Closing the Ring*, 363.
90. ER, 180.
91. *Ibid.*
92. *Ibid.*
93. *Ibid.*
94. *Ibid.*
95. *Ibid.*
96. Although Molotov was present during this discussion, he contributed nothing to the conversation. Elliott Roosevelt would later describe him as "gray and colorless," more Stalin's servant than his advisor. *Ibid.*, 129.
97. FDR-LOG, November 29, 1943.
98. It is interesting to note that whereas several dozen members of the American press contingent had complained to Hopkins in Cairo about efforts to impose a total news blackout, there was little effort to challenge the censorship of the press in Teheran.
99. FDR-LOG, November 29, 1943.
100. *FRUS: C/T*, 534–535.
101. *Ibid.*, 538.
102. *Ibid.*, 538–539.
103. *Ibid.*, 539.
104. *Ibid.*
105. *Ibid.*
106. *Ibid.*
107. FDR-LOG, November 29, 1943.
108. *Ibid.*
109. *Ibid.*
110. *FRUS: C/T*, 553.
111. Churchill, *Closing the Ring*, 373.
112. *FRUS: C/T*, 554.
113. *Ibid.*
114. *Ibid.*
115. According to a distinguished British diplomatic historian, Churchill suspected that Roosevelt hoped to use the United Nations to advance his anti-colonial views. This explained why Roosevelt advanced the idea that China was a co-equal of the Anglo-American Allies. Courting Chiang Kai-shek would guarantee his "faggot vote" against colonial interests when the question of the fate of colonial empires was addressed by the U.N. after the war. Christopher Thorne, *Allies of A Kind* (New York: Oxford University Press, 1978), 305–312.

Chapter 11

1. BCOS, 25.
2. *Ibid.*
3. *Ibid.*
4. *Ibid.*
5. *Ibid.*
6. *Ibid.*
7. *Ibid.*
8. CCOS, 70.
9. *Ibid.*
10. In a diary entry made later that day, Alan Brooke attributed Marshall's support of Operation Anvil as a sure sign that Roosevelt wished to give Stalin the impression that the Americans were wholeheartedly committed to the Second Front in Europe. ABP, November 30, 1943.
11. CCOS, 70.
12. *Ibid.*
13. *Ibid.*, 70–71.
14. *Ibid.*, 71.
15. *Ibid.*
16. ABP, November 30, 1943.
17. *Ibid.*
18. Ziegler, *Mountbatten*, 263.
19. Admiral Louis Mountbatten, *Report to the Combined Chiefs of Staff by the Allied Supreme Commander Southeast Asia: 1943–1945* (London: His Majesty's Stationary Office, 1951), hereafter referred to as MR, 28.
20. Ziegler, *Mountbatten*, 263.
21. *Ibid.*
22. Churchill, *Closing the Ring*, 375.
23. *Ibid.*
24. *Ibid.*
25. AH, 278.
26. *Ibid.*
27. *Ibid.*
28. Churchill, *Closing the Ring*, 375–376.
29. *Ibid.*, 376.
30. *Ibid.*
31. *Ibid.*

32. *Ibid.*, 377.
33. *Ibid.*
34. *Ibid.*
35. *Ibid.*, 376.
36. *Ibid.*, 378–379.
37. *Ibid.*, 378.
38. *Ibid.*, p 379–380.
39. FDR-LOG, November 30, 1943.
40. *FRUS: C/T*, 565.
41. *Ibid.*, 566.
42. *Ibid.*
43. *Ibid.*
44. *Ibid.*, 567.
45. *Ibid.*
46. *Ibid.*
47. *Ibid.*, 568.
48. FDR-LOG, November 30, 1943.
49. Churchill, *Closing the Ring*, 384–385.
50. John Boettiger, the president's son-in-law, kept minutes of the dinner party which may be found in *FRUS: C/T*, 582–585. Churchill's account of the evening, written after the war, may be found in the fifth volume of his history of the war, *Closing the Ring*, 384–389.
51. FRUS:C/T, 583.
52. *Ibid.*
53. *Ibid.*, 584.
54. Churchill, *Closing the Ring*, 387.
55. *Ibid.*
56. Admiral Andrew Browne Cunningham, *A Sailor's Odyssey: The Autobiography of Admiral of the Fleet, Viscount Cunningham of Hyndhope* (New York: E. Dutton, 1951), 588.
57. Churchill, *Closing the Ring*, 387.
58. *Ibid.*, 388.
59. FDR-LOG, November 30, 1943.
60. ABP, December 1, 1943.
61. FDR-LOG, December 1, 1943.
62. *Ibid.*
63. This comment is contained in Bohlen's minutes of December 1, 1943, which may be found in *FRUS: C/T*, 587.
64. *Ibid.*, 587.
65. *Ibid.*
66. *Ibid.*
67. FDR-LOG, December 1, 1943.
68. *FRUS: C/T*, 838.
69. The full text of the final text of the Teheran Declaration may be found in *FRUS: C/T*, 640–641.
70. The full text of this secret agreement, known as "Military Conclusions of the Teheran Conference," may be found in *FRUS: C/T*, 652.
71. Churchill, *Closing the Ring*, p 404–405.
72. ER, 185.
73. *Ibid.*
74. FDR-LOG, December 1, 1943.
75. *Ibid.*
76. Churchill, *Closing the Ring*, 408.

Chapter 12

1. FDR-LOG, December 2, 1943.
2. BCOS, 26.
3. *Ibid.*
4. *Ibid.*
5. *Ibid.*, 27.
6. *Ibid.*
7. JSD, December 3, 1943.
8. CCOS, 74.
9. *Ibid.*
10. *Ibid.*
11. ABP, December 3, 1943.
12. Bryant, *Triumph in the West*, 857.
13. Leahy, *I Was There*, 213.
14. *Ibid.*
15. *Ibid.*
16. Warren I. Cohen, *America's Response to China: An Interpretive History of Sino-American Relations* (New York: Knopf, 1970), 220–221.
17. Thomas McCormick, *America's Half-Century: United States Foreign Policy in the Cold War* (Baltimore: Johns Hopkins University Press, 1989), 33.
18. Churchill, *Closing the Ring*, 410–411.
19. *Ibid.*, 409–410.
20. BCOS, 32.
21. ABP, December 4, 1943.
22. *Ibid.*
23. *Ibid.*
24. 2*Ibid.*
25. Churchill, *Closing the Ring*, 413.
26. Somerville to Ismay, December 3, 1943, IP: IV/Som/2.
27. ABP, December 4, 1943.
28. Davies to Gauss, Stilwell Papers, December 16, 1943.
29. This editorial and other like it can be found in a collection of clippings in the Hornbeck Papers dated December 6, 1943.
30. *Ibid.*
31. CKS, December 4, 1943.
32. CCOS, 31.
33. *Ibid.*
34. *Ibid.*, 32.
35. *Ibid.*
36. *Ibid.*
37. *Ibid.*
38. *Ibid.*, 33.
39. *Ibid.*
40. *Ibid.*
41. *Ibid.*, 33–34.
42. *Ibid.*, 34.
43. *Ibid.*
44. *Ibid.*

45. *Ibid.*, 35.
46. *Ibid.*, 35.
47. *Ibid.*
48. *Ibid.*
49. *Ibid.*
50. *Ibid.*
51. CCOS, 79.
52. *Ibid.*
53. *Ibid.*
54. *Ibid.*
55. *Ibid.*, 81.
56. ER, 201.
57. CCOS, 82.
58. *Ibid.*
59. *Ibid.*
60. *Ibid.*
61. *Ibid.*
62. *Ibid.*, 84.
63. *Ibid.*
64. *Ibid.*
65. *Ibid.*
66. *Ibid.*
67. The text of these summaries may be found in CCS Report 432/2, CCOS, 283.
68. *Ibid.*
69. FDR-LOG, December 5, 1943.
70. CCOS, 35.
71. *Ibid.*, 36.
72. *Ibid.*
73. *Ibid.*
74. *Ibid.*, 38.
75. *Ibid.*
76. *Ibid.*, 39.
77. *Ibid.*, 38.
78. *Ibid.*, 39.
79. FDR-LOG, December 5, 1943.
80. FDR-LOG, December 5, 1943.
81. *Ibid.*
82. *FRUS: China: 43*, 179.
83. *Ibid.*
84. FDR-LOG, December 5, 1943.
85. Leahy, *I Was There*, 213.
86. Pogue, *George C. Marshall*, 322.
87. *Ibid.*
88. Leahy, *I Was There*, 213.
89. Churchill, *Closing the Ring*, 412.
90. *FRUS: C/T*, 803-804.
91. ER, 201.
92. *Ibid.*
93. *Ibid.*
94. Pogue, *George C. Marshall*, 322.
95. *Ibid.*
96. Sherwood, *Roosevelt & Hopkins*, 800.
97. *Ibid.*
98. ER, 203.
99. *Ibid.*, 204.
100. ER, 207.
101. Davies, *Dragon by the Tail*, 280.
102. *Ibid.*
103. Liang, *Stilwell in China*, 165.

104. JSD, December 6, 1943.
105. This comment is noted by Liang, *Stilwell in China*, 165, and Davies, *Dragon by the Tail*, 280.
106. JSD, December 5, 1943.
107. *Ibid.*
108. Schaller, *U. S. Crusade*, 152.
109. Churchill, *Closing the Ring*, 412.
110. Bryant, *Triumph in the West*, 76.
111. ABP, December 6, 1943.
112. Churchill, *Closing the Ring*, 419.

Chapter 13

1. ER, 213.
2. MR, 29.
3. *Ibid.*, 29-30.
4. *Ibid.*, 30.
5. The text of Chiang's cable to Roosevelt, dated December 9, 1943, may be found in FDR-MR/10.
6. *Ibid.*
7. *Ibid.*
8. *Ibid.*
9. JSD, December 15, 1943.
10. *Ibid.*
11. JSD, December 16, 1943.
12. Davies to Gauss, "Memorandum of Conversations with Dr. Wang Chung-hui and Sun Fo," December 16, 1943, Stilwell Papers.
13. *Ibid.*
14. An undated copy of this dispatch may be found in the Soong Papers, Cable File, December 1943.
15. FDR-LOG, December 18, 1943.
16. SD, December 18, 1943.
17. *Ibid.*
18. *Ibid.*
19. *Ibid.*
20. FDR to CKS, December 20, 1943, FDR-MR-10.
21. *Ibid.*
22. CKS to FDR, December 23, 1943, FDR-MR-10.
23. *Ibid.*
24. FDR to CKS, December 27, 1943, FDR-MR-10.
25. A complete translation of the text of Chiang's speech may be found in the Hornbeck Papers in a box of newspaper clippings marked 4-5 January 1944.
26. Gauss to Hornbeck, December 27, 1943, HP.
27. Cordell Hull, *The Memoirs of Cordell Hull* (New York: Macmillan, 1948), Volume II, 1587.
28. TVS to Hopkins, January 1944[undated], TVS.

29. Sherwood, *Roosevelt and Hopkins*, 805.
30. TVS to Victor Hoo, January 19, 1943, TVS.
31. *Ibid.*
32. *Ibid.*
33. CKS, December 2, 1943.
34. Blum, *Morgenthau Diaries*, 104.
35. *Ibid.*
36. *Ibid.*
37. Churchill's racism is well documented in Thorne, *Allies of A Kind*, Chapter 1, 3–57.
38. FDR to CKS, January 5, 1944, Department of State, Decimal File, China, hereafter referred to as DF, 893.51/7727A.
39. *Ibid.*
40. CKS to FDR, January 16, 1944, DF, 893.51/7731.
41. ER, 163–165.
42. *Ibid.*
43. *Ibid.*, 164.
44. Roosevelt's change of heart vis-à-vis Chiang and the Kuomintang regime after the Cairo conference was gradual, not sudden, and the president's rhetoric, albeit toned down, gave no cause for alarm to the generalissimo's most ardent supporters in the United States. There is little if any evidence that members of the China lobby understood that the Cairo conference marked a critical turning point in Sino-American relations. For a fuller account of this issue see Ross Koen, *The China Lobby in American Politics* (New York: Octagon Books, 1974).
45. Dorn, *Walkout with Stilwell*, 228–230.
46. "Memorandum of a Conversation with Cordell Hull," March 25, 1944, TVS.
47. *Ibid.*
48. *Ibid.*
49. *FRUS: China: 1944*, 240.
50. JSD, December 6, 1943.
51. Mao Tse-tung, "How Yu Kung Removed the Mountains," *Selected Works of Mao Tse-tung* Volume IV, (Peking: Foreign Language Press, 1956), 317–318.
52. *Ibid.*
53. At the time of the Cairo conference, thirty Chinese divisions had been supplied with new American arms and sent for special training in India under the supervision of General Stilwell. Sixty divisions had yet to be retrained and provided with new equipment.
54. After the Cairo conference, T. V. Soong was frequently treated to Chiang's tirades against Roosevelt's abandonment of the Kuomintang. Soong's papers contain numerous references to these "fusillades." Listening to Chiang berate the president must have been both amusing and painful to Soong given the fact that he had been cut out of any role at the Cairo conference at Chiang's instructions. Soong believed that his absence from the conference had cost Chiang dearly, but he could hardly blame the generalissimo for his own failure and maintain his position in the Kuomintang leadership. Such was Soong's dilemma and the dilemma of others of independent mind in Chiang's entourage.

Bibliography

Personal Records

Haydon Boatner Papers	Hoover Institution Stanford University Stanford, California
Alan Brooke Papers	Liddell-Hart Archives King's College University of London London, England
Chiang Kai-shek Diaries	Hoover Institution Stanford University Stanford, California
Claire Lee Chennault Papers	Hoover Institution Stanford University Stanford, California
Andrew Cunningham Papers	Liddell-Hart Archives King's College University of London London, England
Lauchlin Currie Papers	Hoover Institution Stanford University Stanford, California
John Dill Papers	Liddell-Hart Archives King's College University of London London, England
Chang Hsin Hai Papers	Hoover Institution Stanford University Stanford, California
Maxwell Hamilton Papers	Hoover Institution Stanford University Stanford, California
Victor Hoo Papers	Hoover Institution Stanford University Stanford, California
Harry Hopkins Papers	Franklin D. Roosevelt Library Hyde Park, New York
Stanley Hornbeck Papers	Hoover Institution Stanford University Stanford, California

Hastings Ismay Papers	Liddell-Hart Archives King's College University of London London, England
V. K. Wellington Koo Papers	Butler Library Columbia University New York, New York
H. H. Kung Collection	Oral History Project Columbia University New York, New York
Paul Linebarger Papers	Hoover Institution Stanford University Stanford, California
George C. Marshall Papers	George C. Marshall Library Lexington, Virginia
Henry Morgenthau Papers	Franklin D. Roosevelt Library Hyde Park, New York
Louis Mountbatten Archives	Mountbatten Estate Broadlands, England
Franklin D. Roosevelt Papers	Franklin D. Roosevelt Library Hyde Park, New York
Laurence S. Salisbury Papers	Hoover Institution Stanford University Stanford, California
T. V. Soong Papers	Hoover Institution Stanford University Stanford, California
Joseph W. Stilwell Papers	Hoover Institution Stanford University Stanford, California
Henry L. Stimson Papers	Sterling Library Yale University New Haven, Connecticut
Albert Wedemeyer Papers	Hoover Institution Stanford University Stanford, California
Raymond Wheeler Papers	Hoover Institution Stanford University Stanford, California

Government Records and Published Documents

Churchill and Roosevelt: The Complete Correspondence (Warren Kimball, ed.). Princeton: Princeton University Press, 1984.
Embassy in China Files, 1941–1945, RG 84
    United States, Department of State
    National Archives and Federal Records Center
    Suitland, Maryland
First Lady of China: The Historic Visit of Madame Chiang K'ai-shek to the United States. New York: International Business Machines Corporation, 1943.

Foreign Relations of the United States: 1942: China. Washington, D.C.: Government Printing Office, 1956.
Foreign Relations of the United States: 1943: China. Washington, D.C.: Government Printing Office, 1957.
Foreign Relations of the United States: 1944. Washington, D.C.: Government Printing Office, 1966–1967.
Foreign Relations of the United States: The Conference at Cairo and Teheran. Washington, D.C.: Government Printing Office, 1960.
Foreign Relations of the United States: The Conference at Washington, 1941–1942 and Casablanca, 1943. Washington, D.C.: Government Printing Office, 1968.
Foreign Relations of the United States: The Conferences at Washington and Quebec, 1943. Washington, DC: Government Printing Office, 1970.
Foreign Relations of the United States: The Conference at Quebec, 1944. Washington, DC: Government Printing Office, 1972.
Foreign Relations of the United States: Relations with China, 1944–1949. Washington, DC: Government Printing Office, 1949.
Prime Minister's Office: Files Concerning the Far East. London: Public Records Office.
Report to the Combined Chiefs of Staff by the Supreme Allied Commander Southeast Asia, 1943. London: Her Majesty's Stationery Office, 1951.
Sextant Conference: Minutes of Proceedings at Cairo and Teheran between 22 November and 7 December 1943. London: War Cabinet, 1944.
Sextant: Records of British Chiefs of Staff Proceedings at Malta, Cairo, and Teheran between 18 November and 7 December 1943. London: War Cabinet, 1943.
Sextant: Combined Chiefs of Staff Memoranda Circulated at Cairo and Teheran between 24 November and 7 December 1943. London: War Cabinet, 1944.
Stalin's Correspondence with Roosevelt and Truman: 1941–1945. New York: Capricorn, 1965.

Memoirs, Diaries, Autobiographies, and Published Papers

Alsop, Joseph. *I've Seen the Best of It*. New York: Norton, 1992.
Arnold, Henry H. *Global Mission*. New York: Harper, 1949.
Blum, John M. *From the Morgenthau Diaries: Years of War, 1941–1945*. Boston: Houghton Mifflin, 1967.
Bohlen, Charles. *Witness to History: 1929–1969*. New York: Norton, 1973.
Cadogan, Sir Alexander. *The Diaries of Alexander Cadogen, O.M.* New York: Putnam, 1972.
Carton de Wiart, Sir Adrian. *Happy Odyssey*. London: Jonathan Cape, 1950.
Chiang Kai-shek. *China's Destiny*. New York: Roy, 1947.
_____. *Soviet Russia in China*. New York: Farrar, Strauss and Giroux, 1965.
Chou En-lai. *Selected Works of Chou En-lai*. Beijing: Foreign Language Press, 1981.
Churchill, Sarah. *Keep on Dancing: An Autobiography*. London: Weidenfeld and Nicholson, 1981.
Churchill, Sir Winston. *The Collected Works of Sir Winston Churchill*. London: Library of Imperial History, 1973.
_____. *The Second World War: Closing the Ring*. Boston: Houghton Mifflin, 1951.
_____. *War Speeches*. London: Cassell, 1972.
Davies, John P. *Dragon by the Tail*. New York: Norton, 1972.
Dorn, Frank. *Walkout with Stilwell in Burma*. New York: Crowell, 1971.
Eden, Sir Anthony. *The Reckoning: The Memoirs of Anthony Eden: Earl of Avon*. Boston: Houghton-Mifflin, 1965.
Harriman, W. Averell. *Special Envoy to Churchill and Stalin*. New York: Random House, 1975.
Hull, Cordell. *The Memoirs of Cordell Hull*. New York: Macmillan, 1948.
Ismay, General Hastings. *The Memoirs of Lord Ismay*. New York: Viking, 1960.
Keiji Furama. *Sho Kai-seki Hiroku (From the Private Files of Chiang K'ai-shek)*. Tokyo: Sankei Shimbun, 1976. Abridged and translated as *Chiang K'ai-shek: His Life and Times*. Translated by Chun-ming Chang. New York: St. John's University Press, 1981.

Kung Hsiang-hsi. *The Reminiscences of H. H. Kung.* New York: Columbia University Oral History Project, 1967.
Leahy, Admiral William. *I Was There.* New York: Whittelsey House, 1950.
Li Tsung-jen. *The Memoirs of Li Tsung-jen.* Translated by T. K. Tong. Boulder: Westview Press, 1979.
Macmillan, Harold. *War Diaries: Politics and War in the Mediterranean, January 1943–May 1945.* London: Macmillan, 1984.
Roosevelt, Elliott. *As He Saw It.* New York: Duell, Sloan, and Pearce, 1946.
Service, Grace. *Golden Inches: The China Memoir of Grace Service.* Berkley: University of California Press, 1989.
Service, John S. *The Amerasia Papers.* Berkeley: University of California Press, 1971.
_____. *Lost Chance in China: The World War II Dispatches of John S. Service.* New York: Random House, 1974.
Soong, T. V. *Organizing the New World Order for Victory and Peace.* Chungking: United China Relief, 1942.
Tong, Hollington. *Chiang Kai-shek's Teacher and Ambassador: An Inside View of the Republic of China: 1911–1958.* Edited by Walter C. Mih. Bloomington: AuthorHouse, 2005.
_____. *Chiang Tsung T'ung Chuan (Selected Works of Chiang K'ai-shek).* Taipei: Academy Sinica, 1952.
_____. *China and the World Press.* Shanghai: World Press, 1948.
_____. *Dateline: China.* New York: Rockport Press, 1950.
Wales, Nym. (Helen Foster Snow). *My China Years: A Memoir.* New York: Morrow, 1984.
White, Theodore. *In Search of History: A Personal Adventure.* New York: Harper and Row, 1978.
_____, and Annalee Jocoby. *Thunder Out of China.* New York: William Sloan, 1946.
Willkie, Wendell. *One World.* New York: Simon & Schuster, 1943.

Newspapers

Boston Globe, 1943
Chicago Tribune, 1943
Hollywood Reporter, 1943
Hsin Hua Jih Pao (Chungking), 1941–1945
Los Angeles Times, 1943
National Herald (Chungking), 1941–1945
New York Herald Tribune, 1941–1945
New York Times, 1941–1945
San Francisco Chronicle, 1943
Shanghai Evening Post and Mercury (Chungking), 1943–1944
Su Tung Pao (Chungking), 1943–1944

Secondary Sources

Black, Conrad. *Franklin Delano Roosevelt: Champion of Freedom.* New York: Public Affairs Press, 2005.
Borg, Dorothy. *Uncertain Years: Chinese American Relations, 1947–1950.* New York: Columbia University Press, 1980.
_____. *The United States and the Far Eastern Crisis of 1933–1938.* Cambridge: Harvard University Press, 1964.
Brinkley Alan. *The Publisher: Henry Luce and His American Century.* New York: Knopf, 2010.
Bryant, Arthur. *Triumph in the West: A History of the War Years Based on the Diaries of Field Marshall Lord Alanbrooke.* New York: Doubleday, 1959.
Chi Ch'ao-ting. *Wartime Economic Development of China.* New York: Garland, 1980.
Chi His-sheng. *Nationalist China at War: Military Defeat and Political Collapse, 1937–1945.* Ann Arbor: University of Michigan Press, 1982.
Chou Min-chih. *Hu Shih and Intellectual Choice in Modern China.* Ann Arbor: University of Michigan Press, 1984.

Chu Pao-chin. *V. K. Wellington Koo: A Case Study of China's Diplomat and the Diplomacy of Nationalism, 1912–1966.* Hong Kong: Chinese University Press, 1981.
Chu, Samuel, ed. *Madame Chiang Kai-shek and Her China.* New York: East Gate, 2005.
Cohen, Warren. *America's Response to China: A History of Sino-American Relations.* New York: Columbia University Press, 1990.
———. *The Chinese Connection: Roger S. Greene, Thomas W. Lamont, George E. Sokolsky and American East Asian Relations.* New York: Columbia University Press, 1983.
Craft, Stephen B. *V.K. Wellington Koo and the Emergence of Modern China.* Lexington: University Press of Kentucky, 2004.
Cumings, Bruce. *Child of Conflict: The Korean-American Relationship, 1943–1953.* Seattle: University of Washington Press, 1983.
———. *The Origins of the Korean War.* Princeton: Princeton University Press, 1981.
Danchev, Alex. *Very Special Relationship: Field Marshall Sir John Dill and the Anglo-American Alliance, 1941–1944.* London: Brassey's Defense Publishers, 1986.
De Long, Thomas A. *Madame Chiang Kai-shek and Miss Emma Mills: China's First Lady and Her American Friend.* Jefferson, NC: McFarland, 2007.
Denning, Margaret B. *The Sino-American Alliance in World War II.* Berne: P. Lang, 1986.
D'Este, Carlo. *Warlord: A Life of Winston Churchill at War, 1874–1945.* New York: Harper, 2009.
Dower, John. *War Without Mercy.* New York: Pantheon, 1986.
Eastman, Lloyd. *Seeds of Destruction: Nationalist China in War and Revolution.* Stanford: Stanford University Press, 1984.
Endicott, Stephen L. *Diplomacy and Enterprise: British China Policy, 1933–1937.* Vancouver: University of British Columbia Press, 1975.
Fairbank, John K. *China Perceived: Images and Policies in Chinese American Relations.* New York: Knopf, 1974.
Feis, Herbert. *The China Tangle.* Princeton: Princeton University Press, 1953.
———. *Churchill, Roosevelt, Stalin: The War they Waged and the Peace they Sought.* Princeton: Princeton University Press, 1957.
———. *The Road to Pearl Harbor.* Princeton: Princeton University Press, 1950.
Fenby, Jonathan. *Chiang Kai-shek: China's Generalissimo and the Nation He Lost.* New York: Da Capo Press, 2005.
Gardner, Lloyd C. *Architects of Illusion: Men and Ideas in American Foreign Policy, 1941–1949.* Chicago: Quadrangle Books, 1970.
Gilbert, Martin. *Winston Churchill's War Leadership.* New York: Vintage, 2004.
Grayson, Benson L. *The American Image of China.* New York: Ungar, 1979.
Hastings, Max. *Winston's War: Churchill, 1940–1945.* New York: Knopf, 2010.
Heinrichs, Waldo. *American Ambassador: Joseph C. Grew and the Development of the United States Diplomatic Tradition.* New York: Oxford University Press, 1986.
Heinrichs, Waldo. *Threshold of War: Franklin D. Roosevelt and American Entry into World War II.* New York: Oxford University Press, 1988.
Hunt, Michael. *The Making of a Special Relationship: The United States and China to 1914.* New York: Oxford University Press, 1983.
Iriye, Akira. *Across the Pacific, an Inner History of American East-Asian Relation.* New York: Harcourt, Brace, and World, 1967.
Iriye, Akira. *The Origins of the Secret World in Asia.* London: Longman, 1987.
———. *Power and Culture: The Japanese-American War 1941–1945.* Cambridge: Harvard University Press, 1981.
Kahn, E. J. *The China Hands: America's Foreign Service Officers and What Befell Them.* New York: Viking, 1975.
Koen, Ross Y. *The China Lobby in American Politics.* New York: Octagon Books, 1974.
Lauren, Paul G. *The China Hands: Legacy, Ethics, and Diplomacy.* Boulder: Westview Press, 1987.
Leong, Karen J. *The China Mystique: Pearl Buck, Anna May Wong, Mayling Soong and the Transformation of American Orientalism.* Berkeley: University of California Press, 2005.

Li, Laura Tyson. *Madame Chiang Kai-shek: China's Eternal First Lady*. New York: Grove Press, 2007.
Liang, Chin-tung. *General Stilwell in China, 1942–1944: The Full Story*. New York: St. John's University Press, 1972.
Lohback, Don. *Patrick J. Hurley*. Chicago: Henry Regnery, 1956.
McCormick, Thomas. *America's Half Century: United States Foreign Policy in the Cold War*. Baltimore: Johns Hopkins University Press, 1989.
May, Gary. *China Scapegoat: The Diplomatic Ordeal of John Carter Vincent*. Prospect Heights: Waveland Press, 1982.
Pakula, Hannah. *The Last Empress: Madame Chiang Kai-shek and the Birth of Modern China*. New York: Simon & Schuster, 2009.
Pogue, Forrest. *George C. Marshall: Organizer of Victory, 1943–1945*. New York: Viking, 1973.
Reardon-Anderson, James. *Yenan and the Great Powers: The Origins of Chinese Communist Foreign Policy, 1944–1946*. New York: Columbia University, 1980.
Roberts, Andrew. *Masters and Commanders: How Four Titans Won the War in the West*. New York: Harper, 2010.
Sainsbury, Keith. *The Turning Point: Roosevelt, Stalin, Churchill, and Chiang K'ai-shek, 1943*. New York: Oxford University Press, 1985.
Shai, Aron. *Britain and China, 1941–1947*. New York: St. Martin's Press, 1984.
_____. *Origins of the War in the East: Britain, China and Japan, 1937–1939*. London: Croom and Helm, 1976.
Schaller, Michael. *The United States and China in the Twentieth Century*. New York: Oxford University Press, 1990.
_____. *The US Crusade in China, 1938–1945*. New York: Columbia University Press, 1979.
Sherwood, Robert E. *Roosevelt and Hopkins: An Intimate History*. New York: Harper and Row, 1950.
Smith, Gaddis. *American Diplomacy During the Second World War*. New York: Knopf, 1985.
Smith, Jean Edward. *FDR*. New York: Random House, 2007.
Taylor, Jay. *The Generalissimo: Chiang Kai-shek and the Struggle for Modern China*. Cambridge: Harvard University Press, 2009.
Thorne, Christopher. *Allies of a Kind: The United States, Britain, and the War Against Japan: 1941–1945*. New York: Oxford University Press, 1978.
_____. *The Issue of War: States, Societies, and the Far Eastern Conflict of 1941–1945*. New York: Oxford University Press, 1985.
Tsou Tang. *America's Failure in China (Volume I)*. Chicago: University of Chicago Press, 1963.
_____. *America's Failure in China (Volume II)*. Chicago: University of Chicago Press, 1967.
Varg, Paul. *The Closing of the Door: Sino-American Relations, 1936–1946*. East Lansing: Michigan State University Press, 1973.
Young, Arthur. *China and the Helping Hand, 1937–1945*. Cambridge: Harvard University Press, 1965.
_____. *China's Wartime Finance and Inflation, 1937–1945*. Cambridge: Harvard University Press, 1965.
Young, Marilyn B. *Rhetoric of Empire*. Cambridge: Harvard University Press, 1968.
Ziegler, Philip. *Mountbatten*. New York: Knopf, 1985.

Index

Acheson, Dean 46
Aeronautical Affairs Commission 55
Africa 92
Agra, India 54–55
Air Transport Command 107
Aleutian Islands 44
Alexander, Gen. Sir Harold 59
Alexandria, Egypt 51
American Legation (Teheran) 117, 119–120, 122
American Volunteer Group (AVG) *see* Flying Tigers
Andaman Islands 108–109, 114–115, 118–119, 131, 144, 148–149, 153
Arnold, Gen. Henry A. 26–27, 62–63, 67, 75, 78, 88–89, 97, 106–107, 144
Astaire, Fred 30
Atcheson, George 33
Axis powers 21, 27, 35, 44, 134–136

Baldwin, Hanson 49–50
Balkans 133, 137
Bay of Bengal 72–74, 77, 91, 108–109, 111, 119, 130, 133, 141
Bennett, Joan 30
Bergman, Ingrid 31
Big Three powers 125–126, 136
Birse, Maj. Arthur 136
Boettiger, John 101–102, 120
Bohlen, Charles 120, 122, 126, 134, 136
British Chiefs of Staff (BCOS) 63–64, 70–71, 74–78, 83–84, 91, 97, 109, 116, 118–119, 129–131, 138–141, 146–147, 153
British Empire 121
British Legation (Teheran) 117, 124, 134, 138
Brooke, Gen. Alan 61–68, 70–71, 74–78, 80–81, 85–89, 95–97, 104, 108–111, 118–119, 123–127, 129–131, 135–136, 139, 141–143, 145–147, 153
Buck, Pearl 6, 28, 40
Burma 4, 21, 41–42, 44, 54, 64, 70–77, 80–81, 85–86, 88, 90–92, 96–98, 100, 105–106, 108–109, 111–112, 115–116, 119, 123, 131, 141–142, 144–145, 154–155, 157, 162–163

Cadogan, Lord 93
Cagney, James 30
Cairo Declaration 113, 134, 136, 149, 168
Canton, China 54–55, 76–77, 103
Casablanca, Morocco 40, 42–43
Central Daily News 142
Chan, Charlie 28
Chaplin, Charlie 30
Ch'en Cheng 44
Ch'en Kuo-fu 39
Ch'en Li-fu 18, 39
Chennault, Gen. Claire 18, 43, 55, 60, 67, 82–83, 86, 164
Chicago, Illinois 28
Chiang Kai-shek, Generalissimo 1–4, 7–12, 14–19, 21–22, 32, 34, 36–37, 39–82, 84–100, 102–115, 117–120, 124–125, 127, 129–133, 137–138, 140–144, 146–148, 150, 152, 154–163, 165–166, 168–169
Chiang Kai-shek, Madame (Mayling Soong) 1, 6, 9, 12–15, 17–19, 21–34, 39–40, 42, 52–55, 60–61, 64–69, 71, 74–75, 79–80, 84, 88–90, 92–94, 97–100, 103, 106–107, 111, 117, 131, 149, 151, 154–155, 159–160
Chiang Wei-kuo 19
Ch'in Shih Huang-ti 27
China 2, 12, 36, 42, 58, 72, 75, 79–83, 85, 88, 90, 92, 95–97, 100–101, 104, 109, 112, 117, 121, 124–125, 134, 148, 154–156, 162–163, 165
China, Bank of 34, 39
China-Burma-India Theater (CBI) 4–5, 11, 15, 17, 20–21, 32, 41, 44–45, 51, 54, 58–59, 70–71, 79–81, 84, 86, 91–93, 103, 105, 115, 147, 151, 157
China Incident 3
Chinese Air Force 76
Chinese Americans 26, 30–31
Chinese Communist Party (CCP) 3, 32, 50, 103, 151, 166
Chinese Embassy (USA) 23
Chinese Nationalists (KMT) 3, 4; *see also* Kuomintang
Chinese News Service 40

195

Chou Chih-jou, Gen. 55
Chou En-lai 18, 166
Chu Shih-ming, Gen. 77
Chungking, China 3, 12–19, 21–22, 27, 33–34, 36, 38–41, 43–45, 47–57, 62, 67, 69, 73, 96, 105, 110, 112, 142, 149, 154–167
Churchill, Clementine 2
Churchill, Sarah 88–89, 100
Churchill, Winston 1–2, 8, 11, 22, 39, 41–42, 51–52, 54–56, 58–75, 80–82, 88–94, 96, 99–101, 103–105, 107, 109–119, 121–123, 125–151, 153–156, 159–160, 162
Cohn, Harry 30
Colbert, Claudette 30
Cold War 1
Columbia-Presbyterian Hospital (New York) 22
Columbia University 5–6
Combined Chiefs of Staff (CCOS) 46, 80, 140, 145–146, 159
Coral Sea, Battle of the 23
Cummings, Bruce 113
Cunningham, Adm. Sir Andrew 58, 63, 70, 108, 130, 135
Currie, Lauchlin 9, 12–17, 21–22, 165

Dairen 134
Davies, John Paton 54, 56, 60, 106, 142, 152–153, 155, 165
Delano, Sarah 5
Delano, Warren 5
Delano, Warren Jr. 5
De Gaulle, Gen. Charles 138, 146
Dewey, Thomas E. 26
De Wiart, Gen. Carton 55–56, 66–67
Dietrich, Marlene 31
Dill, Field Marshal Sir John 63–64, 70, 74, 84
Dorn, Gen. Frank 102, 163

East Asia 141
Eden, Anthony 92–94, 105, 110–111, 122, 126, 136
Eisenhower, Gen. Dwight David 58–59
England 59, 99
English Channel 131
Europe 124, 126, 129

Far East 134
Filipino president 122
Flying Tigers 4, 18
Foreign Affairs Bureau (China) 55
Foreign Ministry (China) 9, 34, 39, 44, 154, 159
Formosa 134
Four Policemen 138
France 99, 119, 122–123, 129, 137–138, 140
Free China 3, 4, 21, 112

Garson, Greer 30
Gauss, Clarence 10, 12–18, 50, 158
Germany 21, 23, 57–58, 82–83, 109, 113, 118, 122–123, 126–127, 129, 133, 136–137
Goldwyn, Samuel 30
Gone with the Wind 30
The Good Earth 6
Great Britain *see* United Kingdom
Greece 119

Haiphong-Yunnan Railroad 4
Harriman, Averell 62, 82–83, 90, 93, 111, 118, 121, 124–126, 132, 136
Harvard University 5–6
History of the Second World War 57
Hitler, Adolf 21, 24, 123
Ho Ying-chin, Gen. 18, 101
Hollywood Bowl 30–31
Hong Kong 54, 76–77, 103, 125, 127, 151
Hopkins, Harry 9, 12–13, 34, 41–43, 46, 58, 63, 66–67, 78, 90, 101–102, 112, 118–120, 122, 126, 136, 150–151, 156–160, 164
Hornbeck, Stanley 45, 47, 94, 158
Hsin Hua Jih Pao 50
Hu, Victor 38, 159
Hu Shih 9–11, 14–15
Hughes, Howard 30
Hull, Cordell 9, 13, 16–17, 33–34, 45, 47, 82, 158, 164
Hump 72, 81, 88, 97, 101, 107, 115, 157
Hurley, Gen. Patrick 51, 53
Huston, Walter 31

India 15, 72, 80, 85, 103, 120–121, 131–132, 148
Indian Ocean 71–73, 81, 131
Indochina 4, 120
Inonu, Ismet 139, 149
USS *Iowa* 56–58
Iran 63, 117
Ismay, Gen. Hastings 58, 63, 66, 75, 104, 118, 129, 131
Italy 41, 92

Japan 21–22, 43, 50–51, 53, 65, 72–74, 76, 78–83, 91, 103–105, 110, 112–113, 121, 129, 133–134, 143, 145, 148, 151, 155, 161, 164, 166, 169
Japanese Imperial Air Force 148
Joint Chiefs of Staff (JCS) 57–58, 63–67, 70–71, 75–78, 81–83, 85–88, 90–91, 96–97, 100, 107–111, 114, 116, 118–120, 122–124, 126, 130–132, 134, 138–140 142, 144–151

Kerr, Archibald 122, 136
Khartoum, Egypt 58
King, Adm. Ernest 62–63, 65, 67, 78, 91, 110, 144–145
Kirk, Alexander 62

Index

Koo, Wellington 44, 64, 92–93
Korea 112–113
Kung, H.H. 6, 9–11, 14, 18–19, 48, 52–54, 106
Kunming 90, 164
Kuomintang (KMT) 2–3, 5, 10–11, 14, 16–17, 22, 24, 32, 34, 39, 44, 48–50, 55–56, 61, 79, 105, 142, 151–152, 159–160, 162–164, 166–169; *see also* Chinese Nationalists

La Guardia, Fiorello H. 26
Lampson, Sir Miles (Lord Killearn) 60–61
Lashio 75
Lattimore, Owen 165
Leahy, Adm. William 65–67, 75, 77, 80, 109–110, 118, 120, 140–141, 145–147, 150
Ledo Road 101, 108
Lend-Lease 7, 9, 11–12
Libya 62
Life 6–7
Lodge, Henry Cabot 50
London, England 44
Los Angeles, California 30
Luce, Henry 6–7

MacArthur, Gen. Douglas 53, 81
Madison Square Garden 26
Malaya 4
Malta 58–59
Manchuria 3, 73, 125, 134, 161
Mandalay, Burma 85
Mao Tse-tung 166
Marshall, Gen. George C. 11–12, 37, 57, 61–63, 65–66, 71, 77–78, 80, 84–86, 88, 91, 95–98, 100, 104, 109–111, 119, 123, 126–127, 129, 140, 144–147, 150–151, 160
Maximoff, M.A. 118
Mayer, Louis B. 30
McIntyre, Marvin H. 90
Mediterranean 64, 70, 109, 118–119, 123–124, 126, 129, 131, 133, 136, 139–140
Mena House Hotel (Cairo) 61–64, 66, 68, 70–71, 75–76, 83, 86, 96, 107, 139–140, 169
Merrill, Frank D. 56, 60, 78
Middle East 51
Midway, Battle of 23
Military Affairs Commission 55
Molotov, V.M. 118, 122–126, 136
Molotov–Von Ribbentrop Pact 123
Morgenthau, Henry 5, 32, 34–35, 37, 159, 161–162, 164
Moscow Foreign Ministers Conference 82
Mountbatten, Adm. Lord Louis 47, 61–62, 66, 70–77, 79–80, 83, 85–88, 90, 96–98, 100, 104–107, 114–115, 123, 131–132, 142–145, 148–149, 154
Munitions Board 46

Nanking, China 6–7, 161
National Defense Council 107
Nazi Party 7, 21
Near East 92
Neutrality Acts 6
New Delhi, India 51
New York City 22, 27, 28; City Hall 26, 30
New York Herald Tribune 24
New York Times 49, 94
North Africa 15, 41
Northern Expedition 55

Oakland, California 28
Open Door 141
Operation Anvil 129–130, 133–134, 137, 139–141, 143, 145, 147, 151
Operation Buccaneer 108–111, 114–116, 118–119, 123–124, 126–127, 129, 131, 133, 136–137, 139–141, 143–155, 163
Operation Ichigo 164
Operation Overlord 84, 90, 108–109, 116, 120, 123–126, 129–130, 132–134, 137, 139, 141, 143, 145, 147, 151, 154, 160
Operation Tarzan 141, 146–147, 157

Pacific Theater 70, 73, 77, 81, 109–110, 121–122, 124–125, 136, 142, 144–145, 161
Pacific War Council 42–45
Paoting Military Academy 55
Pavlov, V.N. 122–123, 135–136
Pearl Harbor, Hawaii 3–4, 9–10, 21, 34, 79
Persia 52
Pescadores 134
Philippines 4, 35
Pickford, Mary 31
Pin-Yin system 2
Pogue, Forrest 110
Poland 123
Portal, Air Chief Marshall Sir Charles 63, 109
Potemkin village 168
Power, Tyrone 30
propaganda 16, 37–39, 43, 50, 168
Publicity Bureau 39–40

Quarantine speech 6
Quebec, Canada 45–47

Rabe, John 7
Ramgarh, India 115, 131–132
Rangoon, Burma 75
Reader's Digest 49
Red Army 134
HMS *Renown* 59
Republicans 7
Rhodes 108, 119, 131, 136, 139, 141
Rock of Gilbraltar 152
Rockerfeller, John D. 26
Rogers, Ginger 30
Roosevelt, Eleanor 2, 22, 25

Index

Roosevelt, Elliott 80–82, 88–90, 96, 98–99, 101–103, 113, 125, 137, 145, 150–152, 154, 162
Roosevelt, Franklin D. 1–3, 7–16, 19–22, 24, 29, 31–33, 35, 37–38, 40–43, 45–47, 49–50, 52–60, 62–63, 65–72, 74–76, 78–83, 88–103, 105–107, 109–114, 116–127, 129–139, 141–146, 148–155, 157, 159–163, 165–169; administration 7, 32, 34–35, 54; cabinet 25–26, 34
Roosevelt, James 5
Rossi, Angelo J. 29
Royal Family 75
Royal Navy 70, 73–74, 77, 91, 108, 135
Russell and Company 5
Russian Legation (Teheran) 118, 120, 122–123, 125–126

Saint James, Court of 59
San Francisco, California 29; Civic Auditorium 29–30
San Francisco Chronicle 29
Selznick, David O. 30
Shang Chen, Gen. 55, 62, 77–78, 86–88
Shanghai 29, 77, 103
Shanghai, Battle of 6
Sherwood, Robert 151
Sicily 73
Singapore 101, 127
Sino-American relations 2, 4, 9, 13–15, 40, 47, 49–52, 59, 154, 162, 168–169
Sino-British relations 17
Sino-Japanese War 3, 9
Sino-Soviet relations 82
Somervell, Brehon 51–52, 67
Soong Ailing (Madame H.H. Kung) 6
Soong Chingling (Madame Sun Yat-sen) 6
Soong, T.V. 6, 9–15, 22, 26, 33–42, 44–54, 67, 69, 107, 154, 156–160, 162, 164–165, 167–168
South China Sea 76
Southeast Asia Command (SEAC) 64, 70, 72–76, 80–81, 83–85, 91–92, 99–101 103,105, 114–15, 119–120, 122, 124, 126, 129–132, 134, 139–140, 142–143, 145–147, 149–150, 152, 154–156
Soviet Legation (Teheran) *see* Russian Legation (Teheran)
Soviet Union 44–46, 53, 65, 79, 82, 121–123, 135, 137, 148, 151
Sphinx 89–90, 112
Stalin, Joseph 1, 21, 43, 52–53, 57, 59, 63, 71, 79, 82, 84, 91, 93–94, 109, 112–113, 116–118, 120–127, 129–130, 132–138, 141, 145, 148–149, 151
Stanwyck, Barbara 30
Stilwell, General Joseph 5, 11–13, 15, 36–37, 41, 43–44, 46–47, 52–56, 60, 62–72, 74, 76–80, 83–85, 87, 90, 97–98, 100–102, 104, 106–107, 114–115, 140, 152, 155, 163, 165–167
Stimson, Henry L. 5, 11–12, 24–26, 34–35, 37, 40, 47, 51, 156, 159, 161–162, 164
Straits of Formosa 76
Straits of Gibraltar 58
Straits of Malacca 73
Straits of Sunda 73
Su Tung Pao 142
Sulzberger, Cyrus 94
Sun Yat-sen 48, 55
Sunderland, Gen. Riley 95–96
Sympathy Hall 28
Szechwan 3, 164

Ta Kung Pao 49
Taft, Sen. Robert 7
Tashkent, Russia 16
Teheran Conference 1, 57, 63, 82–83, 91–92, 94, 100, 109, 113–114, 116–118, 120, 122, 124–126, 128–129, 132, 134, 136–141, 145–146, 149, 154, 156
Teheran Declaration 136–137
Tibet 127
Time 6–7
Tobin, Maurice J. 28
Tokyo 79
Tong, Hollington 16–17, 19, 22, 24, 26, 28–29, 33, 54–55, 60, 69, 159–160
Too Much Wishful Thinking About China 49
Treasury Department 157, 160
Truman, Harry 168
Tuchman, Barabara 60
Tunis 63
Turkey 136

Union Station, Washington D.C. 22, 30, 160
United Chiefs of Staff (UCS) 83–84
United Kingdom 2, 45–46, 83–84, 122, 124, 127–128, 132, 137
United Nations 127, 138, 141
United States 2, 83, 122–124, 158, 161–163, 165, 167–168; Army 95; Army Air Force 26, 72, 76, 83, 89, 107 151; Capitol 23; Congress 6, 50, 157; House of Representatives 23–24, 27; presidential election campaign (1940) 17; Senate 50; State Department 9, 13, 19, 46, 79, 168; War Department 9, 14, 35, 37, 79
United States Legation (Teheran) 117
Urumchi, China 16

Vichy regime 123
Vincent, John Carter 165
Vladivostok, Russia 83, 134
Voroshilov, Marshal Kliment 123–124
Vyshinsky, Andre 71

Index

Wade-Giles system 2
Waldorf Astoria Hotel (New York) 26
Wallace, Henry 9, 164–167
Wang Ch'ung-hui 54–55, 107, 155, 159, 161
Wang Shih-chieh 64, 111
Warner, Harry 30
Warring States period 27
Washington, D.C. 10–12, 14–16, 22, 25, 35–36, 38, 51, 53, 158–160, 162, 165, 167–168
Washington Conference 41, 43
Watson, Thomas J. 26, 58, 90, 101, 120
Wedemeyer, Gen. Albert 67, 71, 78, 167
Wei Tao-ming 14
Welles, Sumner 5
Wellesley College 6, 28

Wheeler, Gen. Raymond 64, 71
White House 6, 23–24, 34, 41, 51, 152, 156, 160
Willkie, Wendell 7, 9, 15–22, 26–27, 33, 159, 165
Winant, Charles 62
Winart, John 58
World War II 1, 59, 95

Yale University 5, 54
Yalta Conference 1
Yee Ming 40
Yenan 162–164, 166
Y-Force 163
Yunnan, China 3, 77, 85, 163–164

www.ingramcontent.com/pod-product-compliance
Ingram Content Group UK Ltd.
Pitfield, Milton Keynes, MK11 3LW, UK
UKHW021833140426
5217IPUK00021B/1430